W. H. G. Kingston

The two supercargoes

Adventures in savage Africa

W. H. G. Kingston

The two supercargoes
Adventures in savage Africa

ISBN/EAN: 9783743306448

Manufactured in Europe, USA, Canada, Australia, Japa

Cover: Foto ©ninafisch / pixelio.de

Manufactured and distributed by brebook publishing software
(www.brebook.com)

W. H. G. Kingston

The two supercargoes

THE TWO SUPERCARGOES

OR

ADVENTURES IN SAVAGE AFRICA

By

W. H. G. KINGSTON

THOMAS NELSON AND SONS
LONDON, EDINBURGH, DUBLIN
AND NEW YORK

PREFACE.

A FRICA will probably continue for a generation or
more, as it has been from time immemorial, a land
of mystery, although the veil which has shrouded it from
the eyes of the civilised world is gradually being drawn
aside.

When the two young Supercargoes and their naval
companions visited it, excepting on the seaboard, it was
comparatively but little known. Whether or not their
adventures will be considered as thrilling and romantic
as those of Stanley and Cameron, I must leave my
readers to decide; but I shall be satisfied if the following narrative induces any of my youthful friends to
take an interest in the long-neglected and fearfully
ill-treated inhabitants of that benighted land, and to
assist those who are so heroically labouring for their
amelioration with their contributions, if not by their
personal efforts. I would advise them also, when they
have finished the adventures of the Two Supercargoes,

to read the narratives of the above-mentioned explorers, and they will see how judgment, courage, and perseverance can conquer dangers and difficulties which might have induced many a stout heart to turn back and abandon the enterprises which they have successfully achieved.

W. H. G. K.

CONTENTS.

CHAPTER I.

CHAPTER II.

CHAPTER III.

CHAPTER IV.

CHAPTER V.

CHAPTER VI.

CHAPTER VII.

CHAPTER VIII.

CHAPTER IX.

CHAPTER XII.

CHAPTER XIII.

CHAPTER XVL

LIST OF ILLUSTRATIONS.

I saw the canoe lifted high in the air.

No it moved by some mysterious ill force sprung upon him

THE TWO SUPERCARGOES;

OR,

ADVENTURES IN SAVAGE AFRICA.

—◆—

CHAPTER I.

The office of Crank, Trunnion, & Swab—Harry Bracewell reports the arrival of the "Arrow"—History of Nicholas Swab—The slave trade—Our firm gives up all connection with it—Captain Roderick Trunnion—Something about myself and friends—Interview between Mr. Trunnion and Godfrey Magor, mate of the "Arrow"—An unexpected arrival—A strange accusation—Suspicions of Captain Trunnion—Mrs. Bracewell and her daughter Mary.

"THE 'Arrow' has come in, sir, from the Coast of Africa, under charge of Mr. Godfrey Magor, the second mate," I heard Harry Bracewell, one of our shipping clerks, say, as I was seated on a high stool, pen in hand, leaning over my desk in the office of Messrs. Crank, Trunnion, & Swab, general merchants, of Liverpool.

Harry addressed the senior partner, Mr. Peter Crank, who had just then stepped out of his private room with a bundle of papers in his hand into the counting-house, where I, with a dozen other clerks, senior and junior, were driving our quills as fast as we could move them over the paper, or adding up columns of figures, or making calculations, as the case might be.

As I turned my head slightly, I could see both Mr. Crank and Harry. They afforded a strange contrast. Harry was tall, well-built, had a handsome countenance, with a pleasant expression which betokened his real character, for he was as kind, honest, and generous a young fellow as ever lived—the only son of his mother, the widow of a naval officer killed in action. She had come to Liverpool for the sake of giving a home to Harry, who had been for some time in the employment of the firm. The difference between Mr. Crank and Harry was indeed most conspicuous in their personal appearance. Whereas Harry was tall, Mr. Crank was short and stout; he had a bald head, shining as if it had been carefully polished, a round face, with a florid complexion, and a nose which was allowed by his warmest friends to be a snub; but he had a good mouth, bright blue eyes, often twinkling with humour, which seemed to look through and through those he addressed, while his brow exhibited a considerable amount of intellect. Had not he possessed that, he would not have been at the head of the firm of Crank, Trunnion, & Swab.

"Brought home, did you say, by Godfrey Magor? What has happened to Captain Rig and the first mate?"

"Both died from fever while up the Nunn, as did all hands except himself and three others. So Mr. Magor told me; and the survivors were all so weak, that he could not have brought the vessel home had he not shipped six Kroomen. He had also a narow escape from pirates, who actually boarded his vessel, when a man-of-war heaving in sight, they made off without plundering her or killing any one."

"Bless my heart! I'm sorry to hear about Captain Rig's death. The poor man remained longer up the river than he should have done, no doubt about that. I have over and over again charged the masters of our vessels to be careful in that respect, but they won't attend to what I say. Let me see! that makes the fifth who has lost his life during the last two years. I'm thankful he got clear of the pirates. Those rascals have long been the greatest pests on that coast. It is time the British Government should take effectual steps to put a stop to their depredations by sending a squadron into those seas. Have you brought the manifest and the other papers with you?"

"Yes, sir," answered Harry, producing them. "Mr. Magor will be on shore himself in an hour or two, when he has seen the vessel made snug, for he has no one to leave in charge; he himself is still suffering from the fever, and two of her white crew are in their bunks."

Mr. Crank, taking the documents, retired with them into his room, to run his eye over the list of articles brought by the "Arrow," and to calculate their present market value. The result I know was satisfactory. I had afterwards to note down the prices which they fetched. Merchants who could make so large a percentage on all their cargoes were certain to grow rich. It was at the cost, however, of the lives of a great number of human beings; but that was not my employers' look out, nor did they allow the matter to trouble their consciences. They could always obtain fresh masters to take charge of their vessels, and fresh crews to man them.

In a short time Mr. Trunnion, who had heard on 'Change of the arrival of the "Arrow," came in to learn what news she had brought, expecting to find her master, who was wont, immediately he came on shore, to put in an appearance at the office. Mr. Trunnion expressed himself much shocked at Captain Rig's death.

"Poor fellow! he used to boast that he was acclimatised, but it is a proof of the old adage, 'that the pitcher which goes often to the well gets broken at last.' We might have lost a worse man;" and with this remark Mr. Trunnion passed into his room, in which he sat to receive visitors on private business.

Mr. Trunnion, although the second partner, was the youngest in the firm. He was a good-looking, urbane, well-mannered man, who, if not always loved by those under him, was much liked and respected in the social circle in which he moved, he being also one of the magnates of Liverpool.

For my own part, I had reason to like and be grateful to Mr. Swab, the junior member of the firm. He had formerly been a clerk in the house, but by diligent attention to and a thorough knowledge of business and strict honesty, he had some years before been made a partner. To him I felt that I owed all the knowledge I possessed of commercial affairs, as from my first entrance into the office he took notice of me, and gave me the instruction I so much required. My chief friend was Harry Bracewell, who was also a favourite with Mr. Swab, and had received the same instruction from him that I had obtained. Mr. Swab was not at all ashamed of his origin. He used to tell us that he had risen, not from the gutter, but from the mud, like other strange animals, having obtained his livelihood in his early days by hunting at low tide for whatever he could pick up along the shore, thrown overboard from the lighters or similar vessels unloading at the quays. At length it was his good fortune to pick a purse out of the mud containing ten golden guineas, and, as he used to tell us, being convinced that he should never have a find like it, he resolved to quit his occupation, for which he had no particular fancy, and endeavour to obtain a situation where he might have a prospect of rising in the world. Though he could neither read nor write, he was well aware that those acquirements were necessary for his advancement, as also that a decent suit of clothes would greatly contribute to his obtaining a respectable place. These objects were now within his reach. The most easily attained was the suit of clothes, and these he bought, with a cap and a good pair of shoes, at a slopseller's, including three shirts, a necktie, and other articles of clothing, for the moderate sum of £2, 13s. 6d. He had taken good care not to let the slopseller know of his wealth; indeed, that fact he kept locked in his own bosom, as he did his purse in a place in which no one was likely to discover it. The balance of the ten pounds into which he had broken he expended in supporting himself while he acquired the first rudiments of knowledge, with the aid of a friend, the keeper of a second-hand bookstall, a broken-down schoolmaster, who, strange to say, still retained a pleasure in imparting instruction to the young. Nicholas Swab first bought a spelling-book, and then confessed that he should find it of no use unless Mr. Vellum would explain to him the meaning of the black marks on the pages.

"Then you do not know your letters, my poor boy?" said the old man in a tone of commiseration.

"No, sir, I don't; but I soon will, if you'll tell them to me," answered Nicholas in a confident tone.

"Sit down on that stool, and say them after me as I point them out to you," said Mr. Vellum.

With great patience he went over the alphabet again and again.

"Now I want to put them together, sir," said Nicholas, not content with the extent of the first lesson. All day long he sat with the book before him, and then took it with him to his home. That home, the abode of his mother, a widow, with a pension of five shillings a week, which enabled her to live, although too small to afford subsistence to her son, was in a small garret up a dark stair in one of the poorest of the back streets of Liverpool. Nicholas set working away by the flame of a farthing rushlight, and at dawn he was up again poring over his book.

Old Vellum was so pleased with the progress made by his pupil, that he continued to give him all the assistance in his power, not only teaching him to read but to write. In a few weeks young Nicholas could do both in a very creditable manner. Having thus gained the knowledge he desired, dressed in a decent suit of clothes, he went round to various offices in Liverpool offering to fill any vacant situation for which he might be considered fit. Although he met with numerous rebuffs, he persevered, and was finally taken into the small counting-house of which Mr. Peter Crank's father was the head. To the firm, through all its various changes, he had remained attached, and though frequently offered opportunities of bettering himself, had refused to leave it. "No, no; I'll stick to my old friends," he always answered; "their interests are mine, and although I am but a poor clerk, I believe I can forward them."

From the first, during all his leisure moments, of which he had not many, he continued to study hard, and to improve himself, spending a portion of his wages in books, which he obtained from Mr. Vellum, who allowed him also the run of his library. He was raised from grade to grade until he became head clerk, and during the illness of Mr. Crank and the absence of Mr. Trunnion, he so well managed the affairs of the firm, that they felt bound to offer him a partnership in the business, to the success of which he had so greatly contributed. Notwithstanding his rise in the social circle, Nicholas Swab continued to be the same unostentatious, persevering, painstaking man which he had been from the first—upright in all his dealings, and generous to those who required a helping hand.

Some of the transactions of the firm would not, it must be confessed, stand the test of the present code of morality. The slave trade had, until lately, been lawful, and the firm had engaged in it with as little hesitation as it would in any other mercantile business. It had been in the habit of buying negroes in the cheapest market, and disposing of them in the dearest, without for a moment considering how they were obtained. When the traffic was pronounced illegal, it withdrew its own vessels, but still had no hesitation in supplying the means for fitting out others which it knew were about to proceed to the African coast, although no particular inquiries were made on the subject. It was not very long before the time of which I speak that the fact dawned on the minds of the partners that the traffic was hateful in the sight of God, as well as in that of a large number of their countrymen, and that it was the main cause of the cruel wars and miseries unspeakable from which the dark-skinned children of Africa had long suffered. Being really conscientious men, they had agreed to abandon all connection with the traffic, and to employ their vessels in carrying on a lawful trade on the coast. To do this, however, was not at first so easy as might be supposed. One of the vessels especially, which they had contributed to fit out and to supply with goods, although not belonging to them, was commanded by Mr. Trunnion's brother—a Captain Roderick Trunnion, of whose character I had heard from time to time mysterious hints thrown out not much to his credit. He occasionally made his appearance at Liverpool. He seemed to me to be a fine, bold, dashing fellow, ready to do and dare anything he might think fit. He was like several privateer captains I had met with, who set their own lives and those of their followers at slight value, provided they could carry out their undertakings. He gave, I believe, his brother, Mr. Thomas Trunnion, the partner in our firm, considerable cause for anxiety and annoyance. The last time he had been on shore, in order to recover his brother's confidence he endeavoured to make himself agreeable to the other partners. Mr. Swab, however, I know, did not trust him, as he privately told Harry Bracewell on one occasion. "And don't you," he added; "he is without principles; he always did what he chose regardless of God or man. And he doesn't believe in God, or that any man has a grain of honesty, nor does he, except when it suits him, boast of having any himself."

Captain Trunnion, however, appeared to have insinuated himself into the good graces of our senior partner, at whose house he was a frequent visitor. He had a strong attraction there; for Lucy, Mr. Crank's, only child, was a sweet, amiable, pretty girl, and Captain Trunnion believed that, could he win her, he should not only obtain a charming wife, but become possessed, some day or other, of Mr. Crank's property. Which influenced him most I cannot say. All I know is, that he did not make any progress in the affections of Miss Lucy, for a very good reason, which he was not long in suspecting—that she had already given her heart to some one else. That some one was my friend Harry Bracewell. Captain Trunnion had, however, gone away without suspecting who was his rival.

My father and mother resided in Chester, so that I was received into the house, as a lodger, of Mrs. Bracewell; thus it was that I became more intimate with Harry than I might otherwise have been. I also had an opportunity of being constantly in the society of the widow's only daughter, Mary—a charming little unaffected girl, full of life and spirits, who treated me as her brother's friend, almost like a brother. For a long time I also thought only of her as a sister, although, somehow or other, I began at last to entertain the hope that, when I had by steady industry obtained the means of making her my wife, she would not feel it necessary to refuse me; and as my family was a respectable one, I had no reason to fear that any objection would be raised by Mrs. Bracewell or Harry. Of my own family I need not speak, except of one member—my brother Charley, who had gone to sea before I entered the office, and was now a midshipman of some years' standing. He had lately joined the "Rover" frigate, employed on the African station. Charley and I had been fast friends and companions, as brothers should be, when we were together, and when separated we constantly corresponded with each other. I cannot say that I had any special fondness for mercantile pursuits, or at all events for the work of an office, having to sit for ten or twelve hours of the day on a high stool at a desk, but yet I was thoroughly impressed with the fact that I must gain my own livelihood, and that by working hard alone could I expect to do so. Had the choice been given me, I should have preferred a life in the open air, with the opportunity of travelling about and seeing the world; but my father did not wish to have more than one son in the navy, and Charley had been devoted as an offering to Neptune. I was, however, very happy in my situation. Understanding what I was to do, I took a pleasure in doing it well; and I spent my evenings happily in the society of Mrs. Bracewell and her son and daughter. We had generally music and singing, now and then two or three visitors. Occasionally we went out to Mr. Crank's parties and those of other friends, so that our lives were in no respects dull.

I enter into these details in order that more interest may be taken in the rest of my narrative than might otherwise have been the case.

About an hour after Harry had reported the arrival of the vessel, as I was engaged in Mr. Trunnion's private room in taking down letters at his dictation, the mate of the "Arrow" was announced. As Mr. Crank was out, Mr. Trunnion desired him to come in and give an account of his voyage. As I was not desired to quit the room, I continued transcribing the notes which I had taken down, but I glanced round at the mate as he entered. His appearance showed that he had suffered from the fever which had carried off so many of his shipmates. His cheek was pale and hollow, his eye dull, and his figure emaciated ; even his voice sounded weak and hollow.

"Sit down," said Mr. Trunnion in a kind voice, showing that he was struck by the sickly look of the poor mate. "I should like to hear full particulars of your voyage. It has been a successful one judging by the manifest, which I have been looking over, although fatal to so many long in our employment. You have managed well, too, in bringing home the 'Arrow.' We are well satisfied—I can tell you that at once."

The mate then began an account of the transactions connected with the vessel from the time of her arrival on the Coast of Africa, the number of places visited, and the trade transactions at each. They were very interesting to me I know at the time, but I did not note them. Mr. Magor then described how one after the other the captain and crew died, until he and three others were alone left. "I doubted indeed whether I should have been able to bring the vessel home," he continued. "We had a narrow escape of being captured by a picarooning craft which swept alongside us during a calm. A number of the crew, headed by their captain, had actually made their way on board, and having bound me and three of my men, were proceeding to get off the hatches to take the cargo out of the hold, when a man-of-war, bringing up a strong breeze from the south, hove in sight. The pirates on discovering her hurried on board their own craft, carrying away two of my Kroomen, and casting off the grapplings with which they had made her fast alongside, got out their long sweeps and pulled away for their lives. As soon as the remaining Kroomen had set me and the other white men free, we ran out our guns and began firing at her. She returned our shot ; and as she had more guns and heavier metal than ours, we judged it prudent not to follow her. When the breeze came, which it did soon afterwards, she stood away under all sail before the wind. She showed that she was a fast craft, for she had almost got out of sight before the man-of-war came up with us. The latter pursued her, but whether she was overtaken or not I cannot say, as we continued our voyage towards England, and I saw no more of either of them. The pirates who had boarded us were of all nations, Spaniards, Portugese, and French, and there were several Englishmen among them. That their leader was one I could swear, for I heard him speaking English to several of the villains ; and what is more, as he gave me a good opportunity of marking his features while I was bound to the mainmast, I should remember him were I ever to meet him again."

"I hope that you may never fall in with him again under similar circumstances," remarked Mr. Trunnion. "Should you do so, he will probably make you walk the plank before he begins discharging your cargo into his own craft."

While the mate was narrating his adventures I heard a strange voice speaking in an authoritative tone in the outer office. Suddenly the door was burst open, and a tall powerful man, dressed in riding-boots, his clothes bespattered with mud, yet having in other respects a nautical cut about him, entered the room. Mr. Trunnion gazed on him without speaking.

"What, Tom! don't you know me?" exclaimed the new-comer advancing and putting out his hand. "My beard has grown, and I have become somewhat sunburnt since we parted."

"Bless my heart! is it you, Roderick?" exclaimed Mr. Trunnion. "I own that I did not recognise you, and was surprised at the intrusion of a stranger."

Roderick Trunnion, giving a laugh, threw himself into a chair opposite his brother, who reassumed his usual cold and dignified demeanour as he took his seat. From my desk I could observe what was going forward. I saw the mate start and narrowly scan the countenance of the new-comer with a look of extreme astonishment, while the latter, who did not appear to remark him, leaned forward and gazed at his brother, whose manner seemed to irritate him.

"Where in the world have you come from, Roderick?" asked Mr. Trunnion.

"From Falmouth last, where I left the 'Vulture' to refit. We met with a somewhat heavy gale, in which she was fearfully knocked about, and had we not kept the pumps going she would have foundered to a certainty. As I wanted to see you and other friends, I took horse and rode night and day to get here. The business I have got to speak of brooks of no delay, and is such as you and I can talk about best alone."

Turning round as he spoke, he cast a glance at Mr. Magor. For a moment, it seemed to me that his eye appeared to quail, but he quickly recovered himself.

"Have you finished your business here?" he asked in a bold tone, looking at the mate. "If so, you will leave me and your employer alone—for I presume that you are the master of one of his vessels. And that youngster—you do not wish him to take down our conversation, I suppose," he added, first looking at me then round at his brother.

"Really, Roderick, you have been so accustomed to command, that you forget that you are not on your own quarter-deck," observed Mr. Trunnion, who was evidently annoyed at the authoritative tone assumed by his brother.

The mate rose and looked first at Mr. Trunnion then at Captain Roderick.

"I have met that man before," he said, "and it is my duty to tell you when and how it was. It was not long ago, on the high seas, when he boarded the 'Arrow' at the head of"——

Mr. Trunnion, as the mate spoke, looked very much agitated, and I naturally fancied that something extraordinary was about to be said. Captain Roderick alone appeared perfectly cool. Fixing his glance on the mate, he exclaimed in a loud tone, interrupting him—

"You, my good fellow, may have met me half-a-dozen times for what I know to the contrary, or half-a-dozen men whom you may mistake for me, although I cannot say that I ever set eyes on you before. However, go on and tell Mr. Trunnion what I did when you fancy that you saw me, and I shall then know whether you are mistaken as to my identity."

The mate looked greatly confused.

"I can only hope that I am mistaken, and unless Mr. Trunnion desires me, I shall decline at present stating where, as I believe, I last saw you."

Mr. Trunnion was silent for a minute, and seemed lost in thought. Suddenly looking up he said—

"You have been suffering from fever, Mr. Magor, and your recollection of events, very naturally, is somewhat clouded. A few weeks' quiet and rest will restore your health. I would advise you not to repeat what you have just said. I'll send on board and relieve you of charge of the brig as soon as possible, and you can go to your friends in the country."

Mr. Magor, making a nautical bow to Mr. Trunnion, and giving another glance towards Captain Roderick, left the room.

"Westerton," continued my employer, turning to me, "you have heard all that has been said, and if it were repeated, although the poor man is under an hallucination, it might be the cause of disagreeable reports. You are discreet, I can trust you. Let not a word on the subject escape your lips. You can now go and finish those letters at your own desk."

I did as I was ordered, and gathering up the papers, followed the mate out of the room, leaving the two brothers together. What followed, I of course cannot say. For an hour or more they were closeted together. At last Captain Roderick came out, and returned to the inn where he had put up his horse. All I know is, that Mr. Trunnion did not invite him to his house. It seemed to me suspicious, and I could not help thinking about the matter, and wished that I could have consulted Harry Bracewell. Two evenings afterwards we went to a party at the house of Mr. Crank. Shortly after we arrived, who should walk in but Captain Roderick. By the way Mr. Crank and Lucy received him, I felt convinced that Mr. Trunnion had said nothing to prejudice the senior partner against him. He made himself at home as usual, treating Miss Lucy with great deference, and it seemed to me that he was gaining ground in her good graces.

His appearance was greatly improved since the day I had seen him in the counting-house. His face was carefully shaved, and his dress was such as to set off his well-made active figure. His aim was evidently to play the agreeable, not only to the young lady of the house, but to all the ladies present, and with some—especially with the dowagers—he appeared to be as successful as he could desire. He cast an indifferent glance now and then at me, as if he had never set eyes on me before, and appeared perfectly unconscious of the accusation—for such I considered it—brought against him by Mr. Magor. When I observed his apparent success with Lucy Crank, I felt a greater desire than ever to tell Harry what I had heard, and to advise him to warn her and her father of what I believed to be the real character of the man. His brother, I supposed, from fraternal affection or family pride, had said nothing to his senior partner to warn him, and, of course, even to Harry I could not venture to say what I thought about Captain Trunnion. I could only hope that Lucy would remain as indifferent to him as she had always before appeared to be, and that he would quickly again return to the " Vulture." I was surprised, indeed, that he had ventured to be so long absent from his vessel, as his presence would be necessary while she was refitting. Perhaps, after all, his statements about her might not be true; she might not even be at Falmouth, although his mud-bespattered appearance on his arrival showed that he had ridden a long distance.

CHAPTER II.

NOTWITHSTANDING the very grave suspicion cast on him by the mate of the "Arrow," Captain Roderick Trunnion did not immediately quit Liverpool, as I supposed he would have done. He was, as far as I could judge, not on friendly terms with his brother, as he lived at an inn, although there was ample room for him at Mr. Trunnion's house, where he seldom went, nor did he again appear at the office. I met him, however, frequently walking about Liverpool, dressed in shore-going clothes, booted and spurred, and carrying a riding-whip in his hand.

Notwithstanding, I should have known him at a glance to be a seaman. I found also that he very frequently called at Mr. Crank's residence at times when he well knew that the old gentleman would be at his counting-house. I did not suppose, however, that he received any encouragement from Miss Lucy, but he always had some excuse for paying a visit, either to show some curiosity which he said he had brought from abroad, or to leave a book or other articles which he had obtained for her. The fact was, that he had got into the good graces of Miss Deborah

Crank, Mr. Crank's maiden sister, who resided with him to look after Miss Lucy and keep his house in order. I met the Captain there at two or three evening parties to which the Bracewells and I were invited, and on each occasion he was evidently paying court to the young lady. When not with her, he was making himself agreeable to Miss Deborah.

Harry appeared to be in no way jealous or unhappy, which he would have been had he thought that Captain Roderick had the slightest chance of success.

"We understand each other," he said, "and she has assured me that she does not like him, though she cannot be rude to him while her father and aunt invite him to the house."

I did not like to make Harry unhappy by saying that I was not quite so certain about the matter as he was; at the same time I longed to be able to warn Miss Lucy of the character of the man. What surprised me was that Mr. Trunnion should not have spoken to Mr. Crank, or that the latter should not have thought it strange that Captain Roderick never came to the counting-house.

Probably Mr. Trunnion was influenced by fraternal feelings in not warning his partner of his suspicions regarding his brother's character. I did not, however, long entertain fears of Miss Lucy's affection for Harry, from a circumstance which he told me. It was a holiday, and he had arranged to accompany her and her aunt on a visit to some friends in the country. The coach was at the door waiting for Miss Deborah, who was upstairs, not yet naving finished her toilet, while Lucy, who had finished dressing, was seated in the drawing-room with Harry by her side. Suddenly the door opened, the young people expecting to see Miss Deborah enter. What, therefore, was their surprise when Captain Roderick stalked into the room. He stood for a moment gazing fiercely at Harry.

"What business have you here?" he exclaimed in a voice hoarse with passion.

Harry wisely did not answer him; but Lucy, looking up and holding Harry's hand, said quietly—

"Mr. Bracewell has come to escort my aunt and me into the country, and I have good reason for the annoyance I feel at the question you have put to him. My father is from home and will not return for some time, so I cannot invite you to wait for him."

Captain Roderick was not a man to be abashed even by the way Miss Lucy had addressed him. Taking a turn or two in the room, he waited—so Harry thought—expecting Miss Deborah to come down-stairs and invite him to accompany them. Lucy, suspecting his purpose, took Harry's arm and whispered, "Let us go down to the carriage."

Miss Deborah, happening to look out of her window, saw them get in, and being just then ready, she joined them without going into the drawing-room. Lucy, with much presence of mind, just before the carriage drove off, desired the servant, in a low voice which her aunt did not hear, to see Captain Roderick out of the house.

Whatever Captain Roderick might before have supposed, he now discovered to a certainty that Harry Bracewell was his rival. When I heard the account just given, believing that the mate was right in his suspicions, I felt sure that, should he have an opportunity, he would revenge himself on my friend. I told Harry all I could to warn him. I said that I believed Captain Roderick was a bad, unprincipled man, whom no fear of consequences or any right feeling would restrain from committing an act of violence if he thought that it would further his object.

Harry merely laughed, and observed, "When he finds that he has no chance of cutting me out he'll take himself off. I should think his brother, who is so strict and correct in his conduct, would be very glad to get him away from Liverpool."

Knowing what dreadful deeds had been done by men of ill-regulated minds influenced by jealousy, I felt seriously anxious about Harry, lest Captain Roderick should find means to revenge

himself. Had I been able to explain the cause of the dread I
had of him I might have convinced Harry of his danger, and induced him to be careful when going abroad at night; but I could
only tell him that I suspected the man, and that I did not like him:
Harry, however, though he had a true regard for me, either thought
that I was mistaken or needlessly alarmed.

Sometimes I thought of telling my fears to Mr. Trunnion, and
asking permission from him to warn Harry Bracewell; but I knew
that he would feel highly offended were I to speak on the subject
to him. I therefore, whenever Harry went out, made some excuse
for accompanying him, especially when he went to Mr. Crank's
house. On those occasions, instead of going in, I used to walk
about in the neighbourhood, or sit down in an archway where the
dark shadow concealed me from the view of passers-by. On two
different evenings I saw a person pass whom I felt sure by his
figure was Captain Roderick. The second time, when he stopped
before Mr. Crank's house, the light of the moon falling on his
face revealed his features to me, and convinced me that I was
not mistaken. He was dressed as I first saw him at the counting-
house, and he had a hanger by his side, and a brace of pistols in
his belt, with a pair of riding-boots on, as if prepared for a journey.

Fearing that Harry might come out, and that his rival might
attack him, I went up as if I was going to knock at the door; instead of which I stood in the porch, where, concealed, I could
watch Captain Roderick. Perhaps he suspected that I had recognised him; for after waiting a minute, and looking up at the windows, he moved away, and I lost sight of him. I waited until
Harry came out, and then taking his arm, I hurried him along
in an opposite direction to that which he would naturally have
followed as the shortest way home.

"Why are you going by this road?" he asked.

"I will tell you presently," I answered, continuing at a quick
pace. "Don't ask questions just now, for I really cannot answer
you."

Harry did as I wished, and we therefore exchanged few words until we reached home.

"Now," I said, "I will tell you. I am confident that Captain Roderick was waylaying you, and would either have sought a quarrel, or perhaps have cut you down with his hanger, or shot you."

Harry was at length inclined to believe that I was right, but still he added, "Perhaps, after all, he may be going away, and only came to take a last look at the house where Lucy lives; for, from what she tells me he said to her, I cannot help thinking that he must be desperately enamoured."

"If he does go, well and good; but if he remains, I tell you, Harry, that I do not consider your life safe," I remarked. "I must beg your mother and sister to lock you up, and not let you go out at night until the fellow has gone. He is a villain!" I repeated, in my eagerness almost revealing what I was bound to keep secret.

After this I saw no more of Captain Roderick. Whether or not he had left Liverpool I was uncertain, but I hoped he had gone. A few days afterwards, Mr. Magor, the mate of the "Arrow," came to the office, where he was received in a very friendly way by Mr. Swab. He looked completely changed. The sickly hue had left his cheek, and he was stout and hearty, with the independent bearing of a seaman.

"I am glad to see you looking so well, Mr. Magor," said Mr. Swab. "My partners and I have been talking the matter over; and from the way you brought the 'Arrow' home, and the character you received from her late master, we are resolved to offer you the command."

"Thank you, sir. I am proud of your approval; and I may venture to say, as far as navigating a vessel, or handling her in fine weather or foul, I am as competent as most men. I cannot boast, however, of my abilities as a trader, as I am no hand at keeping accounts. In that respect, I do not think that I should do you justice."

3

"Well, well, Captain Magor; we cannot always expect to find a man like Captain Rig, who combined both qualifications. We must therefore send a supercargo, or perhaps two, to help you; and *I* hope, with their assistance, that you will not be compelled to remain long up any of the rivers, and run the risk of losing your own life or of having your crew cut off by fever. You must try and be away from the coast before the sickly season sets in. It is by remaining up the rivers during the rains and hot weather that so many people die."

"As to the hot weather, I don't know when it is not hot on the coast," observed Captain Magor, for so in future I may call him; "but I am ready to brave any season in your service. And I again thank you, sir, for the offer you make me, which I gladly accept, provided you supply me with the assistance you see I require."

"We will try to do that," said Mr. Swab. "Now, without loss of time, look out for a couple of good men as mates, and the best crew you can obtain, and get the vessel fitted out without delay. I will accompany you on board and place you in command."

This was said in the outer office, where Henry and I overheard it.

"I wonder to whom they will offer the berths," said Harry to me. "If I thought that it would advance me in the house, and enable me the sooner to speak to Mr. Crank, I for one should be ready to accept an offer, although it would be a sore trial to go away. I had never dreamed of doing so; but yet, if I was asked, I would not refuse, as, of course, it could not fail to give one a lift; whereas, should I refuse, I should fall in the estimation of the partners."

The very next day Mr. Crank desired Harry and me to come into his inner room, and he then told us, what we already knew, that the firm intended to send out two supercargoes, who might assist each other, and asked if we would go, promising us each a share in the profits of the voyage, and advancement in the house on our return. "I do not hide from you that there is danger from the climate, and in some places from the natives; but the vessel will be well armed, and you must exert all the judgment and discretion you possess. You are both young and strong, and have never tampered with your constitutions, so that you are less likely to succumb to the climate than the generality of seamen." He then entered fully into the subject, telling us how to act under various circumstances, and giving us full directions for our guidance.

We did not appear very elated at the offer, but accepted it, provided Harry's mother and my parents did not object. "Tell them all I have said," observed Mr. Crank, "and let me know to-morrow, that should you refuse our offer I may look out for two other young men who have no family ties to prevent them from going. Our interests should, I think, be considered in the matter."

I judged by the tone of the senior partner's voice that he would be offended should we refuse his offer, and we therefore made up our minds to press the matter with those who had to decide for us. Of course we talked it over as we walked home that evening. We both fancied that we should be absent little more than five months, and that we should come back with our purses well filled, or, at all events, with the means of filling them.

Mrs. Bracewell and Mary were very unhappy when Harry placed the state of the case before them; but they acknowledged that he ought to act as the firm wished. My parents, to whom I wrote, expressed themselves much in the same way, only entreating that I would come and pay them a visit before starting. As soon as I received their letter I placed it in the hands of Mr. Crank, who seemed well pleased.

"You will not have cause to regret going, as far as we are concerned," he observed; "as for the rest, we must leave that to Providence."

Harry and I had, of course, been very often on board vessels, and made several trips down the Mersey, returning in the pilot-boat, but neither of us had ever been at sea. It was necessary that we should both see the cargo stowed, and be acquainted with the contents of every bale. As soon as it was stowed the brig would sail. I therefore hastened over to the neighbourhood of Chester to pay my promised visit to my family. "I shall be gone only five or six months," I said cheerfully, fully believing that such would be the case. "I will take good care of myself, depend upon that. I won't trust the black fellows, and will never sleep on shore."

On my return I found the vessel nearly ready to take in cargo. Harry and I were employed from morning until night in the warehouse, examining and noting the goods. We then both went on board, one remaining on deck to book them as they were hoisted in, the other going below to see them stowed away, so that we might know where each bale and package was to be found. Captain Magor was also on board assisting us, as were his two mates, Tom Sherwin and Ned Capstick, both rough, honest hands, as far as I could judge, who had been chosen by the master simply because they were good seamen and bold fellows in whom he could trust. While we stood by, notebooks in hand, it was their business to stow away the various packages; and as we were together many hours every day, we became pretty well acquainted before we sailed. We had a few hours left after the cargo was on board and the hatches fastened down.

I should have said I had made all the inquiries I could for Captain Roderick, but could hear nothing of him, nor did he ever come near Mr. Crank's house after he knew I saw him waiting at the door. I had another reason for supposing that he had gone. Mr. Trunnion had regained his usual spirits, and looked as cheerful as he did before his brother's appearance.

"You have acted discreetly, Westerton," said Mr. Trunnion to me one day when I was alone with him in his private room. "Whether Captain Magor was right or not in the fearful accusation he brought against that unhappy man. I know not. The

'Vulture' has, I trust, long since sailed. I wish you to under-stand that, although she was once our vessel, she does not now belong to us, and I need not say how I fear she is employed."

I was pleased to receive this commendation from my principal. I merely replied that I hoped to be always able to give him satis-faction in whatever way he might be pleased to employ me. He shook hands with me warmly on parting. "You will receive full written directions from the firm for your guidance while on the coast, and I hope that we shall see you and Bracewell back again well and hearty in a few months with a full cargo. I have great confidence in Captain Magor, into whose character, since he went to sea, we have made minute inquiries, and you will find him a bold and sagacious seaman, and an obliging and agreeable companion."

Before I left the counting-house, Mr. Swab called me into his little den, into which he was wont to retire whenever he had any private business to transact, although he generally sat in the outer office, that he might keep an eye on the clerks and see that there was no idling.

"My dear boy," he said in a kind tone, "I have had a talk with Harry, and now I want to speak with you, and I'll say to you what I said to him: Work together with a will; do not let the slightest feeling of jealousy spring up between you, and give and take. If he is right one time, you'll be ready to follow him the next; while, if your opinion proves correct, he will be ready to follow you. I am sure you will both act as you consider best for the interest of the firm; and remember there is One above who sees you, and you must do nothing which He disapproves of—your conscience will tell you that. You are to be engaged in a lawful traffic. If carried on fairly, it must of necessity tend to advance the interest of the Africans. We did them harm enough formerly when we were engaged in the slave trade, although I for one didn't see it at the time, and was entirely ignorant of the horrors it inflicted on the unfortunate natives. If I thought at all, I thought they exchanged barbarism for civilisation ; and what are called the horrors of the middle passage were not so great in those days as they are now, when the traffic has become unlawful. We had roomy vessels, the slaves were well fed and looked after; and the master had no fear of being chased by a man-of-war, so that they could wait in harbour when the weather was threatening, and run across the Atlantic with a favourable breeze. You will very likely see something of the business, and hear more of it while you are up the rivers ; but you must in no way interfere, either to help a slaver by supplying her with goods, provisions, or water, or by giving information to the man-of-war of her whereabouts, unless the question is asked, and you will then tell the truth. And now about your personal conduct. You must do all you can to keep your health. Be strictly sober. Do not expose yourself to the heat by day nor to the damp air by night, which is, I understand, more likely to prove injurious than even the sun's rays. Never lose your temper with the natives, or any one else, for that matter; and, from what I can learn, you are often likely to be tried. Many people fancy they show their spirit by losing their temper; in reality they always give an opponent an advantage over them, and the negroes are quick enough to perceive that. Do not imagine them fools because they do not understand your language. Indeed, I might say, as a golden rule, never hold too cheap the person with whom you are bargaining or an enemy with whom you are engaged in fighting. You will, of course, be very exact in all your accounts, and endeavour to obtain such information as you possibly can from all directions likely to prove of further use to the firm. Now, my dear boy, farewell. I pray that you and Harry may be protected from the dangers to which you will be exposed."

The worthy man said much more to the same purpose. The "Arrow" had, in the meantime, hauled out into the stream, and Harry and I went on board that evening, as she was to sail at daybreak, the tide being fair, the next morning. Mrs. Bracewel' and Mary accompanied us, very naturally wishing to see the last of us ; and just as we were setting out, Lucy Crank arrived, greatly to Harry's satisfaction.

"Papa did not object to my going, and I thought that Mrs. Bracewell and Mary would require some one to cheer them up," she said.

Mrs. Bracewell smiled, for Lucy did not look as if she was very well capable of doing that. She had evidently been crying, although she had done her best to dry her tears.

Just as we were at the water's edge, Mr. Swab joined us, remarking as he did so, " My partners are not able to come. I wanted to have a few more words with Captain Magor, so that I shall have the satisfaction of escorting you ladies back." I suspected that, in the kindness of his heart, the latter was his chief object.

" Thank you," said Mrs. Bracewell ; " we shall be glad of your protection. We wish to see Harry's and Mr. Westerton's cabin, and the brig, now that she is ready for sea, so that we may picture them to ourselves when they are far away."

The evening was serene, the water smooth as glass, the slight breeze blowing down the river, being insufficient to enable us to stem the flood tide, which had then begun to make up, or we should at once have sailed. Boats were plying backwards and forwards between the shore and the various vessels which lay in that much-frequented river. Some, like the " Arrow," ready for sea ; others only just arrived, or taking cargo on board from lighters. They were either bound to or had come from all parts of the world, the African traders perhaps predominating ; but there were not a few either going to or coming from the West Indies, with which Liverpool had a considerable commerce. There were South Sea whalers, high black vessels, with boats hoisted up on either side, and fast-sailing craft running up the Mediterranean, besides innumerable coasters. Indeed, Liverpool had become a successful rival of Bristol, hitherto the chief commercial port of the kingdom.

The ladies were well pleased with our little berths off the main cabin, for Captain Magor had done his best to make them comfortable. The cabin was well fitted, with a mahogany table, a sofa at the upper end, and two easy-chairs. A swinging lamp was suspended above us, while the bulkhead in the fore part was ornamented with muskets, pistols, and cutlasses ranged in symmetrical order. The brig carried seven guns, three on each side, and one long gun, which could be trained fore or aft to serve as a bow or stern chaser, while all told she had thirty hands, besides Harry and me; so that we were well able to cope with any ordinary enemy we were likely to meet with, either pirate or Frenchman, Spaniard or Hollander. The captain had prepared tea on board, or rather supper. Mr. Swab did his best to keep up the spirits of the party—which poor Lucy certainly failed in doing—by telling stories or cracking jokes, though he soon gave up the attempt when he saw none of us responded. Indeed, I must confess that both his jokes and stories were stale, and it might be added "flat and unprofitable." They did not flow naturally from him. At length he discovered that the time was passing on ; the shades of evening were already stealing over the broad surface of the magnificent stream. The boat belonging to the firm had hauled up alongside, and Harry and I helped the ladies into her, Mr. Swab following, and giving each of us a hearty shake of the hand. As the boat rowed away they waved an adieu with their handkerchiefs, which before they were out of sight all three applied to their eyes, and even then I could dis tinguish Mr. Swab frequently blowing his nose with his scarlet bandana.

Neither Harry nor I slept very soundly ; we had too much to think about to allow "nature's soft nurse," as the poet calls it, to visit our eyelids.

The boatswain's call roused up all hands. Quickly dressing, we were on deck. The dawn was just breaking in the eastern sky, from which direction there came a gentle breeze. The pilot was on board, the anchor hove up, the tide was making down, sail after sail was set, and just as there was light sufficient to enable us to see our way, the brig, under a cloud of white canvas, was standing down the Mersey.

"God bless you all! A prosperous voyage, and a safe and happy return!" was uttered by the pilot, as, having seen us clear of the sandbanks at the mouth of the river, he lowered himself into his boat and paddled off to his cutter, which had accompanied us. We were now left to our own resources, and before evening we were standing down the Irish Channel with a brisk breeze on the larboard tack.

CHAPTER III.

HARRY and I soon got our sea-legs, for although when we sailed the weather was fine, before we were well clear of the Irish Channel it began to blow fresh, and a heavy sea ran, which tumbled the vessel about not a little. We both quickly made the acquaintance of the officers and crew, for we did not consider it beneath our dignity as supercargoes to talk to our shipmates of lower rank. We were well repaid by the confidence they bestowed upon us, and the histories of their lives and adventures which they narrated. Although rough in their ways, they possessed many of the best qualities in human nature. The mates were, as I before said, good steady men, fair navigators, who could be trusted on all occasions, and had been chosen for these qualifications by Captain Magor, to whom they had long been known. Our chief friend was Tom Tubbs, the boatswain. Tom would have risen to a higher rank, but he was destitute of the accomplishments of reading and writing, though having to some purpose studied the book of nature, he possessed more useful knowledge than many of his fellow-men. He, like Tom Bowling, was the darling of the crew; for although he wielded his authority with a taut hand, he could be lenient when he thought it advisable, and was ever ready to do a kind action to any of his shipmates. He could always get them to do anything he wanted; for, instead of swearing at them, he used endearing expressions, such as "My loves," "My dear boys," "My charming lads." Thus, "My darlings," he would sing out, "be smart in handling that foretop-gallant-sail," or "Take down two reefs in the topsails, my cherubs," or when setting studding-sails, he would sing out, "Haul away, my angels," or again, when shortening sail, "Clew up—haul down, my lovely dears." He varied his expressions, however, according to the urgency of the case. If more speed was required, the more endearing were his words. I won't undertake to say that he did not sometimes rap out words of a very different signification, but that was only in extreme cases, when all others seemed to fail, or he had exhausted his vocabulary; but the men did not mind it a bit, for it only showed them that they must exert all their strength and activity if the masts were to be saved or the ship preserved from capsizing, or any other catastrophe prevented. The men were well aware of the motive which induced him to use strong expressions. We had two black men, who, having long served on board merchant vessels, spoke English pretty well. One of them, called Quambo, acted as steward; the other, Sambo, being ship's cook, spent a good portion of his time in the caboose, from which he carried on a conversation on either side with the men who happened to be congregated there. He, as well as Quambo, had to do duty as a seaman, and active fellows they were, as good hands as any of the crew. Sambo, besides his other accomplishments, could play the fiddle, and in calm weather the merry tones of his instrument would set all the crew dancing, making even Tom Tubbs shuffle about out of sight of the officers; for it would have been derogatory, he considered, to have been seen thus conducting himself in public. We had an Irishman, a Scotchman, three Fins, and a Portuguese, who was generally known as "Portinggall." The captain and the rest were Englishmen, two of whom had seen better days. One had been a schoolmaster and the other a lawyer's clerk. There was also a runaway from home of gentle birth, but who had so long mixed with rough characters, that not a trace of the good manners he once possessed remained by him.

We had got into the latitude of the Cape de Verde islands, and were looking out for the African coast, the wind being about east, when about two hours after noon the lookout at the mast-head shouted, " A sail in sight on the larboard bow."

On hearing this, the first mate, with a glass slung over his shoulder, went aloft to have a look at the stranger. He was some-time there, and when he returned on deck I thought by his countenance that he did not like her appearance.

"She's ship rigged, going free, and standing this way, sir," he said to the captain ; "and if we keep on our present course she will be within hail of us within a couple of hours at furthest. She may be a man-of-war cruiser, or an enemy's privateer, or an honest trader ; but were she that, I don't see why she should be standing this way, unless she thinks the wind will shift, and she wishes to get a good offing from Cape de Verde. Or else she may be one of the picarooning craft which we have heard of on this coast, although it has never been my ill luck to fall in with them."

" But it has been mine ; and though I had the good fortune to get clear of the rascal, I never wish to meet with one of her class again ; and so, in case yonder craft should be of that character, or an enemy's privateer, we shall do well to stand clear of her," said Captain Magor ; "and although we may lose a day or two, that will be better than running the risk of being captured or sent to the bottom. All hands make sail—up with the helm—square away the yards. Rig out the studding-sail booms, Mr. Sherwin," he added, addressing the first mate as soon as the ship was before the wind.

The boatswain sounded his whistle. "Be smart there, my sweet lads," he cried out. "Haul away, my lovely cherubs, on the starboard studding-sail halyards. Belay all that, my charmers;" and so he went on whistling and shouting, until we had studding-sails extended below and aloft on either side, and both royals set, and were running along at the rate of some seven or eight knots an hour before a light breeze.

Harry and I on all occasions lent a hand when we thought we could be of use, and Tom did not fail to bestow his approving remarks upon us. The first mate now went aloft to ascertain whether the stranger had again altered her course, or whether she was standing on as before, in which case we hoped to run her out of sight, when we could again haul on the wind. He remained some time aloft. When he came down he looked even graver than before.

"It is as I feared, sir. The fellow has clapped on all sail and is standing after us. It is a question which has the fastest pair of heels. If we can keep well ahead until nightfall, we may then alter our course and get clear of her."

"Perhaps, after all, she is only a British man-of-war, which takes us for a slaver, or perhaps for an enemy's cruiser; for the 'Arrow,' I flatter myself, doesn't look like an ordinary trader," observed Captain Magor.

"That may be, sir," answered the mate, "but we are doing the wisest thing to keep out of her way; and, as you said, it's better to do that and lose a day or two, than be snapped up by an enemy."

The captain ordered all hands to remain on deck at their stations, ready to shorten sail at a moment's notice. I saw him frequently look astern, not so much at the stranger as at the appearance of the clouds.

"Do you think she is coming up with us, Captain Magor?" I asked.

"No doubt about that, though she is carrying less sail than we are. She has got a stronger breeze, and I am watching lest the wind should come down on us harder than our sticks can stand."

A few minutes afterwards, as I moved to the fore part of the quarter-deck, where the boatswain was standing, the captain cried out, "All hands shorten sail."

In an instant Tom's whistle was at his mouth, and didn't he stamp and shout.

"In with the studding-sails, my lovely lads; let fly top-gallant sheets, my sweet angels. Haul down, trice up, my pretty boys." Though what between the orders issued by the captain and mates, and repeated by him, with the howling of the wind and the whistling of his shrill pipe, the rattling and creaking of the blocks, and the fluttering of the sails, it was difficult for ears unnautical to comprehend the actual words uttered. All to me seemed hubbub and confusion. The men flew here and there, some going aloft, while others came tramping along the deck with the ropes. Even Captain Magor and the mates were pulling and hauling. Harry and I caught hold of the ropes they gave us, and ran along with them to gather in the fluttering canvas, which seemed as if it would be blown to shreds before it could be secured. As it was, a foreroyal was carried away and a studding-sail boom was snapt off. Before we had time to stow the lighter canvas the squall came down thick and strong on us. The order was given to clew up the courses and take a reef in the topsails. The wind, though coming off the land, quickly beat the ocean into wild tossing waves, through which the brig dashed forward with lessened sail, yet still with increased speed. A thick misty appearance, caused by a fine impalpable sand brought off the land by the squall, soon hid the stranger from sight.

"It's an ill wind that blows nobody good," observed the mate; "and I hope we shall be in luck, and get out of the way of that fellow; I don't like his looks, that I don't."

What Captain Magor thought about the matter he did not say. He kept the brig away, running as before, which showed that he considered the stranger was still in pursuit of us. Harry and I looked out for her, but she was nowhere to be seen.

"Perhaps the squall took her unawares and carried away her masts; if so, and she is an enemy, we may thank the wind for the service it has rendered us," observed the first mate.

"There's little chance of that, I fear," said Captain Magor. "When it clears up again we shall see her all ataunto, or I am much mistaken."

We all continued looking out anxiously over the taffrail, while the brig ploughed her way through the fast rising seas, which hissed and foamed around her.

The captain paced the deck, now looking aft, now aloft, waiting for the moment when he could venture to make sail again. The men stood with their hands on the halyards, ready to hoist away at the expected order, for all on board knew the importance of keeping ahead of the stranger should she be what we suspected. Still the atmosphere remained charged with dust off the coast, which, as the rays of the sun fell upon it, assumed a yellowish hue. At any moment, however, it might dissolve, and already it had sunk lower than when it first came on. Before long we had evidence that the captain's surmise was correct, for just over the thick bank astern we caught sight through our glasses of a fine perpendicular line against the sky, which he asserted were the royal masts of the stranger, with the royals still furled. If he was right—and of that there appeared little doubt—she must have gained rapidly on us. The best we could hope for was that the mist would continue until nightfall and shroud us from her sight. The setting sun, it should be understood, cast its light upon her masts, while ours were still in the shade. We were doomed, however, to disappointment; suddenly the mist cleared off, and the bright rays of the sun exposed to view the topsails and courses of our pursuer.

"We may still keep ahead of her, and when night comes on give her the slip," observed Captain Magor; "if not, we will fight her. The men, I hope, will stand to their guns, and show that they are British seamen. It will be a disgrace to knock under to piratical villains, such as I fear are the crew of yonder craft."

"The men are staunch, I'll answer for that," observed Mr. Serwin. "Tubbs has had a talk with them to try their tempers, and he is as true a fellow as ever stepped."

"That he is; and if you and I and the second mate should be killed, he will fight the ship as long as a stick is standing," answered the first mate, showing his appreciation of the boatswain's character. Harry and I, as we walked the deck, agreed that we would fight to the last, though we heartily wished that we might escape the stern necessity. Before long the captain shouted—

"Shake out the reefs in the fore-topsail, my lads."

The topmen flew aloft and the sail was hoisted. Soon afterwards the captain gave the order to set the foretop-gallantsail.

"We must get preventer braces on it," he observed to the first mate; "it won't do to run the risk of carrying away the spar."

The additional ropes were quickly secured by the active crew. As they stood aft watching the sail, it seemed as if at any moment it would carry away the mast and spar, as, bulging out with the strong breeze, it strained and tugged in its efforts to free itself, but the sticks were tough and the ropes which held them sound, and with increased speed the brig flew before the gale. Two of the best hands were at the wheel, for any carelessness in steering might in an instant have produced a serious disaster. The effects of the additional sail were satisfactory, as the stranger was no longer gaining on us, as she had hitherto done. Still, as I felt the violent blows given by the seas, now on one quarter, now on the other, the brig now pitching into a hollow ahead, now rising rapidly over another sea, then rolling from side to side, I feared that the masts must be jerked out of her. Harry and I found it scarcely possible to walk the deck without being tossed about like shuttlecocks, so that our only resource was to hold fast to the stanchions, or, when we wanted to move, to catch hold of the bulwarks. As night approached, however, the wind began to decrease, and the sea, having no great distance to run, went down. Whether this was likely to be an advantage to us or not was now to be proved. As the last rays of the sun ere he set glanced horizontally across the ocean, they fell on the stranger's canvas down to the foot of her courses. Still our stout-hearted captain did not despair.

"We will do what we can to give the fellow the go-by, and may outwit him, clever as he thinks himself," he said, laughing. "Aloft there, and set the fore-royal," he shouted; and this being done, the foretopmast studding-sails were again rigged out, thus exhibiting a broad sheet of canvas to the eyes of our pursuer, which would probably make him suppose that we intended to continue our course directly before the wind. The sun had now sunk, but we could yet distinguish through the fast gathering gloom the sail astern. Captain Magor now ordered the mainsail to be hauled out, and the main-topsail and maintop-gallant-sail to be set. By the time this was done, not even the outlines of the stranger could be perceived astern.

"Take in studdin'-sails," cried the captain.

These by the united efforts of the crew, wildly fluttering, were hauled down without a spar being lost. The fore-royal was then furled. "Starboard the helm," was the next order given. "Haul on the starboard fore and main braces," he then sang out, and the brig was brought to the wind on the larboard tack. No sooner did she feel its power, as the yards were braced sharp up, the tacks hauled down, and the braces and bowlines sheeted home, than she heeled over to the force of the wind, which was still considerable, although it did not appear so when we were running before it.

"If the stranger does not discover our change of course, she will be well away to leeward before morning, and we shall see no more of her," said Captain Magor, addressing Harry and me. "I don't want to expose the lives of you young gentlemen to danger, or to risk the loss of our cargo. I daresay you felt not a little anxious, but you may turn in and sleep soundly, with the prospect of making the coast of Africa in another day or two at furthest. We will have some food first though, for you have been on deck ever since dinner; you'll be hungry. Quambo!" he shouted, "let's have some supper on table as soon as possible."

"Him dare 'ready, captain," answered the black steward, "only wait de young gen'lemen to cut him."

The captain, leaving the deck in charge of the first mate, descended with us, and did ample justice to the plentiful meal Quambo had spread on the table. The captain, before going on deck again, advised us to turn in. We were, however, too anxious to do so, notwithstanding his assertions that all was likely to go well, and we therefore soon joined him on deck. We found him looking out over the larboard quarter, the direction in which the stranger was most likely to be seen. Although we swept the ocean with our glasses round two-thirds of the horizon, she was nowhere visible. At length, trusting that the captain really was right, with our minds tolerably relieved, we went below and turned into our berths. Still, though I slept, I could not get the thought of the pirate out of my mind. I dreamed that I was again on deck, and that I saw our pursuer, like some monster of the deep, her canvas towering high above our own towards the sky, close to us. Then she poured forth her broadsides, her shot with a crashing, rending sound passing across our deck. Still we remained unharmed, and I heard the captain say, "Give it them again, my lads—give it them again." Our crew sprung to their guns; but there came another broadside from the enemy which carried away our masts and spars, pierced our bulwarks, knocking our boats to pieces. Still Harry and I stood on deck uninjured, and our crew appeared as undaunted and active as before. I have often heard of people "fighting their battles o'er again ;" but in this instance I fought mine before it occurred. I was awakened by the stamping sound of the feet of the watch overhead as they ran along with the halyards; then came the cry, "All hands on deck." I jumped out of my berth, and found Harry slipping into his clothes. No one else was in the cabin. We hurried on deck, where the officers and the watch below with the idlers had assembled. I was surprised to find the brig once more before the wind and the crew engaged in making all sail. The captain was standing aft issuing his orders, while the mates and boatswain were aiding the men in pulling and hauling. We joined them without asking questions. Some of the crew were aloft setting the top-gallant-sails and royals. I wondered why this was done, but there was no time to ask questions. At last, all the sail the brig could carry was set. I then, having nothing further to do, went aft and asked the captain the reason of the change of course.

" If you look astern you will see it," he said.

Shading my eyes with my hand, I gazed into the darkness, and there I at length discovered what the more practised eyes of the captain had long seen—the shadowy form of the stranger coming up under all sail towards us.

"You see now why we have kept away," observed the captain. " Before the wind is our fastest point of sailing, and I wish that we had kept on it from the first. That fellow out there must have hauled his wind soon after we lost sight of him."

" Do you think she will come up with us ? " I asked.

" There is a great likelihood that she will," answered the captain ; "but a stern chase is a long chase, as every one knows. Perhaps we may fall in with a man-of-war cruiser, when the tables will be turned; if not, as I said before, we must fight her."

" With all my heart," I answered ; and Harry echoed my words.

The stranger had by this time approached much nearer to us than before, or we should have been unable to see her. We could thus no longer hope for an opportunity of escaping by altering our course.

"It is my duty to stand on as long as I can, to give ourselves every chance of meeting with another craft, which may take a part in the game," observed the captain. "At all events, it will be daylight before we get within range of her guns, and you young gentlemen may as well turn in in the meantime and finish your night's rest."

Neither I nor Harry had any inclination, however, to do this. The dream I had had still haunted my imagination, and I felt pretty sure that were I to go to sleep it would come back as vividly as before. Stepping into the waist, I found Mr. Tubbs, the boatswain.

"Well, Tom, what do you think about the matter?" I asked. "Shall we have a brush with yonder craft which seems so anxious to make our acquaintance?"

"No doubt about it, Mr. Westerton, and more than a brush too, I suspect. That ship out there is a big fellow, and will prove a tough customer. We shall have to show the stuff we are made of, and fight hard to beat him off. I don't say but that we shall do it, but it will cost us dearly; for his people, we may be sure, know how to handle their guns; and from the height of his canvas I should say that he was twice our size, and probably carries double as many guns as we do, and musters three or four times more men."

"Then I'm afraid that we shall have but a poor chance of beating him off," I observed.

"There are always chances in war, and one of them may be in our favour; so it is our business to fight hard to the end. A happy shot may knock away his masts and render him helpless, or enter his magazine and blow him up; or we may send half a dozen of our pills between wind and water, and compel him to keep all hands at the pumps, so that he will have no time to look after us."

"But the same may happen to us," observed Harry.

"Granted; those belong to the chances of war," answered Tom. "I was only speaking of those in our favour. We must not think of the others; if the worst comes to the worst, we can but go to the bottom with our colours flying, as many pretty men have had to do before."

On the whole, Tom's remarks did not greatly increase our spirits. Harry and I walked aft together.

"One of us may fall, Dick," said Harry to me in a grave tone. "If I do, you will carry my last fond love to my mother and sister and poor Lucy, and say that my last thoughts were about them."

"That I will," I answered. "And should I fall and you escape, you will see my parents, and tell your mother and sister Mary how to the last moment of my life I thought of them—how grateful I am for all their kindness to me."

The expressions we exchanged were but natural to young men who were about to engage for the first time in their lives in a desperate battle—for desperate we knew it must be, even should we come off victorious, if the stranger astern was, as we supposed, a pirate. We paced the deck together. The suspense we were doomed to undergo was more trying than when we were engaged in making or shortening sail, and the gale was blowing and the vessel tumbling about.

Now we were gliding calmly on, with nothing to do except occasionally to take a look astern at our expected enemy. I began to long for daylight, and wished even to see the stranger come up within shot, so that we might ascertain to a certainty her true character. At length a ruddy glow appeared beyond her in the east, gradually increasing in depth and brightness until the whole sky was suffused with an orange tint, and the sun, like a vast ball of fire, rose rapidly above the horizon, forming a glowing background to the sails of our pursuer, who came gliding along over the shining ocean towards us. Already she was almost within range of our long gun, which the captain now ordered to be trained aft through one of the stern-ports. The gun was loaded and run out.

"Shall I fire, sir?" asked Tom Tubbs, who acted as gunner as well as boatswain, running his eye along the piece.

"Not until we can see her flag," answered the captain; "she may, after all, be a man-of-war. If we fire she may take us for a pirate, and we should get small credit for our bravery. We shall see her colours presently if she yaws to fire at us. Wait until I give the word."

In the meantime the magazine had been opened and powder and shot brought up on deck; the guns were loaded and run out, the arm-chest was also got up, and Harry and I, as did all on board, girded hangers to our sides and thrust pistols into our belts.

The captain shortly afterwards issued the order for all hands to be ready to shorten sail as soon as no chance remained of escaping without fighting. Even now there was a hope that we might get away, or that the stranger might after all prove a friend instead of a foe; every rope was therefore kept belayed. "Long Tom," as the boatswain called his gun, was run out, it should be understood, under the poop on which Harry and I stood. The captain had taken his post near the mizen rigging, so that he could see all parts alike, and his voice could be heard by Tom and the crew of the gun below him.

The mates were at their stations ready to shorten sail. I had my spyglass turned towards our pursuer, endeavouring to get a glimpse of her flag should she have hoisted one, which she very certainly would have done were she a King's ship. As I watched her, I could see that she was gaining upon us. Objects which at first appeared indistinct were now clearly visible. I could make out the men on the forecastle, but I saw no gun there with which she could return the compliment our "Long Tom" was about to pay her. So far this was satisfactory.

"Were she a King's ship she would have fired a gun without altering her course, as a signal for us to heave to," observed the captain.

Scarcely had he spoken than the stranger yawed—a gun was fired, and a shot came towards us, striking the water and sinking close under our counter. At the same moment, raising my glass, I caught sight of the British ensign flying from the end of the peak.

"Hurrah!" I exclaimed; "she's a King's ship, and we are all right."

"We must not be too sure of that," observed Harry; "pirates can hoist false colours. We want better proof of her honesty before we heave to. Had she been well disposed, she would not have sent that iron messenger after us."

For some time longer the "Arrow" stood on her course, while the stranger, keeping directly astern, did not alter hers. I expected every moment to hear our captain give the word to fire, but he refrained from doing so. Suspicious as was the behaviour of our pursuer, still I thought it possible that, after all, she might be a King's ship, and had shown her proper colours. Presently, however, she yawed, her studding-sails fluttering as she did so, being almost taken back. Two spouts of flame, followed quickly by a couple of round shot, issued from her bow-ports. That the shot were fired with evil intent was evident, for one struck our larboard quarter close below where I was standing, and knocked away the carved work, while the other, flying high, passed close above our heads, and fell into the water not a dozen fathoms from the ship. Before her helm could again be put up, Captain Magor shouted, "Give it them, Tubbs," and our "Long Tom," with a loud roar, sending forth a spout of flame, pitched a shot right through the fore part of her bulwarks, and I could see the splinters fly as it struck them.

"Load and fire away as fast as you can," cried the captain; "if that's a King's ship, she fired first, and must take the conse quences."

I should have felt more satisfied had I been convinced that the captain was right, but still I could not help fancying that she was a royal cruiser, and that we might be committing a terrible mistake. Shot after shot was now aimed at our pursuer. Tom Tubbs and his men hauling in and loading the gun with a rapidity which only well-trained hands could have done. Few of our shots—as far as I could judge—appeared to be so successfully aimed as the first had been. Still I heard Captain Magor shouting out, "Well done, my lads; never saw a gun better served. Wing her if you can; knock away her foremast, and twenty golden guineas shall be yours."

The stranger all this time did not return our fire, for she could not bring her foremost guns to bear without yawing, and by doing so she would have lost ground. She was still gaining on us, and I observed at length that she had slightly altered her course, so as to be creeping up on our starboard quarter, though so slightly, that at first the alteration was not perceived. Captain Magor took two or three short turns on the poop, then suddenly stopping, he shouted, "In with the studding-sails, send down the royals," and presently afterwards, when this was done, "Furl top-gallant-sails." He had evidently made up his mind that escape was impossible, and was determined to fight the stranger should she prove an enemy. Active as were our crew, some minutes passed before sail was shortened, by which time the stranger had crept up on our quarter. She had hitherto kept all her canvas standing. We were still running before the wind. I saw the captain give a steady look at her.

"I know her now. She is the 'Vulture,' and we can expect no mercy if we are taken," he exclaimed, turning to Harry and me, his countenance exhibiting the anxiety he felt in the discovery, although the next moment he spoke in the same firm tone as usual. "The men stationed at the starboard guns be ready to fire," he cried out. "Brace the yards to larboard."

Before, however, the words were out of his mouth, the stranger's crew were seen swarming aloft. The yards and tops were covered with men, and with a rapidity far excelling anything we were capable of, the studding-sails were taken in, the royals and top-gallant-sails furled, and just as our helm was put down, and we were about to luff across her bow, she luffed up and let fly a broadside of ten guns in return for our three. At the same moment, as I looked aft, expecting still to see the ensign of Old England flying from her peak, I beheld a black piratical flag with the death's head and cross-bones, which had evidently been hoisted to strike terror into the hearts of our crew. At that instant I heard the same crashing, rending sounds which had disturbed my slumbers, as the shot tore their way through our bulwarks, some striking the masts, others cutting away the shrouds and knocking a boat to pieces. I saw one man fall at the after-guns, while two more were binding handkerchiefs round their arms, showing that they had been struck either by shot or splinters. Having missed the opportunity of raking the enemy, we were now placed in a disadvantageous position to leeward. Still Captain Magor was not the man to give in. He ordered "Long Tom" to be dragged from its present position, and run through the foremost port.

"If the enemy have more guns than we have, we must make amends by firing ours twice as fast as she does," he cried out in a cheerful tone. "Cheer up, my lads. Toss the pieces in, and give the villains more than they bargain for."

Harry and I hastened to one of the guns, at which three of the crew had already been killed or disabled, and we exerted ourselves to the utmost. I confess that I have a somewhat confused idea of what now occurred. I was thinking only of how I could best help in loading and running out the gun at which I had stationed myself. All my thoughts and energies were concentrated on that; but I remember hearing the cries and groans of my shipmates as they were shot down, the tearing and crashing of the shot as they struck our devoted craft, the blocks falling from aloft, the shouts of the officers, and the occasional cheers of the men, and seeing the ropes hanging in festoons, the sails in tatters, wreck and confusion around us, with wreaths of smoke. Then I remember observing the pirate ship, which had approached us closer and closer, come with a louder crash than any previous sounds alongside. Grapplings were thrown on to our bulwarks, then a score or more of ruffianly looking fellows with hangers flashing leapt down on our decks. We fired our pistols and drew our own blades, and for a few minutes fought with desperation; then Harry and I, with Tom Tubbs and the captain, were borne back towards the poop, where, as we stood for a few seconds, keeping our enemies at bay, we saw that, overwhelmed by numbers, all hope of successful resistance was vain. Captain Magor shouted to us to sell our lives dearly, but just then I heard a voice exclaim, "Drop your weapons and you shall have your lives, for you have fought like brave fellows." Gazing at the speaker, whom I had not before recognised among the boarders, I beheld one whose countenance I knew. Yes! I had no doubt about the matter, he was Captain Roderick Trunnion. At his heels followed a huge mastiff, who growled fiercely as his master was addressing us. Whether or not Captain Roderick recognised Harry or me, we neither of us could tell.

"We had better make a virtue of necessity," said the captain, dropping his sword; and I with the rest of the party did the same, for we could not suppose that our captors intended afterwards to slaughter us. One of the officers of the pirate, stepping up, took our weapons, which we handed to him; and as our assailants now separated, apparently to plunder the vessel, the fearful condition of our deck was exposed to view. In every direction were our poor fellows dead or wounded, including the two mates, one of whom had his head knocked off, while the other was cut almost in two by a round shot. Planks were torn up where the shot had ploughed their way along them; blocks, entangled ropes, shattered spars, fragments of the bulwarks and boats, and pieces of sails, were scattered about amid large splashes of blood. The pirates, now masters of the vessel, began at once to heave the dead overboard, several still breathing, who might have recovered, being treated in the same way. Every moment I expected that the miscreants would compel us to walk the plank, but for a wonder they appeared satisfied with their victory.

Captain Trunnion did not appear to recognise us, though he fixed his eyes on Captain Magor in a very ominous way.

"I know you," he said, approaching him; "you once did me a good turn by picking me out of the water. I should probably otherwise have served for a dinner to a hungry shark close at my heels; but you counterbalanced that by the scurvy trick you endeavoured to play me at Liverpool. However, as no harm was done, except that my brother was not quite so affectionate as he might have been, I'll overlook that, and I tell you I don't wish to have your blood or that of any other man on my hands. Now, listen to me, and if you are a sensible person, you will accept my offer and save your life. I happen to have no one on board whom I can spare capable of navigating the vessel. I intend to put a prize-crew on board this craft, and leave you some of your own men, and if you take her and them safe into the Sherbro River, you shall have your liberty and go wherever you like after the vessel has sailed. I must send a man on board to act as mate who will stand no nonsense. If you prove true, he'll be civil; but if not, you may expect to have your brains blown out at a moment's notice. You understand me?"

I watched Captain Magor's countenance, to judge whether he would accept the offer or not. I hoped that he would do so, and that we should be allowed to accompany him. He placed his hand on his brow as he paced several times up and down the deck.

"I accept your offer." he said at length. He did not, I

remarked, address Captain Roderick by his proper name. "You will, I hope, allow my two passengers to accompany me, and the boatswain, who, although not a navigator, is a first-rate seaman, and will be of great assistance to me."

" No, no, my friend. I intend these two young gentlemen, who, by the way they fought, have shown themselves to be fine spirited fellows, to accompany me; and the character you give of the boatswain makes me wish to have him on board my craft, where, to tell you the truth, I have not got too many able seamen. You may consider yourself very fortunate at being allowed the privilege I offer you, so say no more about the matter."

These remarks destroyed the hopes Harry and I had entertained that we might get free of the pirate and erelong obtain our liberty. Poor Tubbs looked very much cast down. Knowing him well, I was sure he was not a man who would join with the pirates, although Captain Roderick might employ every means to win him over. We were not long left in suspense as to our fate.

" Now, my lads," exclaimed the pirate captain, addressing Harry and me, "make your way on board my ship, and you follow them," he added turning to Tubbs.

We had just time to shake hands with Captain Magor, whose countenance showed the sorrow and anxiety he felt, when, at a sign from Captain Roderick, several of his men seized us by the shoulders, and hurried us on board the "Vulture." Tubbs then, giving an involuntary shrug of his shoulders, as if resigned to his fate, followed us; the savage growls of the dog making us dread that he would seize one of us by the leg, and so I have no doubt that he would have done at a sign from his master. The deck of the pirate presented much the same scene as did that of the "Arrow." Our shot had done no little damage to the hull and rigging, while several of her crew were dead or dying. Their shipmates were in the act of heaving the bodies overboard, although they did not treat those who were still breathing as they did our poor fellows. A few of them, more compassionate than the rest, were endeavouring to staunch the blood flowing from the limbs and sides of the wounded men. Harry, Tubbs, and I, finding that no one interfered with us, knelt down beside three of the men who were unable to move on the after part of the deck. The wretched beings were crying out for help and mercy. Two of them were evidently suffering fearfully from thirst.

"I'll get some water ; it will do them good," said Tubbs, and making his way to a water-cask which stood on deck, from which he filled a tin mug, he brought it back to the men. They all drank eagerly, one of them, however, in the very act, fell back and expired. The others cast a look at their shipmate. Such might be their fate. "Take him away," groaned one of them. "I cannot help casting my eyes on him, and he is terrible to look upon." In truth, the man's countenance, distorted with pain, bore a horrible expression. We dragged the body forward, that his shipmates might dispose of it as they thought fit. We were so eagerly engaged in attending to the wounded men, that we did not observe that the vessels had been cast loose from each other, and that Captain Roderick had returned on board. We were aroused by hearing his voice issuing orders to his crew to make sail. We cast a look over the bulwarks, where we saw the "Arrow," from which we were greatly increasing our distance, her people busily employed in repairing damages, knotting and splicing the running rigging, getting fresh yards across, and bending new sails. The work was still going on when the "Vulture," having made sail and steering to the south-east, ran her out of sight.

CHAPTER IV.

WE were treated with more leniency than we could have expected on board the " Vulture," in consequence, I believe, of our having attended to the wounded.

" We have no doctor on board, and you and your friends may look after those fellows, and try to patch them up," said the pirate captain to me the day after the action. " I cannot spare the boatswain, as he is wanted to do duty as a seaman. Remember that I might have clapped you down in the cable tier, or, had I chosen, made you walk the plank, as many have done before ; but I don't want to have the deaths of more men than I can help at my door, even though I run the risk of losing my life in consequence of my leniency."

" We will continue to look after the wounded as long as we are able," I answered. I thought it prudent not to expend any thanks on him, for which he would not have cared, nor to show any very great satisfaction at being left at liberty, as he might have suspected that we were contemplating plans for our escape, nor would he have been far off the truth. Harry and I, when we were certain that no one was listening, had discussed the matter, intending to let Tom Tubbs into our plan, and invite him to join us. At present, however, we had no means of holding communica- tion with him. He was sent forward, while we remained either on the quarter-deck, or in a sort of cockpit to which the wounded had been carried. It was a dark, close place, its only advantage being that it was out of the way of shot in action. In the course of a few hours, death removed all but six of our patients and Harry and I had enough to do to attend to them. They were groan- ing and complaining all day long, and constantly calling out for liquor, though, when we supplied them with water instead, they drank it greedily, sometimes fancying that it was what they had asked for. We kept them constantly supplied with liquid, which, although often hot and tepid, appeared like nectar to their fevered lips. No one interfered with us. How the poor fellows would have fared had they been left to themselves I know not, but I suspect that they would have been allowed to suffer with very little com- miseration felt for them. Still all this time our position was far from comfortable. I was doubtful how Captain Roderick might treat Harry. I had no doubt that he knew who he was, though he had never addressed him by name; indeed, after having spoken to us about the wounded men, he took no further notice of us, allow- ing us to take our food in the cockpit, and to sleep in a couple of hammocks which were slung there, which had belonged to two of the men who had been killed. We had to do everything for our- selves, the seamen being either surly to us or rude. Harry and I separately, on two different occasions, endeavoured to speak to Tubbs, but a man immediately stepped up and asked us what we wanted, he having, I suppose, been directed by the Captain to watch us and Tubbs, to see that we held no communication, while Growler—for so we found that the captain's dog was called—came snuffing and growling round and round us, ready to fall to and tear us to pieces at the word of command. We fortunately had fine weather as we continued our voyage towards the Bight of Biafara, for which we were bound. All this time we did not lose the hope of falling in with a British man-of-war by which we might be rescued. Day after day passed by, but not a sail hove in sight. That Captain Roderick thought such might be the case seemed probable, as he was constantly on the watch, and exercising his men both at the guns, and with small arms and cutlasses ; and I felt certain that, sooner than surrender, he would fight to the last, and then blow up the ship. It appeared to me that he had become more desperate than he had been when he last paid a visit to Liverpool. Indeed, he must have known that he could never again show his face there, should either Harry or I, or Captain Magor, or the boatswain, find our way back. Probably, however, he counted on our never doing so. It was not a pleasant feeling to know that he might consider his interest advanced by effectually preventing us from again seeing our native land. The wounded men made fair progress towards recovery under our care, but when not attending them, Harry and I found time hang very heavily on our hands. We had no books, and were afraid of conversing except on indifferent subjects, for fear of being overheard. Even the men we were attending might betray us should we say anything at which the captain might take offence. Our life was therefore, as may be supposed, anything but a pleasant one. We went on deck occasionally very early in the morning or after sunset, when the shades of night prevented our being observed, and generally managed to get a few turns together to stretch our legs and breathe the fresh air ; for had we always remained in the close hold, I do not suppose that we could have retained our health. Our chief amusement was endeavouring to win our way into the good graces of Growler, and gradually we succeeded in doing so, though we of course took good care not to let it be seen that we were on friendly terms with him. We were very thankful when at length, early one morning, we heard the cry from the look-out at the mast head—

"Land, oh !"

Both Harry and I felt a strong impulse to run aloft and have a look at it, but this we dared not do. It was some time, therefore, before we saw the shore from the deck. We could then make out a line of mangrove-trees, with blue hills rising to a considerable height in the distance. The mangrove-trees marked the entrance of the river up which we were bound. We stood on until within about four miles of the shore, when it fell a dead calm. There the brig lay, rolling her sides in the smooth burnished water on which she floated. We could now perceive, projecting from among the mangrove bushes, a long spit of white sand, from which to the opposite shore ran a line of foam, marking the bar which we had to cross. The heat was intense, making the pitch bubble up between the seams of the deck, while down below the air was horribly stifling. It seemed surprising that the poor wounded fellows could live in it ; but they had got accustomed to a close atmosphere, I suppose, and were, at all events, saved from feeling the direct rays of the sun. The whites of the crew sough! shelter wherever a particle of shade existed, although the black and brown men, of whom there were several, appeared indifferent to the heat—the black cook and his mate actually sitting on the top of the caboose and smoking their pipes, with the advantage of a fire beneath them. I expected to see them begin to broil, but they were evidently enjoying themselves. Thus it lasted for . a couple of hours, until the sea-breeze set in, when all sail was instantly made, and the ship was headed up for the bar. The breeze increased. As we got nearer we caught sight of a canoe and half a dozen black fellows coming off to assist us. We accordingly hove to, that they might be able to get up the side, when a huge fellow in a broad-brimmed straw hat and a pair of trousers with pink stripes came on deck, and walking up to the captain, shook hands with him as with an old friend.

"Ah, massa cap'n, glad to see you 'gain. You take plent' slavy—him dare all ready," and he pointed up the river.

"All right, Master Pogo. Take care that you don't put my ship ashore though, as you did Captain Watman's. I wonder he did not shoot you through the head for your carelessness. I wouldn't scruple to do so, let me tell you."

Pogo grinned and shrugged his shoulders. "Me take good care, cap'n," he answered; and stepping up to the break of the poop, he took his post there that he might con the vessel. He looked around him and then surveyed the shore.

"Starboard a little," he sung out. "Now steady, dat will do. Now we go in like shot," he added, turning to the captain, who significantly touched the butt of one of the pistols in his belt.

As the line of surf was approached, Pogo became more energetic in his actions. He shouted to the crew, "Stand by the braces, tacks, and sheets!" The wind began to fail, and he knew well that a puff coming down the river might take the ship aback, and drive her on shore before there was time to drop an anchor. For an instant her sails fluttered. He began to dance about and wring his hands, looking at the captain's belt as if he expected every moment to see the pistol sticking in it pointed at his head; but happily for him the sails again filled, and the breeze increasing, the ship, after pitching three or four times, glided on into smooth water. We were now free of all danger for the present. There was nothing very attractive in the appearance of the river. As far as the eye could reach, we could distinguish only mangrove bushes rising apparently out of the water itself. Except a hut or two at the inner end of the sandy point I have described, not a human habitation was to be perceived, and scarcely a canoe dotted the broad expanse of the river as we glided up it, stemming the current with the strong sea-breeze which had now set in. As we got higher up, an occasional opening in the mangrove bushes showed us a more attractive looking country, with cocoa-nut, fig, and other trees, and native huts nestled beneath them; but it was not until we had got about twenty miles from the mouth of the river that any sign of a numerous population appeared. At length we prepared to come to an anchor off a village from which a wooden stage projected into the river. Beyond it were several long sheds of considerable extent, which were ere long discovered to be barracoons or sheds for the reception of slaves brought down from the interior to be embarked. The anchor was dropped, the sails were furled. What now was to be our fate? The captain had interfered so little with us, that we hoped he would allow us to go on shore, and that we might be able from thence to make our way down the river, and get on board a lawful trader or man-of-war. I proposed to Harry that I should at once ask him. Just as I was about to do so, I heard him order the wounded men to be brought up and placed in a boat alongside. I thought that now was a good opportunity.

"I am afraid, sir, that these men are scarcely in a fit state to be removed; unless they have some one to look after them, they are very likely to lose their lives."

"You may accompany them," he said, "but remember that you do not go beyond the village, or you will stand a chance of being knocked on the head. The blacks are not very fond of strange white men hereabouts."

Of course Harry and I did not consider ourselves bound to follow his directions in this instance, nor had we given any promise to do so. Before we left the ship, we found that the crew were preparing her for the reception of slaves. Some were hoisting up her cargo and placing it either on deck or in the after-cabin ready for trade, and others were fixing in a slave-deck fore and aft, while casks of water and bags of farina were being brought on board in large quantities. I was thankful to see Tom Tubbs in the boat which was to convey the wounded men on shore. He gave us a wink as we went down the side, and I saw that he took the stroke oar, so that he would have an opportunity of speaking to us. The ship was some distance off the bank, for there was not sufficient depth of water to enable her to come nearer. It took us, therefore, nearly ten minutes to reach the shore.

"I'll lend a hand to carry one of these poor fellows," observed Tom, giving me a meaning look as he pulled away. "I suppose Mr. Bracewell will help us?"

I turned to Harry, and of course he said "yes." Two of the men were able to walk, but the other three were still too weak to help themselves. The crew of the boat, therefore, took two of the latter up on their shoulders, and Tubbs, Harry, and I lifted the third. Harry carried the man's feet; Tubbs and I supported him by our arms and shoulders.

"We shall be here for more than a week, I suspect," said Tubbs as we walked along. "I must come on shore to see how these poor fellows are getting on, and may be you may fancy a walk into the country, either up the river or down the river, as you wish."

The habitation selected for the accommodation of the wounded was far superior to what I expected to find. It was, indeed, the house of a white slave-dealer and general trader, who, with his clerks, was now away, and Captain Roderick had thought fit to take possession of it. A large airy room in which eight hammocks were slung, afforded quarters for our five patients and to Harry and me.

"I wish that you could occupy the other," I said to Tubbs; "we should be glad to have your assistance. Couldn't you ask the captain's leave, and say that we want you to help us to look after the wounded?"

The boatswain shook his head. "Not much chance of his granting it; he would suspect that there was something in the wind; but I'll keep my weather eye open, and if I have a chance I'll come on shore. If you determine to try and make your escape, it must be just before the 'Vulture' sails, or the captain will be sending to look for you," he whispered. "Good-bye, gentlemen," he added aloud; "glad to see you on board again."

We found a couple of blacks in the house—an old man and a woman, servants of the owner,—left to look after it. They appeared well disposed, and brought us food and everything we required for ourselves and the wounded men. The latter—ruffians as they may have been—were very grateful to us, and one and all declared that they would not have received such attention from their own shipmates.

"I should think you must be pretty well sick of the life you have been leading," I ventured to say in a low voice to one of them, who appeared to be of a better disposition than the rest.

"That indeed I am, sir," he answered, the tears coming into his eyes. "I'd leave it to-morrow if I could, for I know a sudden death or a bowline-knot will be my lot some day or other."

"What do your wounded shipmates think about the subject?" I asked.

"I cannot say positively; but my idea is that they would be glad enough to get free if they had the chance," was the answer.

I did not venture to make any remark in return, but the thought then occurred to me that we might possibly all escape together. If we could procure arms, we should form a pretty strong party, and might fight our way in any direction in which it might be advisable to go. The French had a settlement on that part of the coast, so had the Portuguese further south; but the English had none except a long way to the north. Still, as ships of war and traders occasionally appeared off the coast, could we once reach it, we might make signals and be taken on board. I do not mean to say that Harry or I had much hope of thus escaping, still it was possible, and that assisted to keep up our spirits.

Captain Trunnion appeared much disappointed at not finding the number of slaves he had expected in the barracoons, as it would compel him to wait until they could be obtained from the interior, and his crew he knew were as liable to coast fever as that of any other vessel.

Next to the house in which we lived was a large store where the cargo of the "Vulture" was stored when landed. At a short distance off were several barracoons. I may as well describe one of them. It was a shed composed of heavy piles driven deep into the earth, lashed together with bamboos, and thatched with palm-leaves. Down the centre was another row of piles, along which was a chain. In this, at intervals of about every two feet, was a large neck-link, which, being placed round the necks of the slaves, was padlocked. When I looked in, the barracoon contained only about twenty slaves. Some of them were fine athletic looking men, and were shackled three together, the strongest being placed between two others, and heavily ironed. The walls of the building were about six feet in height, and between them and the roof was an opening of about four feet to allow the free circulation of air. The floor was planked, not, as I found, from any regard for the comfort of the slaves, but because a small insect, a species of chigoe, which is in the soil, might get into the flesh of the poor creatures, and produce a disease which might ultimately kill them. Half a dozen armed men, two being mulattoes, the others blacks, were guarding the barracoon and watching the slaves, so that any attempt to free themselves from their irons was impossible. These slaves were the property of a dealer with whom the captain now commenced bargaining. As there was time to spare, he chose to select each one separately, lest any sick or injured people might be forced upon him, as is often the case where slaves are shipped in a hurry. He and the trader stood at a dignified distance, while their subordinates carried on the active part of the business, a half naked black acting for the trader, while the captain was represented by a mulatto, who felt the arms and legs of each man, and struck him on the chest and back to ascertain that he was sound in wind, before he consented to pay over his price in goods. Another slave was then summoned, and, if found satisfactory, passed at a fixed price; but otherwise, a less sum was offered, or the slave was sent back to await the arrival of some other slaver likely to be less particular. Women and children were treated in the same way, but there were comparatively few of them in the lot now offered for sale.

I had to return on board the "Vulture" to obtain some medicines for our wounded men, and also to get some articles belonging to Harry and myself which we had left on board. Great alterations had taken place in the fitting of the ship between decks. Huge casks called *leaguers* had been placed in the hold; in these were stowed the provisions, wood for fuel, and other stores; above them was fitted a slave-deck, between which and the upper deck there was a space of about four feet. On this the slaves were to sit with shackles on their feet, and secured to iron bars running from side to side. They were divided in gangs, about a dozen in each, over which was a head man, who arranged the place each slave was to occupy. The largest slaves were made to sit down amidships, or the furthest from the ship's side, or from any position in which their strength could avail them to secure a larger space than their neighbours. As I was to see more of the system, I need not now describe it. On my return on shore, I looked into the barracoon hired by Captain Trunnion, in which I saw from forty to fifty slaves assembled, and even more heavily ironed and secured than they had been before. They were mostly sitting with their heads between their knees, bowed down with blank despair. Having seen the ship which was to convey them from their native land to a region they knew nothing of, and observed the savage countenances of the men who were to be their masters during the voyage, all hope of escape had fled. Every day after this, fresh batches of slaves arrived, their hands secured behind their backs, and walking in a long line fastened together by a rope, strictly guarded by blacks with muskets in their hands and swords by their sides, with which they occasionally gave a prod to any of the laggards. The wretched beings were marched, in the first instance, to the trader's barracoons, where they could be sorted and regain some of their strength.   Harry and I were paying all the attention we could to the wounded men, who, enjoying the advantage of fresh provisions, were quickly recovering their health. Caspar Caper, the man who seemed to be the most grateful to Harry and me, was quite himself again, and was certainly fit to return on board, but he begged hard that we would not inform the captain.

"If I had my will, sir, I'd never go back to that craft; nor would you if you knew the dreadful deeds which have been done on board her or by her crew."

"I have no wish to go back, you may be sure of that," I answered ; "but what do your companions say ? "

"Well, sir, three of them are pretty well agreed with me; but there is one, Herman Jansen, the Dutchman, who has a fancy for the buccaneering life we have led, and I don't like to trust him."

This showed me that the man to whom I was speaking, Caspar Caper, had thought the subject over, and was himself fully prepared to try and escape from the pirates.   I told him to speak to his shipmates while Harry and I were out of the way, and not to say that we entertained the idea, but simply to state his belief that we would accompany them if they made up their minds to run off from the slave village.   Before doing anything, I was very anxious to see Tubbs ; but he was so busily employed on board that he could not manage to come on shore. It was very probable, I thought, that the captain would not give him leave, and that he must come at night if he came at all.   I thought again of all sorts of excuses for visiting the ship, although I feared, if I did so, that I might be detained on board.   Several days passed; the "Vulture" was ready for sea, but a sufficient number of slaves to form her cargo had not yet arrived ; others, however, were coming in, sometimes twenty or thirty at a time. It would not take more than a couple of hours to stow them all away on board.   Although by this time all the wounded men had recovered, they pretended to be too weak to get out of their cots. Once or twice the captain looked in to see how they were getting on, when they all groaned and spoke in feeble tones, as if they were very little better.

" I can't say much for your doctoring, young sirs," he observed, turning to Harry and me. " I believe if you had left the men alone they would have got well of themselves. I never have had a surgeon on board my ship, and never intend to have one. Nature is the best surgeon, and if she can't cure a man he must die."

" I don't know what you would say if you were wounded, captain, and there was no one to extract the ball," observed Harry.

" I should have to take my chance with the rest," answered the captain in a tone which showed, however, that he did not like the remark. " But, whether cured or not, these fellows must come on board and try and do their duty," he exclaimed as he left the house.

" I must get some stronger medicines then," I said, the thought suddenly striking me that this would be the best excuse for visiting the ship; for although the captain spoke in the way he did, he had a medicine-chest on board well stored with drugs, with a book of directions for their use.

" I thought that you before took enough physic on shore to cure a dozen fellows," he remarked.

" And so I did, sir, but I remember seeing on the last visit a mixture, the name of which I forget, for restoring strength to people who have been brought down, and that's just what these men want."

I spoke the truth in regard to the drugs, the only question was how much the men required of them. As the captain did not forbid me, as soon as he was out of sight I hurried down to the beach, and got a black fellow to paddle me on board in his canoe. I soon found a big bottle, and made up the mixture according to the recipe, which I took good care to keep in my hand, so that anybody could see what I had been about. I looked round for Tubbs, and when I returned on deck, much to my satisfaction I found him working at the mizen rigging with no one else near. I hastened up to him, and in a low voice said—

"The rest are ready. Will you come to-night or to-morrow night? although I fear if we put it off till to-morrow you may be too late. We will, however, wait for you if you will come."

"Yes," he answered, "wait! I will be on shore an hour before midnight. By that time the black fellows will have turned in. Tell the negro who brought you off that there will be a couple of doubloons for him if he comes alongside at the hour I name. If he fails me, I must swim on shore, although there is a risk of being snapt up by a shark or a stray crocodile. However, I may find another chance before that of getting on shore. Now you'd better be off, for it won't do for you to be seen lingering about talking with me."

I followed his advice, and got into the canoe. As the black paddled me on shore, I asked him if he would like to obtain a doubloon. I knew very well what would be his answer. Being a discreet personage, he asked no further questions, but promised to be alongside at the hour I named.

On landing, I hurried to the house, which was some way up the beach, and told Harry of the arrangements I had made. I then explained more clearly to Caspar Caper than I had hitherto done the plan Harry and I proposed, which was to direct our course to the southward, and then to strike directly for the coast, where we might hope to be taken off, or to find a canoe or craft of some sort, in which to make our way to one of the European settlements. The means of subsistence we hoped to find in the forest if we could obtain firearms. As I had been going about the house one day, I had seen a couple of fowling-pieces, with powder-horns and shot-belts, hanging against the wall. Harry doubted whether we had a right to take them ; but necessity has no law, and in this case we came to the conclusion that we were justified in taking possession of them. Our associates had no scruples on the subject. Caspar fully agreed to carry out the plan we proposed, and now told us that his shipmates were perfectly ready to escape, and try for the future to lead peaceable lives. We did not inquire too minutely into their motives, but I suspected that these arose not so much from their hatred of piracy, as from being compelled constantly to fight with the fear of a rope's end before their eyes. I told the two old blacks that the wounded men required as much food as they could obtain, and they brought us an abundant supply. We accordingly had a hearty supper, but we were to make a scurvy return to them for their kindness. As soon as it was dark, the men got up and dressed themselves. Harry and I groped our way to the room where we had seen the fowling-pieces, which, with the ammunition, were at once secured.

" There's more to be found in the house than those things," observed Jansen. " We shall want a fresh rig out. What say you, mates ? Besides which, if old Dobbo and his wife hear us moving about, they will give the alarm, so we must settle them first." Saying this, he took up the lamp, and, followed by the rest, quitted the room, leaving Harry and me in darkness. Soon afterwards we heard a slight scream, then all was silent. We waited a quarter of an hour or more. The time was approaching when we expected to see Tubbs. Presently we heard a knock at the shutter of the room. Of course there was no glass. I opened it, and Tubbs sprang in. We knew him by his figure, though there was not light sufficient to see his countenance.

" Are you alone ? " he whispered.

" Yes," answered Harry ; " the others have gone to see what they can find in the house likely to be useful on the journey. We secured some fowling-pieces ; we could not defend our lives without them."

" And I have brought off a brace of pistols and a hanger," said the boatswain.

" We shall do very well then ; but I almost wish that we had attempted to escape without those other fellows—they are likely to bring us into trouble by their lawless ways," said Harry.

This was indeed too probable. While we were speaking they returned. They had sense enough to suppress their voices, and as Caspar, who carried the light, entered, I saw that they were all rigged out in the trader's clothes, which they had appropriated. One had got a musket, another a sword, and others richly ornamented pistols, while the legs of another were encased in high boots, and he had on a handsomely embroidered coat, used by the owner on grand occasions.

" The old people will not follow us or give the alarm," said Jansen. " We have gagged and bound them, for we heard them moving about in the next room, and if we hadn't been quick about it they would have given the alarm, and the whole village would soon have been awake."

The men had not returned empty handed. Some had brought in a further supply of provisions which they had found in the house, and several articles they had picked up.

Having made a hearty supper, " Now, my lads," I said, " it is time to start. The people in the village must be fast asleep, and the further off we get, the better chance we shall have of keeping ahead of our pursuers. One of us must act as leader. Who will do so ? "

The men at once unanimously chose Tom Tubbs. Harry and I were glad of this, as we felt sure that he was the best person for the post.

" Well, my lads, if you will obey me, I'll do what I can to lead you well," he said. " Now, the first thing I have to charge you is to keep silence. Follow me ! " He noiselessly opened the door and looked carefully about. Neither seeing nor hearing any one, he gave us the signal to move on. Harry and I went next, and the other men followed in single file. They knew that the slightest noise would betray them. For what they could tell, the captain himself might be on shore ; and should we be caught, he would certainly visit us with severe punishment. We treaded our way silently through the village, keeping at a distance from the barracoons, the guards at which would otherwise have discovered us. The country was sufficiently open to enable us to see the stars overhead, by which we guided our course to the southward. When we approached any huts, we turned aside, taking care not to go through any plantations, where, by breaking down the stalks, we should leave traces of our passage.

After going some distance we stopped to listen. We could hear two or three dogs barking, one replying to the other, but no human voices. This made us hope, at all events, that we were not discovered. Again we went on at a pretty quick rate, considering that five of our party had not been on their feet for several weeks. At last the men called a halt.

"We had better not stop yet, lads," said Tom Tubbs; "we must put a good many miles between us and the village before we are safe. Your skipper is not the man to let any of his crew get away without an effort to bring them back."

A short time, however, served to restore our companion's strength, and we once more set off as fast as our legs could carry us, breaking into a run whenever the ground was sufficiently level for the purpose. We had made good, I calculated, fully twenty miles when morning broke. It was a distance, I hoped, which would prevent the pirates from successfully pursuing us, but it would not do to rest here, for as soon as it was discovered that we had fled, Captain Roderick would be informed of it, and he would certainly send a party after us.

"If he does, I hope that he'll send some of his white crew, for they'll soon get tired and give up the chase," observed Harry.

"I am afraid, sir, he won't trust them," remarked Tubbs;

"he'll get a band of black fellows, who will keep on through the heat of day. I would advise that we should go forward during the cool of the morning, and try and find a place to conceal ourselves."

To this proposal Harry and I agreed, so did our other companions, though they would have preferred resting where they were. After a short halt by the side of a stream to take some food and quench our thirst, we again pushed on, the vegetation in many places being so dense that it was not without difficulty that we could force our way through it. The worst of this was, that while we were thus delayed we should form a road for our pursuers. However, that was not to be avoided should they get upon our track.

We had made good nearly a dozen miles, I should think, when we came upon a broad river, flowing, as we supposed, into the sea.

"If we can find a canoe, or a craft of some sort, we may easily reach the coast, and save ourselves a good deal of fatigue," observed Tubbs.

The rest of the men, who were pretty well knocked up, seemed highly pleased at the proposal. Instead of attempting to cross the stream, we proceeded down it. Harry suggested that we should form a raft if we could not find a canoe, and should a party be sent in pursuit, they would thus be puzzled to know what had become of us. I proposed that, before commencing our voyage down the stream, we should cross to the opposite bank, and there trample down the grass, and make other marks as if we had continued our course to the southward. We had not gone far when we saw a smoke ascending from amid trees on the banks of the river.

"Some native traders or white men are encamped there," observed Tubbs. "They are probably proceeding up the river, and will tell us what sort of people we are likely to meet with on the passage down. If they are traders, they are likely to prove friendly and we may consider ourselves fortunate in falling in with them."

"But suppose they are not traders, suppose they are not friendly, what are we to do then?" asked Harry.

"We muster eight white men with arms in our hands, and are not likely to be uncivilly treated," observed Jansen, flourishing his weapon. "I'll go forward, and see who these people are, and we'll soon settle whether we are to be friends or foes."

As there was no time to be lost, he hurried forward, while we halted to await his return. In a few minutes he reappeared.

"Friends! come on," he exclaimed; and once more moving forward, we reached an open space near the bank of the river, where we saw a tent pitched and two white men and a party of six blacks, two of whom were cooking at a fire, while the rest were seated in the shade. They rose to greet us.

The white men were French traders, they told us. They spoke a little English, and we understood enough of their language to be able to carry on a conversation. As they were inclined to be friendly, and appeared to be honest, we told them that we were escaping from a piratical slave craft, which we described. They appeared to know her well, and seemed greatly to commiserate us. They informed us that they were proceeding up the river to trade with the natives; that one of their number had fallen ill and was now suffering from fever inside the tent. They hoped by spending a day or two where they were that he would recover sufficiently to enable them to continue their voyage. They told us that we were nearly two hundred miles from the sea, and a much greater distance following the course of the river; but still it would be the safest plan to descend it in the way we proposed, until we reached a village where canoes were to be obtained. Though Harry and I and Tubbs were anxious at once to set to work and build a raft, our companions declared that they were too tired to do anything more until they had had a long rest. Our new friends, who had plenty of provisions, kindly bestowed some upon them, and invited us to join them in their repast, giving us some wine, which we found very refreshing. The

Frenchmen, hearing how far we had come, expressed their opinion that the pirates would not attempt to follow us, and that we were perfectly safe from pursuit. We ourselves were glad to get some rest, and lay down in the shade to wait until evening, when we proposed building the raft. The Frenchmen had several axes amongst their goods, and furnished us with three, so that we might cut down any small trees we required for the framework of the raft. After a sleep of some hours we got up much refreshed. Harry, Tubbs, and I immediately began to select trees for our purpose. The other men, whom Tubbs roused up, however, showed no inclination to assist, declaring that they were too tired, and must wait until the next day. Tubbs went back two or three times to speak to them, but without success. At last, on his return to us he said—

" I am afraid these fellows intend to play the Frenchmen some scurvy trick. Their idea is to carry off the canoe, and if you and Mr. Bracewell won't go, to leave you behind."

"We must defeat their treachery," I observed. " I will tell the Frenchmen and put them on their guard; I will at once do so."

Our friends, at first, would scarcely believe that the fellows would be guilty of so abominable a trick, but when I reminded them of the lawless lives they had led, they saw that it was too probable, and promised to keep a guard on their canoe. We laboured away until nightfall, our companions either sleeping or pretending to be asleep all the time. They got up, however, to eat some supper which the Frenchmen had prepared for us. Our hosts then produced some bottles of liquor, looking significantly at each other as they did so. I guessed their object, but said nothing. The seamen fell into the trap, but Harry and I took very little of the spirits, and Tubbs followed our example. The Frenchmen having plied the pirates with more and more liquor, they soon appeared to forget all about their previous intentions; they talked, laughed, and sang, and clapped their entertainers on the back, vowing that they were thorough good fellows. They then became very uproarious, and seemed disposed to quarrel amongst each other, but by degrees they became quiet again, and ultimately crawling to the bank of the river, lay down to sleep, entirely thoughtless of the risk they ran of being snapped up by alligators.

"They will do us no harm at present, at all events," said one of the Frenchmen, "and to-morrow I hope that our companion will be well enough to enable us to continue our voyage. We are much obliged to you for your timely warning, and we would advise you to part company from such lawless associates as soon as possible."

Harry and I assured him that such was our purpose, although we would gladly have enabled the men to escape from the pirates, hoping that they would take to a better course of life. We sat up talking with our friends for some time, and were then glad to lie down outside their hut, having agreed to keep watch with them during the night. We drew lots as to who should keep the watches. Harry had the first, from eight to ten; Tubbs the next two hours; I from midnight until two o'clock, and the Frenchmen the morning watch. Tubbs roused me up and said that all was quiet, and that the ex-pirates were sleeping soundly. I paced up and down between the tent and the boat, in which some of the black crew were sleeping, while the rest were near their master's tent. Frequently I stopped to listen for any distant sounds. I could hear occasionally the cries of wild beasts far away to the eastward, and the shrieks of night birds, the chirping of crickets or other insects, and the croaking of frogs; but no human voice reached my ears. I trusted that we should be able to finish our raft early the next day, and begin the voyage down the river. With this hope, having called up one of the Frenchmen, I lay down to sleep, feeling more drowsy than usual. I had just opened my eyes and discovered that it was dawn, when I was startled by the most fearful yell I had ever heard, and the next instant a hundred dark forms, flashing huge daggers in their hands, leapt out from among the bushes on every side. Harry and Tubbs, who were sleeping next to me, sprang to their feet. Our first impulse was to run to the trunk of a large tree and place our backs against it, so that we might defend ourselves to the last. As the unfortunate Frenchmen were crawling out of their tent, the savages were upon them, while others seized upon the drunken and still helpless seamen, and a fearful scene of slaughter ensued. Three of them we saw killed, while some of the crew of the canoe were also mercilessly put to death. Two of the seamen, however, Herman Jansen and Caspar Caper, seizing their weapons, fought their way out from among the savages, and, we concluded, took to flight, for we saw a party of blacks start off in pursuit. Our enemy, seeing us well armed, had not hitherto attacked us. We expected them to do so every moment. In a few minutes the whole of the party except the two men who had taken to flight and ourselves, were massacred.

"We must fight to the last if we are attacked," said Harry; "but don't fire first. Perhaps the savages, when they see the bold front we show, will think it wiser to let us alone."

Our hopes, however, were soon dashed to the ground; for the negroes, seeing only our small force opposed to them, after shouting and shrieking, and making significant signs, advanced towards us. Although we might have shot down three of them, we should inevitably have been overpowered. Still we would not yield without striking a blow, and we were on the point of firing when a white man appeared, followed by a fresh party of blacks, and as he advanced from the shadow of the wood, I recognised Mr Pikehead, the first mate of the "Vulture." On seeing only Harry, Tubbs, and me together, he exclaimed—

'Put down your arms and your lives are safe. The other

fellows have met the fate they deserved," and he kicked the body of one of the pirates. "They were deserters; but you had a perfect right to make your escape if you could. You have, however, failed, and must come back with me. Our captain will decide what is to be done with you."

"We'll not yield until you call these fellows off," answered Harry; "we shall then be able to treat with you."

The pirate laughed, for he fancied that he had us in his power.

"What shall we do?" asked Harry, addressing Tubbs and me.

"We had better give in, sir," said Tubbs. "The odds against us are too great, and although we might shoot that fellow and a couple of the blacks, we should be certain to lose our lives. If he promises to carry us safe on board the schooner, scoundrel though he is, he will keep his word, and we may have another opportunity of escaping."

"We must make a virtue of necessity," I observed, "and I agree with Tubbs."

In the meantime the mate was shouting to the blacks to fall back, allowing him space to approach us.

"I again promise you your lives, my men," he said, as he stopped a few paces off, still holding a blunderbuss in his hand, pointed towards us. "You are plucky fellows, and I wish to do you no harm, although you have given me a long tramp which I would gladly have avoided."

I felt convinced from his tone that he spoke the truth, and we all three accordingly lowered our weapons. By this time two of the pirate crew and several of the blacks whom we had seen at the village appeared, and by the mate's directions we delivered our arms to them.

"I'll not bind you," he said, "but you must give me your word that you will not run away."

This, of course, as we could not help ourselves, we did. While the mate was engaged with us, the rest of the blacks had been employed in plundering the cargo of the French trader's canoe, over which they soon commenced quarrelling, flourishing their daggers and gesticulating furiously at each other. For some time the mate did not interfere, but I heard him direct his own party to take possession of any provisions they could find : " Leave the rest to the black fellows," he added.

We were not sorry to see some cases of preserved meat, a box of biscuits, and a bag of flour brought up, with a case of tea, some sugar, and other eatables. The fire was quickly lighted, and one of the white men with two of the blacks set to work to prepare breakfast.

By degrees the tumult of the blacks, who had been quarrelling over their booty, subsided ; they had apparently come to some arrangement among themselves without the interference of the mate, and each of them now appeared habited in the various articles they had appropriated—some with pieces of coloured calico round their loins, others in the form of turbans round their heads or over their shoulders, evidently supposing that the appearance they presented was very distinguished. Shortly after-wards, however, the return of the party who had gone in chase of the two pirates, irritated at having failed to overtake them, created a fresh disturbance, each one among them claiming some of the booty.

On this occasion, bloodshed would certainly have ensued, had not the mate interfered, and insisted on the portions claimed being given up. As he and his followers had firearms, and the blacks had only their long knives, they were afraid of disobey-ing him, and order was again restored.

Notwithstanding the unfortunate termination of our adventure, we all ate heartily of the food placed before us. The remainder of the provisions was done up into packages, so that each of us might carry enough to last until we reached the village.

Mr. Pikehead had certainly no wish to be in the company of

his black allies, whom he had instigated to attack the camp, for making them a speech in their own tongue, he sent them off in a different direction to that we were about to follow. He then directed each man to take up his package, gave the word to march, and we set off.

CHAPTER V.

HARRY and I trudged along side by side, feeling dreadfully out of spirits at the ill success of our attempt to escape, as also at the thought of the sad fate which had befallen the good-natured Frenchmen. We also could not help considering ourselves in a degree guilty of the death of the three men we had induced to desert, as well as of that of our friends and their attendants. Tubbs tried to cheer us up.

"Maybe the blacks would have attacked the Frenchmen whether we had been with them or not," he observed; "and as for the rest, it is the fortune of war. We tried to escape but failed; better luck next time, say I."

This, however, was but poor consolation, as we could only expect the harshest treatment at the hands of Captain Roderick, even if he did not put us to death. Whether he would do that or not was doubtful. The mate, however, did not seem inclined to ill-treat us, except that we each had to carry a heavy load, while a dozen men were placed behind and on each side of us; but we were allowed to march as we liked, and to converse freely together. Though we had slept the previous night, we were pretty well tired out when a halt was called and preparations made to bivouac. Supper was prepared by the cooks, and we were allowed as large a share as we required. The mate then told us to lie down together, a couple of black fellows with arms in their hands being placed over us.

"You'll not attempt to run," observed the mate. "I have given orders to these fellows to shoot you if you do; so the consequences be on your own heads."

"No fear of that," answered Harry. "We'll promise to sleep as soundly as we can until we are called in the morning."

"One good thing, we've not got to keep watch," observed Tom Tubbs; "and I hope our black guards will keep a look-out for any snake, leopard, or lion who may chance to poke his nose into the camp; although I wish that Mr. Pikehead had left us our arms to defend ourselves."

We were too tired to talk much, and I believe we all slept soundly until morning, when we were roused up to breakfast and resume our march. It was late in the day when we reached the village. Fortunately for us, the owner of the house we had formerly occupied was still absent, and the theft committed by the pirates was not discovered. Soon after we arrived Captain Roderick made his appearance, a sardonic smile on his countenance.

"You thought to escape me," he said. "You acted foolishly, and must take the consequences. Had you been shot, your blood would have been on your heads, not on mine. I intend to take good care that you shall not play the same trick again. You will now come on board the "Vulture," and it is your own fault that you will not be treated with the same leniency that you were before. My crew will see that I do not allow such tricks to be played with impunity Lash their hands behind them, Pikehead, and bring them along."

The mate, with the aid of three seamen, immediately secured our hands behind our backs, and we were led down, amid the hoots and derisive laughter of the population, to the boat which conveyed us on board the "Vulture." Having been allowed to stand for some minutes in that condition exposed to the view of the crew, we were ordered down below. As we passed near the main hatchway, we saw that the slave-deck was already crowded with blacks, seated literally like herrings in a tub, as close as they could be packed side by side, with shackles round their necks and legs. Our destination was, however, lower down by the after hatchway. As soon as we were below the deck, our arms were released, and we were able to help ourselves down the narrow ladder which led into the cable-tier. Here, in a space which allowed us room only to sit with our knees together, without being able to stand up or walk about, the mate told us we were to remain.

"You may consider yourselves very fortunate, my fine fellows, that worse has not happened to you," he said. "How you'll like it if it comes on to blow, and the hatches are battened down, is more than I can say. You'll get your food though, for the captain doesn't want to take your lives—he has some scruples about that—nor do I. Indeed, you might have escaped as far as I was concerned, although it was fortunate for you I came up when I did, or those Ashingo savages would have put you to death as they did your companions."

"We are grateful for the leniency with which we have been treated, but may I ask what the captain intends doing with us?" I said.

"Why, I suppose that he intends to sell you two young gentlemen as slaves in the Brazils. He will give your faces and bodies a coating of black, and put you with the rest of the negroes," answered the mate. "And as for you," he exclaimed, turning to Tubbs, "you might have been treated as a deserter; and if you don't sign articles and join us, you will probably have to walk the plank. I say this as a hint to you. If you act wisely, you'll be set at liberty as soon as we get into blue water."

"You reckon wrongly if you think I'll join this craft or any other like her," answered Tubbs stoutly. "I'm ready to take the consequences, for turn pirate I won't; so you have my answer."

The mate laughed.

"Many a fine fellow has said that and changed his tone when he has seen the plank rigged or the yard-arm with a running bowline from it. However, I must not waste words on you. I'll send you down your suppers, and you must manage to stow yourselves away in the best manner you can think of for sleep. One of you must needs sit up, and he'll have plenty to do in keeping off the rats and cockroaches, for you'll be somewhat troubled by them, I suspect."

We thanked the mate for the promise of sending us some supper, and wished him good night; and I really believe that, as far as his brutalised nature would allow, he intended to be kind to us. Cramped as we were in the hot stiffling hold, it was a long time before any one of us could go to sleep. We were, I should have said, left in total darkness; not the slightest gleam of light descending into the part of the hold in which we were confined. At length I was awakened from a tolerable sleep by a noise which betokened that the ship was getting under weigh. I did not like to arouse my companions; but Tubbs, who had been sitting on a locker, started up exclaiming—

"Ay, ay! I'll be on deck in a twinkling." The blow he gave his head against the beam above him, roused him up. "Bless my heart! I forgot where I was," he said. "Yes, the ship's under weigh, no doubt about that, and we shall be out at sea in the course of a few hours if we have the tide and wind with us, and don't ground on the bar and get knocked to pieces."

After some time Harry awoke. I told him that the ship was running down the river.

"Our chance of escape for the present is over, then," he said with a deep sigh.

He had naturally been thinking of home and Lucy and his blighted prospects; so indeed had I. Tubbs, as before, tried to cheer us up by talking on various subjects.

"There's many a slip 'twixt the cup and the lip," he observed. "Although the captain fancies his craft faster than anything afloat, he may catch a tartar in the shape of a British man-of-war before we cross the Atlantic. As to selling us into slavery, I don' believe he'll attempt it. He must know that before long we would find means of communicating with a British consul or some other authority, and make our cases known. If he had talked of selling us to the Moors or Turks, the case would have been different. Once among those fellows, we should have found it a hard matter to escape."

"Still he may sell us," observed Harry; "and perhaps months and years will pass before we can let our friends know where we are."

"Well, well, that'll be better than having to walk the plank or being run up at the yard-arm," said Tubbs. "We must not cry out until we are hurt, although I'll own that I'd rather have more room to stretch my legs in than this place affords. I hope Master Pikehead won't forget to send us the food he promised; I'm getting rather sharp set already."

Harry and I confessed that we were also feeling very hungry. Even the talking about food gave a new turn to our thoughts. At last we heard the hatch above our heads lifted, and the black steward came down with a bowl of farina and a jug of water. It was the same food the slaves were fed on, but we thought it wise to make no complaint.

"It shows that the captain has no intention to starve us," observed Harry. "However, this is better than mouldy biscuit and rancid pork, such as I have heard say seamen are too often fed upon."

" You've heard say the truth, sir," observed Tubbs. " Often and often I've known the whole ship's company get no better fare than that, with little better than bilge water to drink. If we get enough stuff like this, we shall grow fat, at all events."

The steward, leaving the bowl between us, quickly disappeared up the hatchway. The only light we had was from a bull's-eye overhead, which enabled us, as Tubbs said, " barely to see the way to our mouths ; " we could not, at all events, distinguish each other's features. Although we could not see, we felt the claws of numerous visitors crawling over us, and smelt them too, and now and then were sensible that a big rat was nibbling at our toes, although, by kicking and stamping, at the risk of hitting each other's shins, we kept them at bay. Notwithstanding this, we managed to sleep pretty soundly at intervals.

Tubbs assured us that the ship was gliding on, although it might be some time before she reached the bar, as it was impossible to judge at what rate she was sailing. Now and then we felt her heel over slightly to starboard, showing that the wind was more abeam, or rather that we were passing along a reach running to the southward ; then, when she came up again on an even keel, we knew that we were standing directly to the westward. At last we felt her bows lift, then down she glided, to rise again almost immediately afterwards, while the increased sound of the water dashing on her sides showed us that we were crossing the bar.

" There is some sea on, I guess, and I know what it is with these African rivers. Should the wind suddenly shift southward, we may be driven on a rock or sandbank, and we and all on board will have a squeak for life," observed Tubbs.

" I hope not, although anything might be better than being carried into slavery," observed Harry. " But we ought not to despair. I have been thinking and praying over the matter, and know that God can deliver us if He thinks fit. We must trust Him; I'm sure that's the only thing to be done in all the troubles and trials of life. At all times we must do our duty, and, as I say, trust Him; even when bound hand and foot as we are at present, all we can do is still to trust Him."

I heartily responded to Harry's remark, and so I believe did Tubbs, who, although nothing of a theologian, not even knowing the meaning of the word, was a pious man in his rough way.

"Ay, ay, sir," he said. "I know that God made us, and He has a right to our service; and if we don't run away from Him and hide ourselves, He'll look after us a precious deal better than we can look after ourselves. That's my religion, and it's my opinion it's the sum total of all the parsons can tell us."

"Not quite," said Harry, "although it goes a long way. We are sinners in God's sight, whatever we are in the sight of men; and if God in His mercy hadn't given us a way by which we can be made friends to Him and saved from punishment, we should be in a bad condition."

"You are right, sir," answered Tubbs; "but to my idea that's all included in what I said."

We sat listening in silence.

"We are pretty well over the bar now, and I don't think we shall be cast away this time," he observed a few minutes afterwards.

That he was right we were convinced by the more regular movement of the vessel, as she slowly rose and fell, moved by the undulations which rolled in towards the coast. We could judge that she was making good way, and Tubbs was of opinion that all sail was set, and that we were standing to the westward. At the time the slaves were fed, we had a bowl of farina brought us, but the man put it down and disappeared again without saying a word. Soon afterwards the mate came down, and told me that I might come on deck for a quarter of an hour to stretch my legs. I was thankful to breathe the fresh air, although there was but little of it, and the ship was almost becalmed. I glanced astern, and could distinguish the shore, although I could no longer make out the mouth of the river. We had, at all events, got a safe offing. When my time was up I was sent below and Harry took my place, and he was succeeded by Tubbs. We were treated, however, with no more consideration than was afforded to the slaves, who were brought up on deck at intervals in the same fashion. The hold felt doubly close and oppressive after the mouthful of fresh air we had enjoyed.

The second night of our captivity was even more trying than the first, for the atmosphere of the hold, into which the horrible odour from the slave-deck penetrated, was becoming every hour more and more unendurable. I feared that should we be kept below during the voyage, I, at all events, would sink under it, for I already felt sick almost to death, and my spirits were at a lower ebb than they had ever before reached. Harry was almost in as bad a condition as I was. Tubbs, who had been well seasoned in the close air of forecastles, held out better than we did.

"Don't give way, young gentlemen, whatever you do," he said very frequently to us. "Cheer up, cheer up! When we get a breeze, some of it will find its way down here perhaps; and if not, I'll ask the skipper if he wishes to kill us by inches, and I'll tell him he'll never land either of us if we are kept shut up in this hold and treated worse than the negroes. They are born to it, as it were, and we are not, and have been accustomed to pure air all our lives."

I did not quite agree with Tubbs as to negroes being born to be shut up in the hold of a slave-ship, but I did not just then contradict him. By a faint gleam, like the light of a glow-worm, which came down from overhead, we knew that it was morning, and soon afterwards we felt the ship heel over to larboard, or port as it is now called. In a short time the increasing motion also showed us that the sea had got up. We heard sounds which indicated that sail was being shortened. We stood on, it might have been an hour, on the same tack, when the ship was put about, and now she heeled over more often, and pitched and tumbled about in a way which showed that it was blowing fresh. The cries of the wretched slaves, unaccustomed to the motion, reached our ears, while the tossing stirred up the bilge water and almost stifled us. Two or three hours passed, when the ship became somewhat steadier. Tubbs averred that the helm had been put up, and that we were running before the wind.

"There's something taking place, although I cannot make out just what it is to a certainty ; but I've a notion that there is some craft in sight which the 'Vulture' wants to escape ; and if so, I hope she won't."

"So do I, indeed," murmured Harry. "I shall die if we remain here much longer."

Another hour of suffering and anxiety passed, when Tubbs roused Harry and me—for we had dropped off in a kind of stupor—by exclaiming—

"Holloa ! What was that ? A shot, or I'm a Dutchman."

As he spoke I distinctly heard the sound of a gun, though it seemed to be at a great distance. We listened with bated breath. Again there came a faint boom, and at the same instant a crash, which told us that the shot had struck the ship.

"Hurrah ! I thought so," cried Tom ; "there's a man-of-war in chase of us, and it is pretty evident that the 'Vulture' has no wish to engage her, or she would not have been trying to get away, as she has been for some hours past."

We waited now with intense anxiety. We knew that the "Vulture" was a fast craft, and that it was too likely she had just passed within range of her pursuer's guns, but might escape notwithstanding. Except by the motion of the vessel, we could not possibly judge how we were steering. In spite of the stifling atmosphere, our senses were wide awake. Again there came the sound of a gun. Although the shot did not strike the ship, yet it seemed to us that our pursuer must be nearer. Another and another shot followed. The "Vulture's" guns were now fired, although I was surprised to find how little noise they appeared to make, and could scarcely believe that they were fired from our deck, had not Tubbs assured us of the fact. Then there came a lull, and we heard a whole broadside fired, the crashing and rending sound showing that the shot had torn through the bulwarks and sides of the ship. The fearful shrieks which rose from the hold made us fear that the miserable slaves had suffered, though perhaps their cries rose from terror as much as from the injuries they had received. A fearful uproar ensued, the roar of the great guns, the rattle of musketry, the shouts of the slaver's crew, the shrieks and cries of the slaves, the groans of the wounded, the rending and crashing of planks mingled, were well-nigh deafening even to us. Presently there came a crash. The ship seemed to reel, a shudder passed through her whole frame.

"They've run us aboard," cried Tubbs, "and maybe the ship with all hands will be sent to the bottom. We must get out of this somehow to try and save our lives. There will be no one on the look-out to stop us."

The boatswain's exclamations made us fear that probably our last moments were at hand.

"We must try and find something to help us to force our way out," cried Tubbs. "If we cannot get the hatch off, we must make our way through this bulkhead. Hurrah! here's an iron bar."

As he spoke, Harry and I laid hold of it to be sure that he was not mistaken. How it came there, of course we could not tell.

"Now, keep behind me, that I may have room to use it," he exclaimed.

We obeyed and he commenced a furious attack on the bulkhead. The crash which followed showed that he had succeeded in driving in some of the planking. He worked away with the fury of despair, fully believing that erelong the ship would be sent to the bottom. The noise he made prevented our hearing what was going forward on deck ; indeed, all sounds were undistinguishable by this time.

"There is room to pass now," he cried.

He led the way through an opening he had formed. We followed him, but still found that there was another bulkhead before us. He quickly attacked that, and in a few seconds had demolished a sufficient portion to enable us to creep through. We found a ladder, which led, we judged, into the captain's cabin. We climbed up it, and were just on the point of springing through a skylight which would have led us on to the poop-deck, when we saw Captain Roderick himself enter, a pistol in his right hand and a sword in the other, his countenance exhibiting rage and despair. He did not observe us. Several casks of powder, which had been brought up to be more ready at hand, were piled in one corner of the cabin. He pointed his pistol, his intention was evidently to blow up the ship and all on board. In another moment his desperate purpose would have been effected. As if moved by one impulse, we all three sprang upon him, Tubbs grasping his right wrist and turning the pistol away, the bullet striking the deck above. Mercifully none of the sparks fell on the powder. Tubbs, grasping him by the throat, and throwing himself with his whole force upon him, brought him to the deck, while Harry and I each seized an arm and knelt upon his body to prevent him from rising. Although we exerted all our strength, it was with the greatest difficulty we could keep him down. He seemed more like a wild beast than a human being. He gnashed his teeth and glared fiercely at us.

"Be quiet, captain, won't you?" exclaimed Tubbs. "We have saved you and ourselves from being blown into the air, and you ought to thank us."

The captain made no answer. I looked round for a piece of

rope or some means of securing him ; for had he been set loose, he would probably have accomplished his purpose, and we, of course, were eager to get on deck and try and save our lives, for we fully believed that the " Vulture " was on the point of sinking. The guns, however, had ceased firing, although there was a stamping overhead, the clashing of hangers, and the occasional sounds of pistols at the further end of the ship.

" The man-of-war's men have gained the after part, and have driven the pirates forward," observed Tubbs ; " we shall soon have some of our people here to help us."

Again the captain gnashed his teeth and made an effort to free himself.

" It's all of no use, captain," said Tubbs. " I don't want to take your life, but if you don't keep quiet, I shall be obliged to draw my knife across your windpipe."

The captain evidently fully believed that the boatswain intended to do what he threatened.

" You've treated us with less severity than we might have expected, Captain Roderick," said Harry. " Will you give us your word that you will not again attempt to destroy the ship, or to attack any of the people who have captured her, and we will conduct you into a cabin where you must remain until to-morrow, or until you are set at liberty? "

Captain Roderick made no reply.

All this time the ship, I should have said, had been rolling and pitching, and it was very evident that she had broken loose from the man-of-war. It might possibly be that the pirates had gained the upper-hand, but the appearance of Captain Roderick below convinced us to the contrary. At length the sounds I have described ceased, although there was a continuous tramping of feet overhead, and the rattling of blocks and yards.

" They are shortening sail," observed Tubbs ; " we shall soon have some one below to relieve us of this gentleman, and I'm thankful to say I don't believe the ship's going down just yet. If he had thought she was, he wouldn't have taken the trouble to try and blow her up."

We could see Captain Roderick's eyes glaring at us, but Tubbs held him too tight by the throat to allow him to speak. So violent were his struggles, however, that he nearly got one of his arms loose, on which Tom tightened his grip until the pirate captain was nearly black in the face. In spite of this, giving a sudden jerk, he freed the arm Harry was holding down, when three persons appeared at the door. One was, I saw, a naval officer, by his uniform—the other two, seamen. I shouted to them to come to my assistance, and seeing what we were about, they sprang forward.

"Get some rope and lash this man; he is mad, I believe," I cried out.

"Go and get it," said the officer. One of the sailors sprang on deck, while the two new-comers assisted us in keeping down the infuriated pirate. He was, I fully believed, from the almost supernatural strength he exhibited, mad.

The seaman quickly returned with a coil of rope, with which the officer and his men, aided by Tubbs, soon lashed Captain Roderick's arms and legs in a way which prevented him from moving until he was secured to the mizenmast, which came through the cabin, when we felt that we were safe from his attacks. I had not hitherto looked into the countenance of the officer, nor he into mine. What was my surprise, then, to see a face I well knew.

"Charley!" I exclaimed.

"Dick!" was the answer. "Can it be you?" and my brother and I grasped each other's hands. He had grown into a tall young man, and certainly I should not have recognised him by his figure. I was also greatly altered; besides he would not have recognised me in my present condition—my countenance pale, my dress begrimed with dirt, torn, and travel-stained. I introduced Harry and Tubbs to him, and he shook hands with them both.

There was no time for talking. He told us that the frigate had sighted the slaver, which had refused to heave to, and had had the audacity to fire at his Majesty's ship. A gale coming on, as the only means of securing her, the frigate had run the slaver on board, when he with a lieutenant and eight men had leapt down on her deck, expecting to be followed by more of the crew, but, before they had time to spring on board, the ships parted. The slaver's crew, as he called them, had made a desperate resistance, but a considerable number having been killed and more badly wounded, the survivors had been driven forward and yielded. " Having ceased to resist, the slaver's crew," he said, " had promised to assist in shortening sail, and apparently in good faith, having yielded up their arms, set about doing so. We have now got under snug canvas. There is too heavy a sea running to allow of a boat with more hands being sent to our assistance. However, as we have complete mastery of the people, we can do very well without them. Mr. Hallton, the second lieutenant of the ' Rover,' our frigate, was inquiring for the captain of this craft, when he was told that he must either have been killed or fallen overboard, but one of his crew suggested that he might have gone below. Another then owned that he had heard the captain say, that sooner than fall into the hands of an enemy, he would blow the ship up. On hearing this, Mr. Hallton sent me down below to search for him."

" You would have been too late had we not providentially prevented him from executing his mad scheme," I observed ; and I then told him how we had discovered the captain in the very act of attempting to blow up the ship. " But you mistake the character of this craft," I said ; and I briefly told him how she had captured the " Arrow," and how we had been treated since we fell into Captain Roderick's hands.

" That greatly alters the aspect of affairs," he observed, looking grave. " If you will come on deck with me, we will inform Mr. Hallton. Perhaps he is inclined to treat the crew rather leniently,

and to put more confidence in their promises than he would do
if he were aware of her real character."

Harry on this desired Tubbs to watch the pirate.

"I should be glad to do it, sir, but I should like a sniff of the
sea-breeze," answered Tom. "I want just to pump out all the
foul air I've got down my throat."

"Well," said Charley, laughing, "one of my men shall remain
instead of you. Noakes, stand by this man, and shoot him through
the head if any one approaches to set him free or he manages
to cast off the lashings, although he'll not do that in a hurry, I
suspect."

On going on deck, we found Mr. Hallton, the second lieutenant
of the "Rover," standing aft, giving directions to heave the dead
bodies overboard and to collect the wounded, to attend to
whom he summoned several of the most respectable-looking of
their shipmates. The "Vulture" had not suffered much in her
rigging, and was now hove to under a closely-reefed main-topsail.
She rode so easily that I was not aware until then that a heavy
sea was running, and had been surprised at Charley telling me
that the two ships could not communicate. Charley introduced
me to Mr. Hallton, and briefly ran over the events of which I
had given him an account.

"A pirate, do you say she is?" exclaimed the lieutenant. "I
must really beg leave to doubt that. She is full of slaves, in the
first place, and the captain and his crew very naturally fought to
defend their property. But you say, Westerton, that you have
found the captain. I will examine him and ascertain the state of
the case."

"But my brother here, sir, and Mr. Bracewell, and the boats-
swain of the 'Arrow,' aver that they were taken out of their vessel
and detained by force on board this ship, and there can be no
doubt of her piratical character."

"I beg that you will wait to give your opinion until you are
asked for it, Mr. Westerton," answered the lieutenant in a gruff

tone. "I say that she's a slaver, and, as such, being taken full of slaves, we will condemn her. With regard to her piratical character, that has to be proved."

I was very much surprised at the way in which the lieutenant spoke. Charley told me that the report on board was that he himself had served on board a slaver, if not a pirate, in his younger days, and that he was stubborn and ill-tempered in the extreme. "Whether or not he has found any of his old associates on board the craft I cannot say, but I know that the crew gave in very soon when they saw him leading the boarders across the deck. To be sure he fought like a tiger, and cut down several fellows, so that I cannot suppose that he has any great love for them, at all events."

The cries and groans which ascended from the slave-deck soon drew our attention towards it, and Mr. Hallton sent Charley with four hands down to ascertain their condition. I accompanied him, having procured a brace of pistols and a hanger, without which I should not have liked to venture among them. A dreadful sight met our eyes. Three or four of the frigate's shot had entered and swept right across the deck, taking off the heads of not less than eight men in one row, and wounding others on the further side of the ship in another row as if it had gone through diagonally ; while the legs of a still greater number had been shot away. Most of the badly wounded were dead, but others were still writhing in agony. I need not picture all the horrors we witnessed. Charley told me to go on deck and obtain assistance. The lieutenant replied that I might take some of the slaver's crew, but that he could not spare his own men. I went forward to where they were collected, but found only three, to whom Harry and I had rendered some service in dressing their wounds, willing to give themselves any trouble in performing the task. They, however, got tackles rigged, and we hoisted up three and sometimes four bodies together, all dripping with gore, a terrible sight, and then swung them overboard. Even this took some time. The wounded thought that they were to be treated in the same manner, and we had great difficulty in persuading them that we intended to do them no harm, but rather to attend to their hurts. Altogether, fifty men had been killed, or had died from fright, or succumbed directly they were lifted on deck from their wounds. Charley proposed having the survivors up, so that the slave-deck might be washed and cleaned from the mass of gore and filth collected upon it, but Mr. Hallton replied that it was perfectly unnecessary, and that if the slaves should break loose, we might have to kill them all, or be ourselves overpowered. This I thought very likely to happen, though I felt that a few might safely be brought up while the part of the deck they had sat upon was cleansed. Harry and I, however, did our best to attend to their wants. We carried down water and supplied a cup to each. They mostly received the water scarcely casting a glance of gratitude towards us; but one man exhibited a marked contrast to this behaviour, and, as I handed him the cup, he exclaimed before drinking it—" Tankee, massa, tankee, massa," and then quaffed it eagerly, showing how much his parched throat required the refreshing fluid.

"Do you understand English?" I asked, thinking perhaps that these were the only words he could speak.

"Yes, massa; him talky English, him serve board English ship."

I inquired his name. He told me it was Aboh. I found, however, that although he might understand me, his vocabulary was very limited. I should have liked to have given him another cup of water, but as I knew that the rest of the slaves would consider themselves ill-treated if I favoured one more than another, I refrained from doing so, but I promised to remember him. I then begged that he would speak to his companions, and advise them to be quiet, telling them that we would do everything in our power for their benefit. I heard him shout out what appeared to me to be perfect gibberish, but it had the desired effect, and they at once became far more tranquil than they had hitherto been.

Night was now rapidly coming on; the frigate was hove to about half a mile to windward, and, as Tubbs observed to me, both ships appeared to be making very fine weather of it considering the heavy gale blowing. The frigate showed signal lights, and the lieutenant ordered ours to be hoisted in return.

Captain Roderick had hitherto remained lashed to the mast, but he could not, without cruelty, be left there all night, and it was necessary to decide what should be done with him. Lieutenant Hallton considered that it would be sufficient to shut him up in one of the cabins and place a sentry over him. Charley suggested that his wrists, at all events, should be placed in irons, as in his savage mood it was impossible to say what he might do. The lieutenant was obstinate.

"The man was only acting as he believed right in defending his own ship, and I'm not one to tyrannise over a fallen enemy," he answered in somewhat a scornful tone.

Charley could say no more. The lieutenant went below to look out for a suitable cabin in which to place Captain Roderick— Tubbs, Harry, and I, with three men, accompanied him. To our surprise, we found the pirate quiet enough. His mad fit had apparently passed away.

" I am sorry to give you all this trouble," he said quite calmly. " You young gentlemen will, I hope, return good for evil, and I shall be grateful."

We were, however, not to be deceived by such an address. Charley replied that his orders were to place him in his cabin by himself, and that was better treatment than he might have expected.

"Certainly," answered Captain Roderick, looking quite pleased; " it is a favour I should not have ventured to ask for. If my steward has escaped, I'll trouble you to tell him I should like some food. He is a good cook, and if you order him, he will prepare supper for you, gentlemen. He knows where all the provisions are stowed and will speedily carry out your directions."

On this being reported to Mr. Hallton, he immediately ordered supper to be prepared in the chief cabin.

As I moved across the deck, the only difference I could see between the man-of-war's men and the pirates was, that the former were armed and that the latter were not ; but as they still numbered more men than the party from the " Rover," it struck me that they might easily possess themselves of the means of offence and master their captors. During daylight it was not likely that they would venture to do this, as the frigate would quickly have retaken the ship. I clearly remember this idea passing through my mind. As Harry and I had had nothing but farina for the past three days, and for several hours we had been without food, we were very glad when we were summoned into the cabin. Here we found a really handsome repast spread out, everything secured by " fiddles " and " puddings," for the ship was tumbling about too much to allow the plates and glasses otherwise to have remained on the table.

As Tubbs was a respectable man in his appearance, the lieutenant, with more politeness than might have been expected, invited him to supper. It may be supposed that we all did justice to the meal placed before us. Charley had to go on deck until the lieutenant had finished supper ; when he had done so, he went up saying that he would send my brother down to have some food.

Charley, however, had to hurry again on deck, as he said Mr. Hallton wanted him to keep a look-out. The lieutenant had, considering the time he had been occupied, imbibed no small amount of liquor, though it did not appear to have affected his head.

Harry, Tubbs, and I ate our suppers more leisurely. As may be supposed, having obtained but a few winks of sleep the two previous nights, we soon became drowsy Harry proposed turning in.

"If we do, we must keep one eye open and our hangers by our sides," observed Tubbs. "I don't quite like the freedom of the lieutenant with these buccaneering fellows. If we hadn't got the King's ship close to us, they would be playing us some scurvy trick, depend upon that."

As Harry and I could be of no use on deck at night, and Tubbs really required rest, we all lay down, Harry and I each taking a sofa at the further end of the cabin, while Tubbs stowed himself away in a berth which had been occupied by one of the mates who had been killed in the late action. I was just dropping off to sleep when I heard a scuffle, and on looking up, what was my dismay to see two seamen grasping the arms of the lieutenant, who had just before entered the cabin, while two others were hauling Charley along. The sentry, instead of attempting to assist Mr. Hallton, presented his musket at us, exclaiming—

"If you interfere, gentlemen, I am ordered to shoot you."

As we saw several other men at the entrance of the cabin with muskets in their hands, we knew that resistance was useless. I was indeed too much astonished and confused, suddenly awakened as I had been out of my sleep, to say or do anything. I fancied for some seconds that I was dreaming. Here were the tables turned, and that with a vengeance. It was very evident that the pirates had tampered with the man-of-war's men, who were probably a bad lot, as was too often the case on board King's ships in those days, and that thus they had easily been won over. Mr. Hallton's folly and obstinacy had also greatly contributed to enable the pirates to carry out their project. I should have been less surprised had Captain Roderick been at liberty, but, as far as I could then see, he had had no hand in the business. I had good reason to dread the way he would serve us when he once more found himself in command of the ship and that we were in his power, when he would, I feared, wreak his vengeance on our heads for the way we had treated him.

These thoughts passed rapidly through my mind. Harry and Tubbs, who had been fast asleep, were awakened by the entrance of the party, and now sat up rubbing their eyes, as much astonished as I had been.

Tubbs, who was but partly awake, sprang to his feet and made a step forward as if to interfere, but seeing the sentry pointing his musket at his head, he sat down again.

"Well, this is a pretty go," he exclaimed. "Who commands this ship I should like to know, and then I can settle whether I'll do duty or turn in and go to sleep again?"

"Belay your jaw-tackle, master," growled out one of the pirates who had advanced into the cabin. "You're mighty too free with your tongue, fine fellow as you think yourself. A better man than you commands her, and he'll soon show you whose master."

I must own I cared very little about Mr. Hallton, but I felt the deepest anxiety as to how Charley might be treated. I feared the pirates less than I did the "Rover's" men, who had thus turned traitors to their King and country, for they were too likely to add crime upon crime, and to murder their officers. Had Mr. Hallton and Charley been armed, we might have made an effort to release them, but they had both been deprived of their swords and I felt sure that Harry, Tubbs, and I would be unsuccessful, and only make matters worse.

The seamen, having now bound the arms of the two officers behind them, led them into an inner cabin, where, shutting the door, they locked and bolted it.

"Now, you three, go on deck and help work the ship," said one of the men, whom I recognised as the third officer of the "Vulture," but who had slipped into sailor's clothes, probably to deceive his captors.

I could scarcely suppose that all this time Captain Roderick had any hand in the mutiny, for, to the best of my belief, he had been shut up in the cabin, and was still there. The mate seemed to be of the same opinion, for he bade the sentry open the door. He did so, when Captain Roderick was seen stretched on his couch. At the first glance I thought he was dead, but he was only in a deep sleep, so deep that all the noise outside had not aroused him. The mate shook him by the arm, but it had no effect. I was thankful for this, for I dreaded that, should he awake and find us in his power, he might commit some act of violence. Lest he should be awakened, Harry, Tubbs, and I gladly made our escape on deck. I prayed that no harm would be done to Charley, for I felt more anxious about him than about myself. On reaching the deck, I looked out for the frigate, I could just see her light away to windward, but it seemed to me much further off than before. The gale had abated somewhat, but both ships were still hove to. The mate speedily followed us up, and gave orders to the men to bring some long spars to the quarter-deck. He then got a grating, to which he fixed the spars upright, so as to form a cone-shaped structure; then turning it over, he secured some rather shorter spars in the same way, fixing a shot at the point where they united. Inside the points of the upper end, a ship's lantern was securely hung, when the machine was carefully lowered overboard, the light we had hitherto carried being extinguished. Immediately this was done, the order was given to put the helm up, and the foresail being squared away, we ran before the gale, leaving the light burning at the spot where we had been. There was no doubt about its object; it was to deceive the man-of-war, so that, until the trick was discovered, it was not likely that we should be chased. The hope that I had hitherto entertained that we might, after all, be quickly recaptured, now vanished. The mate assumed the command—the crew seemed willing to obey him. Whether he intended to retain it or not I could not tell, but I thought that he certainly would should he find that Captain

Roderick remained as mad as I was convinced he was when he attempted to blow up the ship.

As the gale slightly decreased, more sail was made, and before morning the "Vulture" had as much canvas packed on her as she could carry. We were kept on deck pulling and hauling until our arms ached. When dawn broke I looked astern. The frigate was nowhere to be seen.

CHAPTER VI.

AS the day advanced the wind decreased, and the ship close-
hauled was headed up towards the coast. How far off we
were I could not tell, but Tubbs told me he should not consider
that we were less than a hundred miles, perhaps more.

"So far that's satisfactory. It is possible that the 'Rover'
may overtake us," I observed.

"If she finds out the course we have steered, sir; but we had
run seventy or eighty miles at least before she was likely to
discover the trick the pirates played her. Besides, to tell you
the truth, I'd rather she didn't overtake us. The fellows on
board would fight with ropes round their necks, and they would
not give in as long as a plank held together, and then we should

have to go down with them. I would rather run the chance of getting on shore and making our escape afterwards."

I at once agreed with him, and we made up our minds that it would be well for us to get out of the ship without the risk of another battle. The mate, I observed, remained on deck, issuing all the necessary orders; the boatswain of the "Vulture" and one of the man-of-war's men, with one of the mutineers, acting as his subordinates. He ordered Harry and me about, treating us like the common seamen, and if we were not as smart as he wished us to be, he sent the boatswain or the mutineer from the "Rover" with a rope's end to start us. Tubbs at once fell into his ordinary duty of boatswain. The mate, it appeared to me, wished to win him over, and always spoke civilly to him, although he was not very particular in regard to his language when he addressed us. The evening was drawing in, we had been on deck all day. I was, of course, very anxious to know how it fared with poor Charley, who was kept a prisoner below. Whenever Harry or I attempted to leave the deck, the mate called us back and told us to attend to our duty. We got some food, however, for the cook, a good-natured black fellow, gave us some at the caboose, or we should have starved. Still, it was much better than being shut up in the dark hold, and, of course, we wished to avoid being sent below to our former place of confinement. I saw some messes of soup and porridge being cooked and carried into the cabin, and I concluded, therefore, that Lieutenant Hallton and Charley would be fed. Harry and I agreed that it would be wiser for us to obey the orders of the mate as long as he thought fit to issue them.

"I shall go and lie down in the cabin," said Harry to me. "I can but be sent up again, and I have no fancy to go and sleep among the men."

Accordingly, as soon as it grew dark, while the mate was looking another way, we slipped into the cabin, and coiled ourselves up on the sofas we had before occupied. Tired as I was,

however, the heat and the cockroaches and the thoughts of
our dangerous position kept me awake, although I tried hard
to go to sleep.   A lamp hung from the deck above, but
the part of the cabin where we were was in perfect shade.
I had not lain long when I saw the door of Captain
Roderick's cabin open, and out he stepped, looking round
him as if trying to recover his scattered senses.   Presently he
advanced across the cabin, when, by the light which fell upon
him, I saw that he held a pistol in his hand; what he was about
to do with it I could not tell.   To my horror, he opened the
door of the cabin in which the lieutenant and Charley were confined.   Although he had looked unusually calm as the light fell
on his countenance, the moment I saw his movements I felt convinced that he had some evil intention.   Springing up, I grasped
Harry by the arm, and rushed towards the open door.   I could
see the lieutenant and Charley standing upright close together,
with their arms bound behind them against the opposite bulkhead.

"Oh, oh!" exclaimed the captain, fixing his eyes on the lieutenant;
"you thought to capture me and hang me at your yard-arm ; but
the yarn's not spun nor the bullet cast which is to take my life.
I might order you on deck and run you up to the yard-arm before
five minutes are over ; but I intend to have the satisfaction of
shooting you myself."

Lieutenant Hallton, unprincipled man as I believe he was,
stood calm and unmoved.   Charley was endeavouring to draw
his arms out of the ropes which bound them.   Twice Captain
Roderick lowered his pistol as if he had changed his mind, but
still he went on taunting the unfortunate officer.   It would have
been prudent in the latter to have held his tongue, but instead he
went on answering taunt for taunt, rather than endeavouring to
calm the rage of the pirate captain, which increased till I feared
every instant that he would pull the trigger.

Harry and I stood ready to spring upon him, but I saw that in doing so we might run the risk of making him fire the pistol, and bring about the very catastrophe we desired to prevent. Charley in the meantime caught sight of us. I made a sign to Harry to get out his knife. I knew that to cut the ropes which bound my brother's hands would be the work of a moment, and I hoped, by the suddenness of the attack we were about to make, to keep Captain Roderick down until that object was effected. We should then be three to one, or four to one if we saved the lieutenant's life.

Harry understood perfectly what he was to do. One bound would carry him to where the pirate stood. The moment came; I sprang forward, and throwing my arms round his neck, kicked him violently behind the knees. Although I was so much lighter, the effect was what I expected. Down he fell, and his pistol went off, the ball grazing the lieutenant's forehead. The lashings which held Charley were cut, and he immediately came to my assistance, while Harry performed the same office for the lieutenant without difficulty. The sound of the pistol would, I feared, bring some of the crew down upon us. Fortunately at that moment a strong breeze had struck the ship. The officers were issuing their orders, so that we had hopes we might be undisturbed. No time, however, was to be lost. We quickly lashed the pirate's arms and legs, and crammed a handkerchief into his mouth. Lieutenant Hallton proposed to throw him overboard, and then, rushing together on deck, to master the officers, and try to recall the crew back to their duty. To the first part of the proposal none of us agreed, but we forthwith dragged the unhappy man back to his cot and lifted him in. He appeared to me to be insensible. At all events, when Charley took the handkerchief out of his mouth, he did not cry out or utter a word, although his eyes glared at us.

"We might have put you to death," said Charley, "but you are safe if you will remain quiet, and not attempt to summon any one to set you free."

The pirate did not reply, and I was doubtful if he understood what was said to him. He must indeed have been surprised at finding himself again a prisoner at the very moment he supposed that he had regained his authority. We had now to decide what to do. We might certainly master one or two officers, but it was a question if the men from the " Rover " would return to their duty, and still less likely that the pirates would yield to our authority. Lieutenant Hallton then suggested that we should drag the pirate up on deck, and, holding a pistol to his head, threaten to shoot him if he did not order the crew to obey us. To this I for one strongly objected.

Charley thought that Captain Roderick was perfectly mad, and I also was very unwilling to injure a brother of Mr. Trunnion's, villain as he was.

" If he is really mad, he will not know what has happened," said Charley. " The best thing you can do is to return on deck, and try and negotiate yourself with the mate, who has now the command, and will probably wish to keep it. Tell him that I am your brother, and as he has no one on board who understands navigation, that I shall be happy to assist him in navigating the ship ; that we have no wish to inform against him and his men if we obtain our liberty, and that all we request is that he will set us on shore at the first place we touch at."

This seemed the only feasible plan, and Harry and I set off to try and find Tubbs and consult him, while Charley and the lieutenant returned to the cabin in which they had been confined. Harry and I, as agreed on, went on deck.

Our absence had not been discovered. Slowly groping now on one side, now on the other, we at length discovered Tubbs. Taking him by the arm, I led him away apart from where any one was standing.

" To my mind, sir, the mate will be very much obliged to you for what you have done. He has no wish to give up the command, I can see that ; and if you can persuade Captain Roderick—should he come to his senses—that such is the case, we should have him on our side. I suspect, also, that there are two or three of the 'Rover's' men who are sorry for their conduct, and would join us. The truth is, I believe, when Captain Roderick is in his right mind, that he wishes he had a better calling, but when the mad fit comes over him, he goes back to his bad ways."

"That may be true," I could not help remarking, "but it is no excuse for him; he must have an evilly-disposed mind to have taken to such a calling; he should seek for strength from Heaven to overcome his wicked propensities. Even the worst men at times regret the harm they have done on account of the inconvenience and suffering it has caused them, but the next time temptation is presented they commit the same crime, and so it goes on to the end."

It was settled, therefore, that the next day Harry and I should go boldly up to the mate and speak to him as agreed on, while we were to see that no one in the meantime came down to set the captain at liberty, though, as Tubbs observed, "The mate would take very good care of that."

Soon after this a fresh watch was set, and as we were supposed to be in the first watch, we took the opportunity, accompanied by Tubbs, of again slipping down below. Scarcely had we stowed ourselves away out of sight, than the mate came down and looked into the captain's cabin. As not a word was spoken by either, we concluded that he had not discovered the state of things; for, locking the door and taking away the key, he returned to his own cabin, which was further forward on the opposite side. Altogether, as must be seen, affairs were in a curious state on board that ship. I at length dropped off to sleep. How long it was after I closed my eyes I know not, when I heard a sound like that of a cable running out. Tubbs started up at the same moment.

"Why, we have just come to an anchor," he exclaimed.

"We must have been closer in with the land than we supposed."

Harry being awakened, we both stole quietly on deck. The crew had furled sails, the night was perfectly calm, the stars shone brightly overhead. Looking over the larboard side, we saw the shore, a high land with a point running from it, off which we lay. By the ripple of the water against the bows, I knew that a strong current was running, which accounted for the ship having been brought up. Looking forward, I saw that a bright light was burning at the bowsprit end, and presently it was answered by a rocket fired from the shore, which rose high in the air, scattering its drops as it fell. Exclamations of satisfaction escaped the mate and several of the crew who were on deck.

"Lower the starboard quarter-boat," shouted the mate.

"She's well-nigh knocked to pieces, and can't swim," was the answer.

"Lower the larboard boat."

This was done, and several of the crew jumped into her, but most of them as quickly hauled themselves on board again. She sank beneath their feet, as she too had been injured by the frigate's shot. The boat getting adrift, one of the men, before he could spring up the side, was drifted away in her, the current of which I have spoken carrying him rapidly astern. The long-boat amidships was in a worse condition, being riddled with shot.

"I hope that the people on shore will send off to us," observed the mate ; "it's very certain we cannot get to them until the boats are repaired."

"They'll not do that in a hurry ; for, as it happens, the carpenter and his crew are all killed, and there is not a man on board able to do the work," I heard Tubbs observe.

In the meantime, the cries of the poor fellow in the sinking boat reached our ears, but it was impossible to render him any assistance. Farther and farther he drifted at a rapid rate, until he and the boat were lost sight of, although, we could hear his shouts every minute becoming fainter and fainter. At last there arose a dreadful shriek, which, although from a distance, was piercingly clear.

"Poor fellow! Jack shark has got him," said Tubbs. "There are plenty of those creatures about here, and I was sure that it wouldn't be long before they had hold of him."

I have not mentioned the poor slaves all this time. The wounded were suffering dreadfully, and since they had again been sent down to the hot slave-deck, several had died. The mate, while waiting for the expected boat, ordered some hands below to overhaul them. Six dead bodies were brought up, which were without ceremony thrown overboard, as if they were so many rotten sheep, and the men reported several more not likely to live out the night. The mate, hardened villain as he was, did not order them to be got rid of, as was sometimes done by slavers to save themselves trouble, and to economise the food the poor creatures might have consumed. He became impatient when, after waiting some time, no boat appeared. The weather, too, although so fine and calm when we brought up, gave indications of a change. The sky was overcast, and heavy undulations began to roll in towards the shore. Though as yet the wind had not increased, our position was becoming dangerous, and I for one wished that we were miles off the coast.

"If there's no harbour into which we can run, we shall be in a bad way," said Tubbs. "I suspect that the mate doesn't know of one, or we should have steered in for it at once."

"What had we better do?" I asked.

"Do, sir! Why, there's nothing we can do but ask God to take care of us. If it comes on to blow, as I believe it will, ten to one but that the ship is driven on shore, and with the heavy surf there will be, before many hours are over, breaking on the coast, and the sharks waiting for us outside, there won't be many who will reach the shore alive. The best swimmers could not help themselves, and that's all I can say."

I was convinced of the truth of what Tubbs said. That he was right with respect to a gale approaching was soon proved, the wind, bursting suddenly on us, striking the ship, and, although all her sails were furled, making her heel over before it, and at the same time the rollers which came in from the offing increased in height, and we could hear their roar as they broke on the shore to leeward. The ship pitched fearfully into them, and every moment I expected to see the cable part. Should such be the case, I was very sure that not many minutes afterwards all on board would be struggling for their lives. I thought of my brother and the lieutenant, and of the unhappy captain. I intended, should the cable part, immediately to rush below and set them all at liberty. Although the captain had so cruelly ill-treated us, I could not reconcile it to my conscience to allow him to perish without a chance of escaping, which he would do were he left bound hand and foot. I told Harry what I thought of doing.

"No doubt," he said. "Should the captain escape, he would scarcely fail to be grateful to us for saving his life; and if he is drowned notwithstanding, we have done our duty."

The mate, who had been below, now came on deck. He evidently did not like the look of things. Two or three times he went forward and examined the cable, at which the ship seemed to be tugging with all her might as she rose on the summits of the heavy foaming swells. He then got another cable ranged to let go should the first part.

"If I were him, I'd get ready to make sail. The sky looks to me as if the wind were coming more to the south'ard; and if so, we may chance to stand off shore should the ship cast the right way."

"I would not hesitate to tell him so," I observed; "when

his life may depend upon it, he may perhaps take your advice, although he will not follow that of any other man."

"At all events, I'll try it," said Tubbs; and going up to the mate, he told him what he thought. I had very little hope, however, that the mate would listen to him.

"You think yourself a better seaman than I am Just go and attend to your duty," was the answer. Not two minutes had elapsed, however, before the mate ordered the crew to stand by the halyards. Presently he shouted, "All hands make sail."

The boatswain went forward, axe in hand, to cut the cable. The topsails, closely reefed, were let fall, the fore-staysail and jib hoisted.

"Cut!" shouted the mate.

The ship cast the right way to starboard, the helm was put to port, and she begun to stand off from the shore.

"She'll do it, and we shall have a new lease of life," observed Tubbs when he rejoined Harry and me; "that is to say, if the wind holds as it is; but if not, the chances of our hauling off the shore are doubtful."

For some minutes the ship stood on with her head to the north-west, all hands anxiously watching the sails, and casting a look every now and then towards the dark outline of the shore, which could be distinguished through the gloom. The current was all this time drifting us to the northward, but it appeared to me that we were getting no farther from the coast. Of that, however, it was difficult to judge by the rate at which we were sailing, as although she might be moving fast through the water, she might really be making but little way over the ground. Tubbs several times went aft to the binnacle.

"She has fallen off two points, I'm sorry to say," he observed; "still it is possible that we may beat off, as the wind may shift again; but I wish that it had kept steady, and we should have done it."

Scarcely, however, had he spoken, when the sails gave a loud flap.

"No higher!" shouted the mate to the man at the helm, "or you'll have her aback."

The helm was put up in time to prevent this danger.

On looking over the starboard side, we now saw that the land was broad on the beam, and that we were thus standing almost parallel with the coast, towards which it was too evident that the heavy rollers were gradually setting us. Still it was possible, as Tubbs thought, to keep off the shore until daylight, when the mouth of a river might be discovered and we might run into it; or the wind might again shift, and we should, once more, be able to stand off, and get to a safe distance from the hungry breakers, which we could hear roaring under our lee. I was struck by the change which had come over the crew. Generally, when on deck together, they were shouting and swearing, and exchanging rough jokes or laughing loudly. Now scarcely a man spoke, all stood at their stations turning their gaze towards the shore. It was evident they were fully aware of the dangerous position in which the ship was placed. I asked Tubbs how long he thought the ship could be kept off the land, standing as she was now.

"Oh, maybe for half an hour, maybe for less," he answered. "The current is sending her along at the rate of two or three knots an hour, and we may fall in with some headland which we are unable to weather, or we may find ourselves standing across a wide bay which will lengthen the time before she drives on shore."

"At all events, I will tell my brother and Mr. Hallton. It will be wrong to let them remain longer in ignorance of the danger we are in. Perhaps we ought to set the captain at liberty."

"No, no, sir; let him stay until the last, we don't know what mad things he will do if he comes on deck. Perhaps he will be shooting the mate or one of us. It will be time enough to let him out of the cabin when all chance of saving the ship is gone."

I saw at once the prudence of this, and settled to act accordingly. Taking an opportunity, I slipped below, and found Charley and Mr. Hallton asleep. Having roused them up, " I have not got very pleasant information to give you," I said ; and I then told them that Tubbs considered the ship would drive on shore in less than half an hour.

Mr. Hallton, though supposed to be a brave man, was much more agitated than was Charley.

" The ship cast on this abominable coast in less than half an hour ! " he exclaimed. " Why, even down here, the sound of the breakers reaches us."

" Well, Dick, if the worst comes to the worst, we must have a struggle for life," said my brother calmly. " You stick to me, and I'll do my best to help you. I am well accustomed to the sort of work we shall have to go through, and I hope that we shall manage somehow or other to get on shore." Of course, they were both unwilling to remain longer below, and as neither the mate nor the crew were likely to interfere, they made up their minds to come on deck with me. I had some hopes that Mr. Hallton, who was a first-rate seaman, might devise some means for escaping. I first consulted Charley about setting the captain at liberty, but he thought that it would not be prudent to do so until the last moment, when it would be right to give him a chance of saving his life with the rest of us. We soon gained the deck. Whether Charley or the lieutenant were observed, I could not tell. I waited anxiously to hear what opinion Mr. Hallton might offer as to the state of affairs.

" If we get much nearer the shore, we must bring up, and perhaps the anchor will hold until the wind moderates. It is the only chance we have of saving the ship. If we were to go about now, we might miss stays. and there is not room to wear without getting perilously close to the breakers," he observed.

At the rate we were sailing, we must have gone over thirty or forty miles from the point where we exchanged signals with the shore, and as most probably the country was inhabited by a different tribe, who might be at enmity with the white men, those of us who might reach the shore would run a great chance of being slaughtered or carried off into slavery. I said as much to Harry and Charley. The same idea had occurred to them.

"It may be the case, but we may fall among friends, and we will hope for the best," observed Charley.

Dawn was at length approaching, but there was no abatement of the gale, while it was too clear that we were drifting nearer and nearer to the coast. Every moment I expected to hear the mate give the word to furl the sails and let go the anchor. I suggested to Tubbs that he should advise him to do so.

"He would not listen to me; although he may know it is the best thing to be done, he'll just put off doing it until it's too late," he answered.

Gradually the coast became more and more distinct, and we could make out the white line of breakers as they burst upon it. We stood watching it with straining eyes, the minutes turned into hours, the ship all the time rushing through the water at a furious rate. Presently a headland appeared on the starboard bow. It seemed impossible that we could weather it. Still the mate issued no order except to the man at the helm.

"Luff all you can," he shouted out; "we don't want to cast the ship away on that point if we can help it."

In a few minutes—how many I cannot say—we saw the breakers close under our lee, the ship was almost among them, but on she stood. Again the land appeared to recede.

"Can there be a harbour in anywhere here?" I asked of Tubbs.

"The mate doesn't think so, or we should be running into it," was the answer.

It was only a small bay across which we were passing. Not a quarter of an hour afterwards another point appeared. As we had succeeded in weathering the first, the mate evidently expected to pass this in the same way.

Mr. Hallton, convinced that we could not do so, shouted out, "Down with the helm—shorten sail—let go the anchor—let fly everything."

"Who dares give orders on board this ship?" cried the mate.

The crew, however, were convinced that the first order was the wisest. The tacks, sheets, and halyards were let go, the stoppers of the cable cut, the helm put down to bring her up to the wind. She pitched into the seas, but the anchor held. The crew now flew aloft to try and gather in the canvas, fluttering wildly in the gale.

"In three minutes more we should have been knocking to pieces on the rocks," observed Mr. Hallton. "It is a question whether the anchor will hold now; if it doesn't, we sha'n't be much better off."

Scarcely had he spoken when a loud report was heard. "The cable has parted!" shouted several voices.

"Let go the last hope."

The anchor so called was let go, and although it brought the ship up in a couple of minutes, it also parted, and the helpless ship now drifted rapidly towards the breakers, which could be seen curling up along the shores of the bay into which we had driven.

"Come aft," said Charley to Harry and me. "The moment the ship strikes the masts will go, and we shall chance to be crushed as they fall."

"The time has come to set Captain Trunnion at liberty," I said.

Charley and I hurried below and burst open the door of the cabin. The unhappy man was still sleeping, with his dog Growler at his feet. Surly as the animal was to others, he was faithful to his master, and he seemed to understand that we had come with no evil intentions, for though he uttered a low bark, he did not attempt to fly at us. By the light of the lamp we saw that the captain had no arms near him. To cut the ropes which bound his limbs was the work of a moment.

"Captain Trunnion," I exclaimed, "we have come to warn you that the ship will be in the midst of the breakers in the course of a minute or two. If you wish to save your life you must come upon deck."

Not, however, until Harry and Charley had shaken him well did he wake up. He gazed around him with a bewildered look.

"What is that you say?" he asked.

In a few sentences I told him.

"Then it is time to look out to save our lives," he said springing up, apparently quite himself. He looked as cool and composed as he had ever been. We were about to return on deck, when there came a fearful crash overhead, followed by several others. The ship had struck and the masts had all gone together by the board. Shrieks and cries arose, but many of the voices were speedily silenced, as the sea, breaking over the ship, washed several men from the deck into the seething cauldron into which she had been driven. The captain, followed by Growler, sprang up the companion ladder, and we saw no more of them. The cries of the helpless slaves below, uniting in one fearful chorus, overwhelmed the voices of the white crew.

"We must set these poor wretches at liberty. It would be a fearful subject of thought if we were to leave them to perish," observed Charley. "There is a hatch, I know, which leads from the main cabin to the slave-deck, although it is kept closed."

"Ay, ay, sir! But we can't do it without the instruments," said Tubbs. Hunting about, he discovered some irons used for the purpose, with which we each supplied ourselves. With this means we soon opened the hatch.

There was great risk in the merciful task we were about to perform, but Charley, setting the example, we quickly knocked off the manacles of Aboh and the slaves nearest to us, and, with the assistance of the former, made them understand that they were to perform the same operation to their fellow-captives. Some obeyed, but others rushed immediately on deck. However, we persevered, and, faster than I could have believed it possible, we contrived to set all the slaves free. Many of the poor wretches enjoyed their liberty but for a few seconds, for they were quickly washed off the deck, or were drowned in a vain attempt to reach the shore by swimming. All the time the sea was striking with terrific force against the sides of the ship. The loud crashing sound overhead showed us that her bowsprit and bulwarks and everything on deck was being rapidly carried away.

While we were thus engaged daylight appeared, and when we reached the deck we saw that the wind had greatly gone down. Although there were rocks on either side of us, there was a clear piece of sand, on which, could a raft be formed, those who could not swim might land. The blacks were mostly clustered aft, the part least exposed to the fury of the seas. Several persons were in the water, some swimming, others floating apparently lifeless. The greater portion of the crew had disappeared; many had been crushed by the falling masts, others washed overboard, and a few on pieces of wreck were trying to reach the beach One thing was certain, there was no time to be lost, as the ship could not long hold together, lashed as she was by the fury of the seas which rolled in from the ocean. The surviving blacks recognised us when we appeared as the persons who had set them at liberty and we made them understand that if they would remain quiet, we would endeavour to provide the means for enabling them to reach the shore. I thought that among the people clinging to pieces of wreck I saw Captain Trunnion, but I was not certain. The mate had disappeared, and had, I concluded, been washed overboard, and, as far as we could learn, Mr. Hallton had shared the same fate. We had reason to be thankful that we had been below, or we also might have lost our lives. We immediately set about forming the raft from some spars which still remained lashed to ring bolts on the deck and from fragments of the bulwarks. Every instant the wind was going down, rendering our task less difficult. The tide too was falling, and as it did so rocks rose out of the water, which further protected us from the fury of the breakers. When the blacks saw what we were about, some of the more intelligent among them offered to assist us. At length a raft capable of holding a dozen people at one time was constructed. We also obtained a rope of sufficient length to reach the shore, so that we might haul it backwards and forwards. This we made the blacks understand that we intended to do, and that we could only take off a certain number at a time. The head men, who had all along held an authority over the rest of their fellow-slaves, now came forward to maintain discipline By this means only the number which the raft could carry were allowed to descend at a time. As soon as we had a cargo we commenced our passage to the shore, and happily landed all those we had taken on board, who at once squatted down on the beach waiting for their companions. We immediately put back and took in another cargo, and thus we continued going backwards and forwards until we had placed the whole of the slaves on shore.

"We must look out for ourselves now," observed Charley. " I saw some firearms in the cabin ; we must secure them, as well as some ammunition, clothes, and provisions. It will not do to trust those black fellows when they at once find themselves at liberty."

Of course we all agreed to Charley's proposal, and climbing up the side, made our way into the cabin. We each got a fowling-piece or musket, a brace of pistols, and a good supply of ammunition. We also found some dollars, which we stowed away in our pockets.

"The money may not be of much use while we are among the savages, but it will come in very handy when we get into a more civilised region," said Charley. "Hurrah! here are some things which will be of immediate use," and he produced a boxful of strings of beads of various colours.

We each stowed away as many of them as we could carry. Under the circumstances in which we were likely to be placed, they would prove of the greatest value.

As the ship it appeared probable would hold together for some time, we hunted about until we found as many things as we could carry likely to be of use. Among others, were a pocket compass, a knife apiece, and other things. Tubbs produced a cooked ham and a box of biscuits, which were divided and put into some canvas bags well suited for the purpose. We were still engaged in our search, when a loud crashing sound reached our ears. We rushed on deck, and found that the sea had made a breach clean through the ship. Fortunately the raft was secured to the after part. We quickly lowered ourselves down on it, and shoved off in time to escape another sea, which came rolling in, and committed further damage, sending fragments of the wreck floating about in the comparatively smooth water between us and the shore. We had great difficulty in avoiding the pieces of timber which were driven towards our frail raft. Every moment it seemed as if we were about to be overwhelmed. On looking towards the beach, we found that the blacks had disappeared, with the exception of one man, who stood ready to assist us in getting on shore. A few more hauls on the raft, and we, with our packs, were able to spring on the sand, the black seizing our hands as we did so, one after the other, and dragging us up out of the seething water, which came foaming up around us.

CHAPTER VII.

OUR first impulse on reaching dry ground was to kneel down and thank Heaven for having mercifully preserved our lives, the black standing by and watching us with a wondering look as we did so. We rose to our feet.

"Where are the rest?" I asked of the friendly negro, whom I recognised to be Aboh, the man to whom I had given water in the slaver's hold, and whom I had just set at liberty.

He pointed over his shoulder, signifying that they had gone inland.

"And you wish to remain with us?" I asked, at once seeing that it would be of importance to have a native with us who might act as our guide and interpreter.

"Yes, massa; me like white man. Once serve board man-of-war; cappen kind, sailors kind; but me went on shore to see me fadder, modder, me brodder, me sister; but dey all get catchee, an' all de oder people run 'way, an' dey take me for slavee."

The beach, which was here of some height, prevented us at first from seeing what had become of the people; but climbing up the bank of fine sand to the summit, we caught sight of some of them making their way towards the forest, about half a mile off.

"They have gone there, poor fellows, to look for food, or perhaps some of them think that they are not far from home, and expect to get back again," observed Tubbs.

This appeared very likely. Before, however, we set off to join our companions in misfortune, we searched about for any of the white men who might have been cast by the surf on the beach. We found several dead bodies, but not a single living person could we discover. On looking eastward, we observed numerous rocks, stretching out to a considerable distance, which, now that the tide had fallen, appeared above water. It was a mercy that the "Vulture" escaped striking on any of them, for, had she done so, she must have been knocked to pieces at a distance from the shore, and probably not one of us would have escaped alive.

We now sat down on the beach and consulted what to do. As it was not likely that any ship, trader, or man-of-war, or even slaver, would willingly come near that part of the coast, we resolved to travel either to the north or the south, hoping to reach one of the French settlements, which existed at the mouths of two or three of the rivers running into the ocean in that region. On looking along the shore on both hands, we saw a wide extent of sand.

"It will never do to attempt travelling over that, gentlemen," said Tubbs. "We shall certainly find no shade, and probably not a drop of water, without which we cannot get along. If you'll take my advice, you'll follow the blacks to the forest. It's water, to a certainty, they've gone to look after; they're thirsty beings, and their instinct has told them where they can find it."

Aboh, who had been listening all the time, evidently under-stood what was said, and nodded his head. We, that is, Charley, Harry, and I, agreed to do as Tubbs had proposed, and we all accordingly set off eastward, accompanied by the black. The forest appeared much further away than we supposed, or per-haps the soft sand, into which our feet sank at every step, made us think the distance longer than it really was. The sun, which was now high in the heavens, beat down with terrific force upon our heads, and as we had on only our sea-caps, which afforded little or no protection, we felt the heat greatly. We found some comfort, however, by shifting our packs on to our heads. Aboh, who saw how much we suffered, offered to relieve us of them. He carried my pack and his own on his head, and another on his shoulders, with perfect ease. I bethought me of a handker-chief which I had in my pocket, and fastened it like a turban over my cap; Harry imitated my example. Charley and Tom, who were stronger than either of us, continued to carry their packs with comparative ease on their heads. We had lost sight of the blacks, the last of whom had disappeared before we commenced our march. At length we reached the outskirts of the forest, and were thankful to sit down and rest under the shade of a tree.

"I have been thinking," said Harry, "that we ought to have a leader who should decide what we should do. It will save a good deal of trouble and discussion."

"You are right, Mr. Bracewell," said Tom, "that's what I've been thinking too; and I propose that we at once elect Mr. Westerton, Mr. Harry's brother. Although I'm older than any of you, he's a naval officer, and I for one shall be ready to obey him."

Of course Harry and I agreed to this, and Aboh, who under-stood almost everything we said, nodded his head, just to show that he also consented to the proposal.

"I will do my best, my friends," said Charley, "although,

had you chosen Mr. Tubbs, I should have been willing to follow him, for I feel convinced that he is a man of courage and judgment."

"Thank you, sir, for your good opinion," said Tom. "You have been more accustomed to command than I have, although I shall be happy to give you any advice whenever you ask it, to the best of my power."

"Well, then," said Charley, "the first use I will make of my authority is to select a northerly route. I have been trying to recall the map of the country, which I frequently studied on board the 'Rover,' and I think we shall, by proceeding as I propose, fall in with the Gaboon River, at the mouth of which there is a French settlement. I remember that three days before the frigate captured the pirate we sighted Cape Lopez, some way to the south of which I calculate we now are, in what I think is called the Pongo country."

"I believe you are right, sir," said Tom. "We shall have to make a pretty long march though, I suspect; but if we can manage to keep near the coast, we may sight a ship, and by making signals, get her to send a boat on shore to take us off; always provided there happens to be no great amount of surf."

"Well then, friends, if you are all rested, we will commence our march," said Charley. "We will first, however, try to overtake the blacks, who, as Mr. Tubbs observes, have been led by their instinct, or rather their knowledge of the country, in the direction where water is to be found; and I daresay you all feel as I do— very thirsty."

"That I do, sir," said Tom. "I feel for all the world as if my mouth was a dusthole, and that a bucketful of hot cinders had been thrown into it."

We confessed that our sensations were very similar to those Tom described. We accordingly all got up and shouldered our packs, for neither Harry nor I would allow Aboh to carry ours any longer; not that we thought he would attempt to run

away with them.   We told him, however, when we camped in the
evening, that we would divide them, so as to give him a separate
package, and thus we should all have an equal load to carry.
Aboh pointed out the direction in which, from the appearance of
the trees, he believed we should find water, and eagerly led the
way.

It was farther inland than we had intended to go, but from
his description we made out that there was a lake or pond fed
by a stream coming down from the mountains of the interior,
and which afterwards lost itself in the sand.   We had gone some
distance when Aboh made a sign for us to note that the ground
had been trampled down by many feet, and that the people who
had passed that way had broken off a number of young saplings,
probably to form spears, and had also torn down the boughs
to serve as other weapons of offence or defence.   After going a
short distance farther, the sound of voices reached our ears.
Aboh shook his head.   " No good, no good," he muttered, and
made us understand that we must advance cautiously.

Presently he again stopped, and advised us by signs to conceal ourselves.   He then crept forward, crouching down beneath
the bushes, so that he could not be perceived by any persons
in front.

" I'll go forward and try and learn what his object is," I whispered to my companions; and Charley not forbidding me, I
imitated Aboh's example and quickly overtook him.   He turned
on hearing my footsteps, and seeing that I was resolved to accompany him, made a sign to me to be cautious.   We had not gone
far when the sounds we had before heard became so loud that I
knew we must be close upon the people who were uttering them.
After advancing a few paces farther, on looking through the
bushes I saw a large party of blacks encamped in an open spot
surrounded by tall trees.   They were evidently in an excited state,
looking up the glade as if they expected some one to approach.
They were mostly employed in sharpening the ends of long poles

in several fires they had lighted. I at once recognised them as
the blacks whom we had assisted to escape from the wreck.
They numbered, however, fewer than those who had landed, and
I concluded, therefore, that some had deserted their companions in
misfortune. Those who had gone away probably belonged to a
tribe in the neighbourhood, and were endeavouring to reach their
own people.

We were not long left in doubt as to the cause of their
excitement. Some distance off we caught sight of another large
party of negroes advancing with threatening gestures, many of
them being armed with muskets and bayonets. On seeing this,
Aboh, seizing me by the arm, dragged me back, and motioned
me to climb into a large tree the lower branches of which we
could reach without much difficulty, he setting me the example and
assisting me up. We soon gained a place where we were completely concealed and protected by the thick boughs. Scarcely
were we seated than we saw the slaves advancing towards the new-
comers, flourishing the spears they had made and shouting savagely,
as if not aware that their opponents had firearms, or fearless of
their effects. They soon, however, discovered their mistake. The
enemy fired a volley which brought several of them to the
ground.

Notwithstanding this they rushed forward, and a fierce hand-to-
hand conflict ensued. The slaves greatly outnumbered their opponents, of whom there were probably not more than fifty or sixty, but
nearly all these had muskets. Some of the firearms, I observed,
did not go off, probably because they had no locks, or it may
have been that their powder was bad. The parties were indeed
more evenly matched than at first appeared to have been the
case. They fought with the greatest desperation. Those who
had muskets which would go off kept at a distance firing at the
slaves, while their comrades either charged with their bayonets,
or holding the barrels in their hands, used their weapons as
clubs.

Several on both sides had fallen, when a fresh party of armed negroes appeared in the direction from whence the others had come. On seeing them, the slaves, who had hitherto fought so bravely, were seized with a panic. The greater number took to flight, making their way westward towards the coast, though they must have looked in vain for succour in that direction. I was afraid that some of them, flying in other directions, might pass by the spot where we had left our friends, who would run a great risk of being killed either by them or their pursuers. Aboh and I were so well concealed that there was not much danger of our being discovered. As may be supposed, we crouched down among the thick leaves, much in the same way that Charles the Second did in the oak after the fight of Worcester. The tide of battle swept by beneath our feet, and a more fearful din of shouts and shrieks and cries I had never heard. Those of the slaves who had been engaged in the front rank, deserted by their companions, were mostly bayoneted or shot down or knocked on the head, but the courageous way in which they fought enabled the rest to get to some distance before their rear ranks were over-taken by their pursuers. At length not a combatant was to be seen, but the ground was strewn with the dead and dying. As I was anxious to rejoin my friends, I immediately descended. Had I possessed a drop of water I would have taken it to the poor wretches, whose moans as they lay expiring reached my ears.

"Do you think we could help some of them ? " I said to Aboh, pointing to the wounded men.

"No good," he said, and made a sign that they would soon be dead. I went up to three or four, and was convinced from the nature of their hurts that I could do nothing for them ; indeed, the spirits of most of them fled while I stood by. Aboh then, seizing my arm, hurried me away.

I found Charley and Harry very anxious about me, for hearing the firing, they supposed that I must have been in the thick of it, and by my not coming back they thought that I was either killed or taken prisoner.

"One thing is certain, we must not remain here a moment longer. The negroes will very likely pass this way, and either kill us all or carry us off into captivity," observed Charley. "I have heard that the black people in this part of the country are among the most savage of the African tribes, and that some—the Fans—are cannibals. I don't know to what tribe Aboh belongs, but I hope he is not a Fan."

"Maybe he is, and intends to deliver us to his country-men, to serve as a feast given to celebrate his safe return to the bosom of his family," said Tom, in a tone half in joke half in earnest.

"He has hitherto shown only good feelings, and we will trust him, at all events," said Charley.

He made signs to Aboh that we wished to move on, and being anxious to find water, we begged that he would lead us to it as soon as possible. He nodded, and pointed to the east. We were too thirsty to hesitate about going in that direction, although we should thus be led farther than we wished from the coast.

We accordingly once more set off, Aboh hurrying us along as fast as we could make our way through the thick forest, stopping at first every now and then to listen as the sound of distant firing was heard, and then apparently to ascertain whether any of the blacks were coming towards us. Aboh's object was evidently to avoid both parties. It was most likely that the slaves whom he had deserted would murder him for having left them, while the people of the other tribe were probably hereditary enemies of his, and would without ceremony have put him to death. We were by this time very hungry as well as thirsty, but our thirst prevented us from eating, and we urged Aboh to endeavour to find water without delay. He merely pointed eastward, and nodded his head as before.

"Well, keep moving, my black angel; whatever you do, keep moving, and lead us to the water," said Tubbs, patting him on the back.

We marched chiefly under the shade of the forest trees, where we found it tolerably cool; at the same time, as Tom observed— "In the opening the sun was hot enough to roast an ox."

At last I felt that I could go on no longer. I threw myself down at the roots of a large tree. Harry, who was marching with me, while the rest were ahead, endeavoured to rouse me up.

"No, no," I said; "go on. If you find water, bring me some, though I doubt if I shall be alive by that time;" and I spoke as I felt.

"Nonsense!" cried Harry. "You are the last person of the party I should have expected to give in. I'll stay by you until you are rested, and then we will hurry on after our friends."

"Perhaps we shall lose them if we are separated," I answered.

The thought made me arouse myself, and rising to my feet, I staggered on. Harry shouted to Charley and Tom, and they came back to give me their assistance. We had not gone far after this, when Aboh shouted out—

"Dere water, water!"

We caught sight of a bright gleam shining through the trees. Though we were in Africa, we knew that it was no mirage, which only appears on dry and sandy deserts. We all hurried on, knowing that our burning thirst would soon be relieved. As we drew nearer, we saw a lake stretching out before us, on the banks of which appeared numberless birds There were long-legged storks, cranes, pelicans, pink-winged flamingoes, ibises, and similar waterfowl of various descriptions. As we appeared, those nearest to us took to flight, the beautiful flamingoes rising in the air with their long legs stretched out behind them. One thought, however, occupied our minds. How to get to the water, for we feared that we should find muddy banks, which might prove impassable. Aboh's quick eye, however, detected a small inlet into which a rivulet fell. He led us down to a hard, gravelly bank, where the water ran as clear as that of an English trout-stream.

We did not stop to consider whether alligators lurked beneath the lilies which floated on the surface, or huge snakes were concealed near at hand waiting for their prey, but kneeling down, we plunged in our heads, and drank huge draughts of the cooling liquid. Cooling it was to us, although probably it would have been thought somewhat tepid in a colder climate. In an instant I was revived, and my companions felt the same sensations.

We could now sit down and enjoy a few mouthfuls of the food we had brought from the wreck, which we took to stay our appetites. We intended, before many minutes were over, to have some of the waterfowl flying round us cooking before the fire. Charley and Harry, being tolerable shots, agreed at once to try and knock over a sufficient number for our wants, while Tom and I collected sticks for a fire. Aboh, seeing them set off, started by himself in an opposite direction.

" We're not likely to starve on our journey, Mr. Westerton, if we are fortunate enough to fall in with as many birds as we see around us just now," said Tom.

" I am afraid that we cannot expect always to camp on the borders of a lake or river," I answered. " It will be plenty one day, and starvation the next. However, if we are prudent, I hope that we shall get along without much suffering. There are probably wildfowl to be found, and then we may fall in with friendly tribes, of whom we can purchase food. At all events, don't let us expect misfortunes until they come."

" That's what I never have done, and never intend to do," answered Tom. " I've always held that there's ' a sweet little cherub who sits up aloft, to take care of the life of poor Jack ; '

and although that may sound like a heathen song, there's truth in it notwithstanding."

We were talking thus while engaged in collecting sticks, cutting some with our axes, and picking up others, until we had made a large pile, sufficient, Tom averred, to roast an ox, when we saw our friends coming back, each loaded with half a dozen ducks. Directly afterwards Aboh appeared, carrying a still greater number, which he gave us to understand that he had captured by swimming out into the lake, his head concealed by a cap of rushes, towards a flock floating unsuspicious of danger near the margin, and that, getting close to them, he had pulled them down under water by the legs. As the slight repast we had eaten had only just taken off the edge of our appetites, we eagerly plucked a bird apiece, and had them spitted in a few minutes before the fire.

" If we only had some pepper and salt, we should do well," said Harry.

" Here they are, sir," said Tom, producing from his knapsack a bag of each.

"We are greatly indebted to you, Mr. Tubbs, for your forethought," observed Charley; "but remember, we must husband these treasures, for it may be a long time before we are able to replenish them."

By the time we had finished our repast, the sun had sunk behind the trees of the forest we had passed through, and as we could not go farther that night, we agreed to camp where we were. It was important to keep up the fire, as we might otherwise receive an unwelcome visit from a lion, elephant, or leopard, or perhaps from a huge species of ape, numbers of which we had reason to supect were in the neighbourhood, though we had not as yet seen any. It was, of course, settled that we should keep watch, each one of us taking it in turns. Not knowing how far Aboh might be trusted, we did not ask him. Before sitting down we collected a further supply of fuel, and cut down some boughs, with which we constructed a rude arbour to shelter our heads and bodies from the night dew, although it would have been of little service in case of a fall of tropical rain. Tom suggested that, as Charley was leader, he ought not to keep watch."

"No, no," said Charley. "I will share with you all in that respect ; " and he offered to keep the first watch. Harry took the second, Tom the third, and I the morning watch.

Tom called me, saying that he had been listening to the mutterings and roars of lions, the occasional cries of deer as they were pounced on by some savage beasts, and the shrieks and other strange noises of night birds. " But you mustn't mind that, sir," he said ; "you'll soon get accustomed to them. If you see anything suspicious, don't mind rousing me up, although you may not wish to awaken the whole party."

I promised to do this, and began to walk about in front of the fire. However, feeling very tired, I sat down, placing my rifle by my side. While thus seated, I confess that, unexpectedly, my eyes closed. It appeared to me but for a moment, although when I opened them daylight had broken, and a bright gleam cast from the orange-tinted sky was thrown over the lake. I was about to spring to my feet and stoop to pick up my rifle, when I found it had gone. On looking round, I saw Aboh holding it in his hand and moving cautiously away from the camp, while he presented it at some object of which he had caught sight a little distance off, and on which his eye was intently fixed. He did not appear to hear me as I followed, when what was my horror to see an enormous serpent, its neck rising in the air, its mouth extended as if about to spring. Aboh stepped behind a small tree, which afforded him some protection, and resting the barrel of the rifle against the trunk, fixed his eye on the creature. It seemed to me about to make its fatal spring, when he, and perhaps my companions and I as well, might have been destroyed. The serpent rose in the air. Aboh fired, its head instantly dropped, although the body continued to writhe and twist along the ground.

The report aroused the rest of the party, who sprang to their feet. They looked greatly astonished when they found it was Aboh and not I who had fired. This, I may say, was the first of many dangers we escaped from the huge monsters of that region. On measuring the snake, we found it full thirty feet in length, with a girth as large as the body of a stout man. Indeed, we agreed that the creature could have swallowed any of us, or all of us in succession, had he been so disposed.

" Good eat," said Aboh, as he cut off the creature's head.

While we cooked the ducks, he roasted a piece of the snake's flesh at the fire, and ate it in preference to them.

We had now to decide what course to pursue, whether to take the eastern or western side of the lake. Charley was disposed to think that we should find the western very marshy, for, looking in that direction, the ground appeared to be covered with tall reeds, while the distance round the eastern side would evidently be much longer. On consulting Aboh, he gave the preference to the eastern side, intimating that the people we had seen, who had attacked the slaves, resided between the lake and the sea, and that probably they would not allow us to pass through their territory without depriving us of everything we possessed, even should we escape with our lives.

" If you'll take my advice, gentlemen, before we start, you'll make some hats to keep the sun off your heads; it won't take us long, and depend upon it, we shall find it very hot along the borders of the lake. Mr. Westerton, I daresay, knows how to make a straw hat as well as I do."

Charley said he did, and he and Tom quickly procured a quantity of dried palm leaves, which, splitting up, they formed into wide rough plaits. Harry and I imitated their example. In a few minutes they had enough plaited to form a hat, when, with some large thorns for needles. and fibre for thread, they stitched the plaiting together as quickly as they made it. Harry and I were longer about our task, for we managed to make only one hat while they put together two, but in less than an hour we were each provided with a very fair straw hat. Some handkerchiefs, which we had brought from on board served to line them, and make them more impervious to the sun.

Our task completed, strapping our knapsacks on our backs and shouldering our rifles, we commenced our march along the shores of the lake.

CHAPTER VIII.

ACCORDING to Aboh's advice we proceeded eastward, with the lake on one side and the vast trees of the forest rising up to an immense height on our right. Frequently the indentations in the shores of the lake compelled us to keep away from the water, when we trudged on completely surrounded by trees. Even at mid-day it was dark and gloomy, not a ray of the sun penetrating to the ground which we trod. Sometimes the silence was profound, when suddenly it was broken by the shrill scream of a parrot, or the chatter of a monkey as he caught sight of us from his leafy covert.

We saw no other animals, though we discovered elephant tracks and other marks on the ground. Aboh, on examining them, said that they were made by leopards, those savage animals abounding in the forest through which we were passing. On the shore of the lake, however, we caught sight of numerous croco diles, some poking their ugly snouts above the surface of the water, others basking on sandbanks, or on the points projecting out into the water.

Once, as we were keeping along the shore, the head of a huge monster rose not ten feet from us. Aboh shouted, " Run, massa, run." His warning came only just in time. Charley, who was farthest from the water, instantly brought his rifle to his shoulder as he saw the crocodile making a dash at Tom, who was nearest to him. Aboh shouted and shrieked to scare the creature. Its jaws were within a foot of Tom's legs, when Charley, knowing that our companion's life depended upon the correctness of his aim pulled the trigger and the ball entered the monster's head through the eye. Tom gave a desperate leap on one side, the crocodile still moved on, and I fancied that Charley must have missed. Harry and I, imitating Tom's example, sprang out of its way. It had not run five yards on dry ground, however, before it stopped, then rolling on its side, began to kick violently. Harry quickly had his rifle ready, and firing down its throat, put an end to its struggles. Aboh proposed cutting some slices out of its body for dinner, but we declined joining him in the repast, as we hoped to catch as many birds and monkeys as we might require. The narrow escape we had had taught us that we must in future avoid marching close to the water, and that it would be prudent to keep a bright look out when near the shores of the lake not to run the risk of being snapped up by a crocodile.

We were disappointed in consequence of this at not being able to sleep securely, as we had expected, close down to the water, so that we might have only one side of our camp to defend. From the experience we had obtained we now saw that we should run a greater chance of being carried off by crocodiles than even by lions or leopards.

We had marched on for about an hour after the occurrence I

have described, when finding that we could cut off a point by proceeding straight on, we had of necessity to leave the shore of the lake, the water of which we had hitherto always had in sight. We had made good some distance, often having to cut away the creepers which impeded our path, and were expecting soon again to catch sight of the water, when loud trumpeting sounds reached our ears.

We stopped to listen, and were soon convinced that the sounds we heard were uttered by elephants, and, moreover, that they were for some cause or other excited by rage. However, as the animals were, we judged, still at some distance on our right hand, we agreed to continue our course, hoping that they would not discover us. In case they should do so, and we should have to defend ourselves, we put bullets into our rifles. The evening was approaching, and it was necessary to look out for a spot sufficiently open to enable us to light the fire, and at the same time not in too dangerous proximity to the lake. That we might have a better chance of finding the spot we were in search of, we separated, Tubbs and Charley going on ahead, while Harry, Aboh, and I searched round on either side of where we then were. We found that we were at no great distance from the lake, the shining water of which we saw between the trees.

"Here's a spot just suitable for us," cried Harry, "but we shall have to cut down the grass that the fire may not spread, otherwise we may create a blaze which would prove very inconvenient."

Just as he spoke the trumpeting sounds we had before heard again reached our ears, but very much nearer. Aboh stopped in an attitude of listening. Presently there came a noise as of the crashing of branches and the tramping of heavy feet on the ground.

"Elephant come dis way," exclaimed Aboh ; "run, massa,

run ;" and he set off in the direction of the lake, pointing to a large tree at no great distance from us.

Harry and I followed his example, hoping that Charley and Tubbs would hear the sounds in time to make their escape. The trumpeting and crashing sounds drew nearer. Presently we caught sight of several huge trunks lifted in the air, with gleaming tusks below them, and the huge heads of the savage monsters among the leaves.

"Here, massa, here, get up !" exclaimed Aboh, reaching the foot of the tree.

As he spoke, seizing a bough, he swung himself up with the agility of a monkey on to a lower branch. I cast my eye behind me, when what was my horror to see Charley coming along with three or four elephants dashing at full speed not thirty yards behind him. It seemed scarcely possible that he could reach a place of safety before he was overtaken. All my thoughts were now turned on Charley, and I regretted that I had not managed to hand my rifle to Aboh before climbing up myself. Charley had dropped his, and came bounding along, the elephants, however, gaining on him. He saw us, and made towards the tree. Aboh and I stooped down to catch his hands and help him up. He was within twenty yards of us, when his foot caught in one of the treacherous vines which crept in snakelike coils over the ground and hung from numberless branches, and he fell. He was instantly, however, again on his feet, and came rushing on as before ; but the delay had enabled the leading elephant to gain on him. We shrieked and shouted to encourage him, or perhaps impelled to do so by our fears. He reached the foot of the tree. In another instant the elephant would have seized him with its trunk or trampled him under its feet. Had he not possessed unusual activity his destruction would have been certain. He grasped the bough nearest him. Aboh sprang down and got him by one hand. I seized him by the other. The elephant's trunk was already touching his leg, which would the next moment have been encircled in its fatal embrace. We tugged and hauled; the animal caught his shoe, which happily gave way, and Charley was out of its reach. We now breathed more freely, for the tree was far too stout to enable the elephants to tear it down. The beast which had so nearly caught Charley stood trumpeting with rage beneath our feet, lifting up his trunk in a vain attempt to reach us.

We, as may be supposed, climbed higher up, so as to be well out of his way. In a few seconds the remainder of the herd came up, surrounding the tree and all trumpeting together. It was a sound sufficient to make our hearts quail. Had we possessed our rifles, we might have quickly put an end to the animals, mighty as they seemed. Fortunately, in their rage they did not discover them, as they were concealed in the tall grass and leaves between the roots. We dreaded, however, every instant that their feet would come down and crush them, when they, in all probability, would have been rendered perfectly useless.

Our thoughts were now turned towards Tom. Charley said that he had lost sight of him just before he saw the elephants, but that he trusted he had sought safety in a tree as we had done. We shouted out, hoping that he would hear us; but the trumpeting of the elephants drowned our voices. However, although we did not get any answer, we still hoped that he might have escaped.

"I wish that I had not lost my rifle," said Charley, "although I think I should be able to find it again if the beasts did not trample upon it, and I don't think they did, for I threw it as far from me as I could into a thick bush."

"If you hadn't thrown it away, both you and it would have been crushed to pieces," answered Harry. "I think it is fortunate that you had presence of mind to get rid of it. But, I say, I wonder whether these beasts are going to lay siege to us all night. I'm getting very hungry. If they don't go away we shall be starved."

"Perhaps the best thing we can do is to climb up higher and hide ourselves, and then, when they don't see us, their rage may abate, and they will go away," I remarked. "They are not likely to remain here all night, and will probably go to the lake to drink, and give us time, at all events, to get down and recover our rifles."

"What does Aboh think about the matter?" asked Charley.

I inquired of the black, making the usual signs by means of which we carried on a conversation with him, and using such simple words as he was likely to understand. He evidently comprehended what I said, and highly approved of our plan of hiding ourselves,-setting the example by climbing up and concealing himself from the elephants below. We three did the same, though I managed still to watch them by peeping through the leaves of the bough on which I had perched myself. The creatures in a short time ceased their trumpeting, but still remained walking slowly round and round the tree, looking up in a sagacious fashion to ascertain what had become of us. At last they appeared either to forget us, or to fancy that we were birds, and had flown away. The biggest elephant, which had so nearly caught Charley, then led the way down to the lake, the rest following him. It was with infinite satisfaction that we saw them go.

"Now, quick, quick! let us get our rifles, at all events, before they come back," whispered Charley.

Aboh, seeing me about to descend, made a sign that he would go himself, and, with wonderful agility, he slipped down the tree, while Charley descended to the lowest bough to reach the rifles as he handed them up. I followed, keeping a little above my brother, that I might pass them on to Harry. I felt very thankful when Aboh handed up my rifle to Charley, who giving it to me, I passed it on to Harry. Aboh then, again slipping down, handed up Harry's. To our infinite relief neither of them were injured, though the feet of the elephants must have trampled the ground on either side.

"Him go get massa officer's rifle," said Aboh, who was delighted to make use of some of the words with which he was best acquainted; and without waiting to obtain our sanction, he darted off in the direction from which Charley came.

"See if you can find Tom anywhere," I shouted.

Aboh turned and made a sign to us to be silent, pointing at the same time towards the lake, where the elephants were drinking. I regretted having cried out, lest my voice should have attracted the creatures' attention, and might cause them to return and look for us. Although Aboh probably thought that Tom was concealed somewhere in the neighbourhood, yet, knowing the importance of silence, he did not cry out to ascertain his position.

We watched him anxiously, for we feared that at any moment the elephants might come back before he could discover the rifle, which might take some time to find. We saw him hunting about, but Charley said that he thought the spot where he had thrown it away was much farther off. At length he was altogether hidden from our sight by the thick foliage.

"Harry, do you climb up and keep a look-out for the elephants, and Dick and I will stand by to help up Aboh when he comes back. If you see the beasts coming, send a shot into the head of the leader; if you don't kill him, it will probably bring him to a standstill or turn him aside, and give the black more time to climb up the tree," said Charley.

"Ay, ay!" answered Harry, taking his rifle; "I'll do my best to stop the brutes coming this way, at all events."

Charley and I waited on the lower branches, my brother being beneath me, watching for the return of Aboh. At last we saw him coming along with Charley's rifle in his hand. At the same instant Harry shouted out—

"Here come the elephants with their trunks turned up, but they are walking leisurely along, as if they had forgotten all about us."

"Don't fire, then, unless they come close to the tree," answered Charley, while he made signs to Aboh to hasten his steps, pointing as he did so towards the lake. Aboh sprang forward, but the quick ears and quick sight of the elephants had detected him, and sticking out their trunks, they begun trumpeting and moving rapidly forward. I scarcely thought it possible that Aboh could escape them. Just then we heard the report of Harry's rifle over our heads. A shriek of rage escaped the leading elephant, and he had, we concluded, been hit. At the same moment Aboh stopped, and levelling his rifle, fired. The ball struck the animal, which, however, still came on, although at a slower pace than before, and Aboh, grasping the rifle, darted up the tree holding it above his head, so that Charley could stoop down and seize it by the barrel. Handing it to me, he was able to assist Aboh, who nimbly scrambled up.

We all then retreated to our former resting-places, out of the reach of the elephants' trunks. The whole herd came on, the leader bleeding but still trumpeting furiously. We, however, had him in our power, and felt pretty sure that his trumpetings would soon be over. My weapon was still loaded, Charley asked me to let him have it, as he was in a better position for firing than I was. I handed it to him, and as the elephants came near he took aim at the leader, waiting until in his circuit round the tree his head presented a fair mark. He fired, the huge monster immediately sank down, and almost without a struggle was dead. We could not resist joining Aboh in the loud shout of triumph he raised as we saw our enemy destroyed. On the fall of their leader, the other elephants became alarmed, and uttering a few trumpetings, more of fear than anger, rushed off together into the forest, crushing down the shrubs and young trees as they went, making a good pathway towards the southward, which would have saved us much trouble to have followed had we wished to go in that direction. We now, feeling sure that they would not return, descended. Our first care on reaching the ground was to reload our rifles.

"I wish that we could carry off the tusks," said Harry. "I'm sure they would be worth no small number of dollars if they were safe on board."

"It is very certain that we cannot get them down to the sea at present, and probably before we can return to fetch them some other hunters will have carried them off," observed Charley.

While we were discussing the subject, Aboh had got out his knife and was working away at one of the animal's feet, which he succeeded in cleverly amputating.

"Him good eat," said the black pointing to the foot he had just cut off.

Although we certainly could not agree with him, we did not contradict his assertion. He then cut some slices out of the back, which had not a more attractive appearance than the foot. The black, however, seemed to think that we had now an ample supply of food. We should have camped on the spot, as the shades of evening were already coming on, had we not been anxious to discover Tom.

"We must find him before nightfall," I observed; "for even although the creatures may not have killed him, he may be injured and unable to rejoin us."

"Certainly, unless he has got to a considerable distance, he must have heard our shouts," remarked Harry.

Charley agreed with us, and we accordingly proceeded in the direction of the spot where Charley had left our companion. As we went on we shouted out his name, while we looked carefully on either side, dreading at any moment to discover his mangled remains. Aboh hunted about with great care, but for some distance the ground was so trampled by the elephants' feet, and the trees and shrubs so torn, that any footsteps of a human being must effectually have been obliterated. Presently, how-ever, we crossed the path formed by the herd as they had made their way towards us, and all traces of them ceased. A short time afterwards we saw Aboh examining the ground, then he pointed ahead and went on at a rapid rate, we following his footsteps. Again he stopped, and stooping down picked up a rifle. We recognised it as Tom's. What had become of its owner? Still Aboh went on.

By this time the forest was so shrouded in the gloom of approaching night that we could with difficulty see anything before us. Again Aboh stopped and cried out, " Him here ! him here!" We hurried forward. There was our poor friend stretched on the ground, his leg caught in a vine below a tall tree with branches coming close to the ground. The dreadful thought seized me that he was dead.

"Tom, Mr. Tubbs, speak to me," I cried out.

I heard a groan. At all events, he was alive. Stooping down, I rested his head on my knee. Charley and Harry quickly came up. We soon released poor Tom's foot. On examining it, we feared that it was dislocated, or at all events severely sprained, and that probably he had fainted from the pain. Having water in our flasks, we poured some down his throat. By wetting his hands and chafing his arms we in a short time brought him to. He looked round him, evidently very much astonished.

"Where am I, mates? What has happened?" he asked at

length. "I was dreaming that a shark or a tiger or some beast or other had bitten off my foot."

"Not so bad as that," said Charley, "although you have hurt it considerably, I fear."

"Ah, now I recollect all about it. I was afraid, Mr. Westerton, that you were caught by the elephants, and I was expecting to share the same fate. As I could not help you, I thought the wisest thing I could do was to run for my life. I confess it, I never was in such a fright before. I somehow dropped my gun, and then, just as I was about to climb up into that tree overhead, I found myself caught with a round turn about my leg, and down I came. The honest truth is, I don't remember anything more of what happened after that."

It would have been unjust to blame poor Tom for the very natural panic which had seized him on finding himself alone in the forest, and, as he supposed, with his companions killed. He had acted as most people would have done under similar circumstances, and endeavoured to save his life. We fortunately found not far off just such an open space as we were searching for. Our first business was to light a fire in the centre of it, after having cut away the surrounding grass.

"We must keep up a good blaze, or we may have some unwelcome visits from wild beasts," said Charley. "It will be necessary to keep an eye towards the lake, or one of those horrid crocodiles may be crawling up in search of some supper when the odour of the roasted elephant-meat reaches his nose."

While Charley and I attended to poor Tom, Harry and Aboh made up the fire as proposed. We had brought an iron saucepan, with which Aboh intimated that he would go down to the lake to get some water, making a sign to Harry to accompany him with his gun.

" If big ting come out of de water, fire at him head," he said, showing that he was fully alive to the danger of approaching the lake, especially of an evening, when the crocodiles are more active than at other times during the day.

We kept the fire blazing up brightly, so that it might scare any wild beasts prowling round about us.   However, not trusting to that alone, Charley and I kept our rifles by our sides and our eyes about us, lest a lion or leopard might spring upon us unawares.   Having got off Tom's boot and sock, we examined his ankle.   It looked blue and swollen, and when we touched it he complained that it pained him much.   Still, as far as we could judge, no bone was broken.

" The only thing I can think of is to bind it up in a wet handkerchief," observed Charley ; " the inflammation may thus be allayed."

While we were speaking we heard a shot from Harry's gun, showing that we must not expect to obtain even a saucepan of water without trouble.   Shortly afterwards Aboh returned with the water.   Charley asked for some of it, and saturating a handkerchief, which he fortunately had in his pocket, he bound up Tom's ankle.   Harry told us that scarcely had Aboh dipped the saucepan into the water, than a crocodile poked its ugly head above the surface and made a dash at him.

" I was too quick, however, and firing, hit the creature in the throat, when it slid off again into deep water," he added, " whether killed or not I cannot say, as it sank immediately."

" You have done so well that we must get you to make another trip as soon as we have eaten our soup, which, I suppose, Aboh intends to make out of the elephant-meat, for I doubt if it will be palatable cooked in any other way," said Charley.

We found that the black had brought several stones from the

shores of the lake. He now, having placed them in the fire, dug a hole near at hand, into which he scraped some of the ashes, and then put in the stones with the elephant's foot on the top of them. Above this having placed some thick leaves, he quickly filled up the hole.

"Him soon good eat," he said.

Harry had in the meantime cut up some pieces of elephant-meat, which he put into the saucepan. Having placed it on the fire, he stuck some other slices on forked sticks as close as they could be placed to the flames.

"We shall have the opportunity of trying the comparative excellencies of three styles of cooking," he observed, laughing.

"I have no great faith in Aboh's mode of proceeding," remarked Charley.

"Nor have I, except to produce any especially excellent soup," said Harry.

Our patience was to be severely exercised. We were all so hungry that Charley consented to serve out a small piece of biscuit to each of us, just to stay our appetites; but that produced a very transient effect. At first I saw him tightening his waist-belt; then I had to tighten mine, as Harry did his. Poor Tom was suffering too much pain to care about eating, and Aboh was well accustomed to endure long hours of fasting.

"When is that mess of yours likely to be ready?" Charley and I kept crying out to Harry.

"I think that it is done to a turn now," said Harry, and he produced five pieces of black-looking stuff.

"A very long turn," said Charley as he took his share. "Why, it's as hard and dry as shoe-leather, and quite as tough, I suspect."

"Chew it, man, chew it," answered Charley, laughing; "it's better than that in the soup."

We all cut off little bits, hunger making us in no way particular; but it was a difficult business to get down a mouthful. At last I took to scraping it with my knife, by which means I was able to swallow more than I otherwise could have done.

We next tried the soup. The warm liquid could at all events be swallowed, and it appeared to do good to poor Tom, to whom we gave several cupfuls. The meat, however, was scarcely an improvement upon the steaks. Aboh had been watching us all the time while he munched his share without showing a sign of dissatisfaction.

" As we shall want some more water for poor Tom's foot, I wish you would go down, Harry, to the lake and fill the saucepan," said Charley.

" I will go with Aboh willingly enough, provided he carries a torch, for otherwise the chances are that we shall not get off as easily as we did before," answered Harry.

Aboh understood what was proposed, and taking a brand from the fire in one hand, and the saucepan in the other, he set off, Harry accompanying him with his rifle ready for instant use. Charley and I, in the meantime, got up and examined the forest around us. Strange noises were issuing from it ; but our ears being unaccustomed to the sounds of an African wilderness, we could not distinguish either the animals or birds which produced them. Here and there we picked up sticks, which we carried to the heap prepared for keeping up the fire during the night. I was stooping down, expecting to take up a thin stick, when I saw it glide away. I had nearly caught hold of a snake by the body. It might have been harmless, but if venomous, I should have probably been fatally bitten. I sprang back, as may be supposed, and was very cautious after this to feel with the pole I carried in my hand before I picked up any other sticks. In a short time Harry and Aboh came back with the saucepan of water, from which we filled our mugs, for the tough elephant-meat made us thirsty. We were all suffering from hunger, and as we expected to find Aboh's dish as unpalatable as ours, we had made up our minds to lie down, if not exactly supperless, as hungry almost as before.

"Now, massa, him 'tink foot ready," said Aboh, and without more ado, he opened the hole and produced the foot hot and steaming. Just taking off the top, as if it had been a piece of pie-crust, what was our surprise and very great satisfaction to find the interior full of a rich glutinous substance. We eagerly hooked it out with our knives, and it was pronounced excellent jelly, although somewhat strong tasted. The single foot contained more than we altogether could eat, although Aboh got through twice as much, as either of the rest of us. We regretted that we had not brought along more of the elephant's feet.

Instead of going supperless to bed, we thus had a more ample meal than we had eaten since we landed. As it was important that Tom should have a night's rest, Charley, Harry, and I agreed to keep watch in turns. We did not ask Aboh, though he would, we felt sure, have proved trustworthy. I had the middle watch. As I walked round and round the camp, my ears were saluted by distant mutterings and the occasional roar of lions, the trumpetings of elephants, or the shrill agonised cry of some hapless deer on which a stealthy leopard had pounced, the shrieks of night birds, the chirp of insects, and the croaking of frogs. Every moment I expected to see some monster shove its nose out amid the dark foliage; but if any came near, the fire prevented them from springing on us. I occasionally stooped down and wetted Tom's bandage, so that his leg was kept cool all the night. Charging Harry to do the same, I at length lay down, and in a moment was fast asleep. Next morning we found Tom better, but utterly unable to proceed. We, therefore, had to make up our minds to camp for another day at least, unless we could manage to find a canoe in which to cross the lake.

Harry and I, as soon as we were on foot, took our guns, accompanied by Aboh, in search of game for breakfast. We soon came upon a number of ducks, and were fortunate in killing half a dozen in three shots, two being brought to the ground each time we fired. We did not forget the crocodiles, nor did Aboh, who was very wary when picking up the birds. As we made our way through the forest, I was especially struck by the variety and luxuriance of the trees and shrubs, the number of vines which hung from the branches in wreaths and festoons, the length of the leaves, some rising from the ground, others forming crowns on the summits of tall trees, surmounted by flowers of bright red or yellow or blue.

"Dere, massa, what you 'tink dat?" said Aboh, throwing himself on the ground as if to contemplate at his ease the magnificent tree before which we stood. "Him 'board ship worth many tusks."

"What tree is it?" I asked.

It was certainly one of the finest and most graceful trees we had yet met with in the African forest. Its leaves were long, sharp-pointed, and dark green, hanging in large clusters. Its bark was also a dark green and very smooth. The trunk rose straight and clean to the height of sixty feet or more, from whence large leafy branches projected to a considerable distance. Aboh pointed to his own skin and then laughed.

"He means that it's an ebony tree, and so I'm sure it is," said Harry. "It is one of those articles we were to have procured."

On examining the tree we found that it was hollow, and Aboh made us understand that the branches also were hollow. On cutting through the bark we came to some white wood, which at first puzzled us. We expected to have found it black, but Aboh made signs that we were to cut deeper into it, and we thus ascertained that the white wood was simply sap wood, and that farther in the wood was perfectly black. We found several others of the same description growing around; and we agreed that if we could fall in with some friendly natives, we would advise them to cut the trees down, and should any navigable river exist running out of the lake, to convey them to its mouth, where they could be embarked. We, however, had to hurry back to cook our ducks for breakfast.

We continued keeping our poor companion's ankle constantly wetted, but, to our disappointment, even the next day he was unable to do more than stand up. The moment he attempted to walk, the pain returned, and we had to make up our minds for a longer stay. Charley proposed that we should cut down a tree and scoop out a canoe in which to cross the lake. When he explained his intentions, however, to Aboh, the black replied that it would take us several weeks, if not months, to construct a canoe, and that we should get round the lake much faster by land.

"That may be the case," said Charley; "but suppose Tom's ankle is broken, or so injured that he is unable to walk, we shall have no alternative. We cannot leave him behind us in this wild forest, and we must try to find a village of friendly natives, where he can remain until he is recovered."

"I'm sorry to keep you back, gentlemen, and if it was a matter of life or death, I'd say go on and leave me behind, but it would be a terrible thing if that were necessary; so I would rather say, let us build a canoe, or, if we cannot, a raft on which we can cross the lake. I don't think it would take as long as Aboh supposes, if we could find a soft tree. He doesn't know what our sharp axes can do; besides, we can clear out the inside with fire. Even if I hadn't sprained my ankle, I again say, provided that we can find the right tree, let us build a canoe."

Charley agreed with Tubbs, and Harry and I had no strong

opinion the other way.   We told Aboh we wished he would hunt about to find a big tree of soft wood.

Aboh agreed to do as we wished, at the same time he shook his head, saying, " Too long, too long."

" No, no," answered Tom ; " we will build a handsome short craft with plenty of beam, so that we may turn her about in any of the narrow streams through which we may have to make our way."

CHAPTER IX.

THE very evening on which we had determined to form a canoe, we commenced our search for a tree suitable for the purpose. In vain, however, we hunted in the neighbourhood of the lake. Aboh pointed to the south. "Find him dere," he said.

We were, however, unwilling to go to a distance from our companion, for we knew not to what dangers he might be exposed should he be left alone, even although he was able to sit up and handle his rifle, and might perhaps have hobbled to a short distance. Still he would have to do that at the risk of again injuring his ankle.

"I will remain with him if you and Charley like to set off with Aboh as a guide," said Harry. "If you can find a tree at no great distance, you can cut it down and shape it where it falls, so that it will not give us much trouble to transport it to the lake."

"More than you suspect, unless we can find a level path down to the water," observed Charley.

Though I agreed with my brother, we notwithstanding made up our minds to start early the following morning, and should we find a tree suitable for a canoe within a mile or so, to cut it down; but if not, to give up the undertaking. We had cooked overnight some waterfowl for provisions, and Aboh, I should have said, had found some fruits, which were highly acceptable. We rose at daybreak, summoned by Harry, who had kept the morning watch, and at once set off, having determined not to wait for breakfast, as we wished to have the whole day before us. Charley and I directed our course to the shore of the lake, to which we had discovered a path, formed probably by elephants, leading directly to the water.

Just as we were approaching the lake, we caught sight through the bushes of a canoe paddled by a single rower skimming lightly over the surface towards us. Wishing to open a communication with the man in the canoe in order to obtain information from him as to the best course we could take to get to the north-ward, or perhaps to induce him to ferry us across, we hid behind the bushes. The stranger, by his movements, appeared not to be aware that any one was in the neighbourhood, and came on without hesitation to the shore, close to the spot where we were hid.

Aboh had remained behind to assist Tom in gathering sticks and lighting the fire, while Harry had settled to come a short distance with us. The black had on no other garment but the usual white cloth, showing that he belonged to one of the wild tribes to the west.

He ran his canoe right up on the bank, and then without hesitation stepped out, carrying a spear in one hand, a quiver of arrows on his back, and a bow in the other. We allowed him to advance some distance, until suddenly he came in sight of Tom and Aboh engaged in making up the fire. Immediately stopping, he was about to fix an arrow in his bow, when Charley and I showed ourselves. On seeing us he retreated a few paces, and then fell to the ground overcome by terror. Charley and I, wishing to reassure him, advanced as Harry came up to him.

The black, seizing his foot, placed it on his neck in token of submission. So sudden was the movement that Harry, who could not prevent him from doing this, was nearly upset, and would have been so had not he supported himself by his rifle. On this I turned round and shouted to Aboh to come and interpret for us. As Aboh approached, Charley and I stooped down and lifted up the negro, who was still trembling with alarm, though we endeavoured by the tone of our voices and our gestures to reassure him.

"Come, Aboh, come; let him know that we are friends," cried my brother.

Aboh hurried up. As he got near he stopped, gazing with astonished looks at the stranger, uttering a few words unintelligible to us. The stranger answered in the same language. Soon they began to speak more rapidly, stepping towards each other; then suddenly with loud exclamations of delight they sprang forward, and throwing themselves into each other's arms, burst out into tears.

"Brodder! him brodder!" shouted out Aboh, turning round to us to signify that he had found a relative.

This was indeed satisfactory, as the stranger would be able to render us all the assistance we required. His canoe, however, was but a small one, and certainly would not convey all the party across the lake.

"We shall still have to build one, unless our friend here can find us another," said Charley.

" I think a better plan would be to get Aboh and his brother to ferry Tom across the lake while we march round and find our way to his village."

On explaining our proposal to Aboh, he had a long palaver with his brother. The result was not satisfactory.

" Bad man dere," he said, pointing to the eastern end of the lake.

" What do you advise, then ? " asked Charley.

" Stay here; Shimbo him go and bring back big canoe," was the answer. When we suggested that Aboh and Shimbo should take Tom across, they at once agreed to do so, Aboh observing that Shimbo's canoe would easily carry three people, but that it would require two canoes of similar size to paddle us all across. Tom had no objection to accompany the blacks, and we were anxious that he should get under shelter as soon as possible. We ourselves proposed remaining where we were and hunting, so that we might carry a good supply of game with us as a present to our friends' tribe.

Instead, therefore, of starting off to look for a tree to make a canoe as we had intended, we all repaired to the fire which Tom had been blowing into a blaze, and soon had a number of wild-fowl roasting before it. As soon as he saw our pot on the fire, Shimbo ran off to his canoe and brought back some plantains, which he set to work to peel; he then carefully washed them, and cutting them in several pieces, put them into the sauce-pan. Then he half filled it with water and covered it over with leaves, on the top of which he placed the banana peelings. The vegetables were boiled by the time the ducks were roasted. He also roasted a few ground-nuts, both of which were very acceptable to us after not having tasted vegetables for so long a time. We thought the boiled plantains were rather insipid, until Shimbo produced a bag full of cayenne pepper, with which he sprinkled them as he hooked them out of the pot, and placed them on some broad leaves to serve as plates. Altogether, we had not had so satisfactory a meal for some time. We told Aboh that we hoped to have plenty of game for his friends, and urged him to come back as soon as possible. Tom looked rather grave as we lifted him into the canoe. Perhaps he was not so confident as we were that he would receive a friendly reception.

While watching the canoe as she skimmed over the calm surface of the lake urged by Aboh's and Shimbo's paddles, we could just see the blue outline of the opposite shore, with here and there what we supposed to be tall trees rising above those of the usual forest growth, but they might be hills or hillocks, so wide was the lake. It would evidently have taken us many a day's march to get round the way we proposed. Then we might have been stopped by the bad people of whom Aboh spoke.

Our meditations on the subject were interrupted by the appearance of the snout of a crocodile, who, swimming by, had taken a fancy to have one of us for his lunch. We shouted loudly; he beat a retreat, looking out, while passing slowly on, for any unwary duck or other wildfowl floating calmly on the smooth water.

"We must keep our promise and get as many birds as we can," said Charley; "so come along. It will be as well, however, not to separate, for we may fall in with a lion or leopard, or a herd of elephants. We ought to be ready to support each other."

Harry and I of course agreed to this. We were very success- ful, and in the course of a couple of hours had shot three dozen ducks. Our difficulty, however, was to preserve them. Even though we hung them up on the boughs of trees, the ants would manage to get at them, or birds of prey were likely to carry them off, or, unless they were placed at a considerable distance from the ground, a leopard or other wild animal might do so; while it was necessary to look out for a shady spot, or they would have become uneatable before the following day. We accordingly set to work and made some baskets of vines, interwoven with thick leaves, which would protect them from all other creatures with the exception of the ants. This occupied us two hours or more, and we agreed that it would be useless to expend a further amount of powder. We then cooked a duck apiece, and the remainder of the roots and nuts which Shimbo had left us.

After dinner we went down to the lake to look out for the canoes, thinking that by this time Aboh might be returning ; but none were to be seen as far as our eyes could reach over the surface of the water. We, therefore, walked along under the shade of the trees, though at a safe distance to avoid danger from the sudden rush of a crocodile. After we had gone some way, we caught sight of a beautiful deer gazing into the waters of the lake, apparently admiring itself, and occasionally stooping down to draw up a mouthful. Retiring behind the trees, we advanced cautiously, hoping to get a shot, and to add the creature to our larder. I was ahead, and having got well within distance, had just raised my rifle, and was on the point of drawing my trigger, when I was startled by seeing a huge crocodile literally leap out of the water, and then, like a flash of lightning, spring back again, holding the unfortunate deer struggling violently in its tremendous jaws. I fired, but my bullet glanced off the side of the scaly monster, which disappeared with its victim. It was much the same to the deer whether it was eaten by us or the crocodile, but we were greatly disappointed at losing it. However, the occurrence made us look out more carefully for deer, as we might hope to catch one or two, and venison we calculated would be highly prized by our friends. Besides which, we ourselves were getting somewhat tired of duck every day.

As we thought it very likely that another deer would come down during the afternoon to drink at the lake, we formed a screen of boughs, which served as a favourable look-out. While two of us kept watch for the deer, the third guarded the rear of our ambush lest a wild beast might carry off one of us for his supper, instead of our supping off deer as we hoped to do. It was very fortunate that we took these precautions. We had not occupied our posts more than a quarter of an hour when Harry, who was on the look-out, whispered—

"There's a creature crawling along not a hundred yards off."

Charley took a glance round. "It's a leopard, and it evidently sees us; we must be ready to fire," he whispered.

"But if we do, we shall frighten the deer; so don't pull a trigger unless it comes nearer," I observed.

The leopard slowly crept by, being apparently itself in search of prey. It soon disappeared, and although we kept a bright look-out, it did not return. After this we waited patiently for nearly an hour, when we saw a small herd of deer coming down the glade. So anxious were we, that we scarcely dared breathe lest we should alarm them. I remembered the leopard, and thought that it might possibly be on the look-out for the deer, and might put them to flight before they could come within shot. On they trotted, however, as if thoughtless of danger. We allowed the leader to reach the water. Charley signed to me to point out the one at which I intended to aim. We each selected one.

The cracks of our three rifles were heard almost at the same moment. Two of the deer fell killed. The third, at which Harry had aimed, attempted to escape, while the rest, looking about them with a startled glance, bounded off. Scarcely, however, had the leader gone a dozen yards than a leopard sprang out, and seizing the creature in its powerful jaws, carried it off through the forest.

"Load, quickly, load," cried Charley.

We did so, and then rushed out to secure the deer we had

killed, fearing that another leopard might have a feast off it. We were not, however, molested, and with infinite satisfaction we dragged the animals one by one up to the neighbourhood of our camp, where we commenced cutting them up, although, I must confess, we were not expert in that part of the huntsman's art. By the time we had finished our task, and hung 'up the deer as near to our fire as possible, the sun had sunk below the horizon.

We again went down to the lake, and were much disappointed at not seeing the canoe Aboh had promised to bring us. As it was not likely, therefore, that he would arrive that night, we made up our minds to camp at the same spot as before. There was no time to lose, and so, collecting firewood, we prepared to pass the night. It might seem an easy task to get a supply of sticks, but it was a dangerous one. Not only did we run the risk of disturbing some venomous snake, but were nearly certain to find scorpions almost as deadly among the dried wood. Our plan, therefore, was to scrape together the sticks with a long staff, and turn them over before attempting to bind them up into faggots for conveying to the camp. I had not long been thus employed, when a big scorpion crept out from a mass of bark ; I laid my stick, which it bit severely, on its back, striking its sting into the wood before I crushed it to death. Having collected a sufficient amount of fuel to last for the night, we put up a lean-to, under which we could shelter ourselves from the night dew, though it would afford but a slight protection against any hungry animal which might venture near, as leopards and lions might occasionally do. We filled our saucepan with water, and made every preparation for the night, not forgetting to cook as much venison as we could possibly eat. Having taken a plentiful supper we were about to lie down, when Charley said that he would first take a look round the camp. Not far off was the huge trunk of a fallen tree, over which bushes had already begun to grow. I saw Charley suddenly sink down behind it, and as I was following him, he made a sign to me to creep along under its shelter. I did so, and presently caught sight of a huge animal advancing in a stealthy fashion along the open ground. I at once knew it to be a leopard. Charley put up his hand, signing me to be cautious. The leopard approached, attracted, I have no doubt, by the smell of the venison, or by the remainder of the carcasses of the deer, which were not far off.

Whether or not it was the same leopard we had seen in the afternoon, I could not tell. The creature moved on in its cat-like fashion, looking cautiously around. Charley and I kept ourselves well concealed, still it apparently suspected that an enemy was near. It got directly in front of us. If Charley missed I must, I knew, take care to bring it down, for if not, it would make nothing of a bound over the tree, and would carry one of us off. Charley levelled his rifle; a sharp crack was heard ringing through the night air, answered by the chattering of numberless monkeys and the shrieks of flocks of parrots and other birds. The smoke for a moment prevented me seeing the leopard; the next instant, what was my horror to observe it approaching. In another instant it would have been upon us. I fired; it leapt high in the air, and rolled over close to the trunk of the tree.

"Well done, Dick!" cried Charley. "I hit it, but my bullet missed the vital part."

The leopard was perfectly dead. We easily found the two bullet-holes. Charley's bullet had struck the edge of a bone, and been slightly deflected. Had he been alone, the result might have been fatal to him. How thankful I felt that he had escaped! It was a lesson to us never to go out hunting singly, and we agreed that we would keep to that rule.

The leopard had fallen just under the bough of a tree, and as we were anxious to preserve its skin, and yet did not wish to spend time in flaying the animal that night, we resolved to try and hoist it up to the bough, where it would remain safe till the morning. We accordingly cut a number of vines which grew near, and under Charley's directions formed a series of tackles, by means of which we succeeded, all hoisting together, in lifting it several feet off the ground. This done, we returned to our camp. While we had been thus engaged, we had run the risk, I suspect, of being attacked by another wild beast, either a leopard or lion, as when I was on watch I heard the mutterings of the last-named savage brutes in the distance. As I walked up and down in front of our fire while my brother and Harry were asleep, I watched the body of the leopard swinging in the air a few feet off, and kept my gun on the cock ready to fire should a lion approach, as I thought would very likely be the case, although I had no particular wish to have another battle that night. However, it so happened that we were left at rest.

At early dawn we let down the carcase, and at once flayed it. Our object in doing so was to present the skin to the chief of the village we expected to visit, as we guessed it would be highly prized ; besides which, the fact that we had killed the creature being known, would raise us in the estimation of the people. Having hung up the skin to dry, Harry and I went down to the lake, hoping to see the canoe of our friend, but we were again disappointed. Charley had, in the meantime, been preparing breakfast, roasting some more ducks, and the remainder of the ground-nuts left us by Shimbo. After this, we employed our time in scraping the inside of the leopard's skin, which gave us enough to do ; we then made a sort of lye from the ashes of our fire, which would have, we hoped, some effect in preserving the skin, though we were aware that the process we adopted was very rude and imperfect. As several hours had passed since Tubbs and the two blacks had left us, we became somewhat anxious about them. If the natives had proved treacherous, Tom would very likely be put to death or kept a prisoner, and we should see nothing more of him. About noon, Harry and I had gone down to the lake to get a sauce-pan of water, when we remarked a tiny speck on the broad shining expanse of the lake, where nothing previously had been visible.

"Hurrah! that must be the canoe at last," he exclaimed.

I was of the same opinion. "If Charley were to have a look at it, he would be more certain about the matter," I observed; and running back, I called my brother.

"Yes, there's no doubt about it; that must be the canoe," he said, after he had watched it attentively.

We now hoped that we should at length get away from the spot where we had spent so much time. After watching for several minutes, though it was still at a great distance, and appeared to be approaching very slowly, we could distinctly make out the canoe. We had gone back to eat our dinners, as we had become hungry, when Harry said that he would go down to the lake to see if the canoe was near the shore. Just as he reached the water, we heard him cry out, " Here they are! here they are!" Charley and I ran down to join him. The next minute Aboh and Shimbo, with two other blacks, stepped out of a good-sized canoe, capable of carrying us three in addition. It was formed very much like the one we had intended to make out of the trunk of a tree. Aboh seemed as delighted to see us as if he had been away for several weeks. Why he had not returned sooner, we could not exactly make out, but we understood that the king of the village, Quagomolo, was very ill, and as the only large canoes belonged to him, Aboh could not see him to obtain the one he wished for. Our friends had brought a supply of plantains and several other things— manioc, sugar-cane, and squashes. There were provisions enough for us and themselves for several days. Before com-mencing the return voyage, they insisted we should cook them and have a feast.

"We have already had our dinner," said Charley.

"Bery good! but we,—we empty stomach. No good go sea without eat," answered Aboh.

By which he let us understand that he and his companions required food, and were not entirely disinterested in pressing us to have a feast on the provisions they had brought. On seeing the deer and the ducks we had shot, their eyes brightened. Aboh and Shimbo were both very good cooks, and immediately set to work to dress both the venison and the vegetables. Their only regret was, that we had not some rum to give them, the taste of which they had acquired from the white traders who occasionally came up to their village. I should have said that Aboh gave us a good report of Tom, who was being well treated by the inhabitants of the village, by whom we also expected to be received in a friendly manner. Aboh and Shimbo were so long in preparing the viands, that by the time they announced that all were sufficiently cooked, we were perfectly ready to fall to. We enjoyed our meal, and as soon as it was over, Charley proposed that we should start without delay.

The ducks and the venison were carried down to the canoe, as well as the leopard skin. By the time we had taken our seats, it appeared to us greatly overloaded; still our black friends were unwilling to leave any provisions behind. Aboh, pointing to the leopard skin, exclaimed, "King, him like much;" so that we hoped our gift would be acceptable to his sable majesty. The day was pretty well advanced, but we hoped to get across the lake before nightfall. All being ready, our black crew seizing their paddles, the canoe began to glide across the lake. Charley took a fifth paddle with which to steer, but he soon found that the blacks could manage the canoe perfectly well without his assistance. The heat was so great on the water that we were all thankful to avoid any unnecessary exertion. The blacks as they paddled sang a low monotonous song, more like a dirge. What it was about we could not tell By looking back we saw that we had got some distance from the land, although we appeared not to have approached nearer the opposite shore, which still remained as indistinct as before. After some time the blacks ceased their song, and I saw them gazing round at the sky, the appearance of which was rapidly changing. The sun suddenly disappeared behind a dark bank of cloud coming up from the west, and a leaden hue overspread the hitherto sparkling water, at the same time that a strong wind began to blow. This soon broke the hitherto tranquil lake into hissing wavelets, which continually toppled over into the canoe. Aboh, turning round, handed to each of us a bason formed from a gourd, and made signs that we should bale out the water as it came in. He and his companions then redoubled their efforts. I caught a glimpse of his countenance as he turned round; it showed that he was far from satisfied with the appearance of the weather. I asked Charley what he thought about the matter.

" I'm afraid that we are going to have a gale ; and if so, a nasty sea will get up, and we shall be obliged to heave our cargo overboard, although we will not do so until it becomes absolutely necessary."

Every instant the wind increased, and the blacks paddled harder and harder. At present it was on our beam, although, should it come ahead, we should make but little progress, or perhaps be compelled to run back to the place we had left. Notwithstanding the threatening aspect of the weather, Aboh and his companions seemed determined to continue their course. The water kept tumbling on board, but we continued baling it out as fast as we could.

" I'm afraid that we must heave the birds and venison overboard," said Charley.

I made Aboh understand what we proposed doing.

" No, no," was the answer; " dat all right."

He and his companions paddled on bravely for another half

hour. By this time it had become perfectly dark, and we could not discover the land ahead, but the black fellows seemed to guide their course by instinct, for I could see no welcoming beacon on the shore. To our satisfaction the wind did not increase, though the canoe tumbled about a good deal, and not for a moment were we able to cease baling. The blacks paddled on bravely through the pitchy darkness. Suddenly a flash of lightning burst from the clouds, followed by a tremendous roar of thunder. I could see the flame dancing along over the water, mercifully avoiding our canoe, leaving all in darkness beyond. The blacks for a moment ceased paddling.

"Go on, go on," I cried out to Aboh; "this is no time to stop; the sooner we reach the shore the sooner we shall be in safety."

Aboh repeated what I had said to his companions, and, thus encouraged, all hands paddled away as before. As no land was in sight, I could not make out how they managed to steer a straight course, but they seemed perfectly satisfied that they were going right. Probably they were guided by the wind on one side. Had it shifted, they would have been thrown out. This I greatly feared would be the case; and after all, might we be paddling up the lake instead of across it. Charley got out his pocket compass, but the wind prevented us striking a light, and it was consequently of no use. He kept it before him, however, in case another flash of lightning should enable him to see it. He had not long to wait. A vivid flash darted directly across the canoe.

"Hurrah!" he exclaimed; "we are all right; we are steering due north."

We had no longer, after this, any doubt about the judgment of our African friends. The thunder rolled, the lightning flashed, and we continued to bale away as the water washed into the canoe. For some moments the lightning ceased, and we hoped the storm was over; but we were mistaken. Another flash darted from the sky, more vivid than its predecessors, with a loud hissing, crackling sound.

"Hurrah! I caught sight of some trees and a hut," exclaimed Charley.

He was not mistaken, in less than a quarter of an hour after this, the canoe ran alongside the bank in a little bay, and our crew, jumping out, welcomed us on shore.

Their loud shouts brought a number of people out of the neighbouring huts, who quickly unloaded the canoe; while we were conducted by Aboh and Shimbo to a hut which they said was prepared for our reception. Within we found Tom seated on a couch formed of bamboos.

"Glad to see you, gentlemen, that I am," he exclaimed. "To say the truth, I had begun to fear that you would never come at all, as I have had some doubts about the intentions of our friends here. They were very kind, howsomever, for they fed me well and tried their skill at doctoring my foot, but I cannot say that they have done it any good; so I hope, Mr. Westerton, that you will again take me in hand."

We were thankful to find that Tom was in such good spirits. Charley, on looking at his foot, said he hoped, as the swelling had greatly gone down, that in a few days it would be as strong as ever. As it was so late at night, we expected to go supperless to bed, but we had not been long in the hut when a bevy of damsels arrived carrying baskets on their heads, containing cooked provisions enough, including some of our venison, to feed a dozen people. We were not sorry to partake of them, as we had become very hungry; but as we had had but little rest the previous night, we begged our entertainers to leave us in quiet, which they did not appear disposed to do. At length Aboh and Shimbo making their appearance, at our request turned all our guests out and allowed us to sleep in quiet.

Next morning we were awakened by great shouting, and on inquiring the cause, ascertained that a famous doctor had come to cure the king, Quagomolo, of his disease, though what that was we could not ascertain. We went out to see this important personage, who presented a most fantastic appearance. His head was adorned with feathers, birds' beaks, and claws of leopards, hyenas, and other savage brutes; half his body was painted red, the other half white, while his face was daubed with streaks of alternate black, white, and red. Round his neck he wore numerous chains and charms, which tinkled and rattled as he moved about.

After having paraded himself through the village to be admired by the inhabitants, he was introduced to the hut of the king, whom he had not yet seen. Finding no one to stop us, we shortly afterwards followed, when we saw the doctor seated on a low stool before a large earthenware pot, into which he was looking intently. This done, having seized a lighted torch smouldering by his side, he whirled it about his head till it burst into a flame. He then waved it over the pot, muttering some mysterious words. He continued this and similar performances for so long a time that we were getting weary of witnessing them, when suddenly a person rose from a couch at the further end of the room, whom we rightly supposed to be King Quagomolo.

"Sit down, your majesty, sit down," exclaimed the doctor. " I'll soon say what's the matter with you."

The king obeyed. Again the doctor waved his torch and gazed into the pot, and then declared that his majesty was bewitched.

"Who are the people who have bewitched me?" asked the king in a trembling voice.

"They are some men and women in your own kingdom, and not far off from this," answered the doctor in a deep bass voice which could be heard outside the hut, where a number of persons were collected.

There was a general howl of alarm, for no one could tell who would be fixed on. The king, on hearing this, announced that the persons implicated must drink the poisoned water, usually given on such occasions. So we learned from Aboh, who had crept into the hut and squatted down beside us.

"We must try to defeat the old rascal," whispered Charley. "Show us where the poison is to be concocted?"

The doctor had now a drum brought him by an attendant, on which he began to beat vehemently, when the king again sank down on his couch. We on this quietly made our exit, and, led by Aboh, entered another hut, where, by the light of a single torch, some old women were concocting the mysterious beverage. We watched them until they had finished, when, leaving the bowl covered up by a piece of matting, they crept out one by one, holding up their hands, taking long, slow strides, and looking truly like witches themselves, and, as Harry observed, "Very bad specimens too."

As soon as they were gone, finding a jug of pure water near at hand, Charley poured out the mixture into a corner, and filled up the bowl again with the harmless liquid. Fortunately, we found a basketful of what was evidently colouring matter, and having mixed some of it in the water, we covered the bowl up again and left the hut. We then went back to our hut. Finding that the king, in spite of the lateness of the hour, was ready to receive us, taking our two black friends, Aboh to act as interpreter, we carried with us the leopard skin, some venison, and three strings of beads of various colours. His majesty was a tall, ungainly looking man, with as hideous a countenance as can well be imagined. His appearance was not improved by the glare of the torchlight and the terror under which he was suffering. Having presented the leopard skin and venison, Charley, who acted as spokesman, threw the string of beads round his neck.

"Tell him," he said to Aboh, "that those are powerful charms, and will quickly restore him to health."

After a short palaver we begged leave to retire, assuring his majesty that he would be quite well in the morning, and that we were very sure that none of his subjects had bewitched him, as would then be proved."

"If we succeed we shall have performed a very good work," said Charley, laughing, as we returned to our hut.

Next morning the whole tribe was collected, and the accused persons brought forward. The bowl was handed round among them. No one to whom it was offered dared refuse to drink from it, although the distortions of their countenances showed the alarm under which they laboured. The king, who had been brought out to witness the ceremony on a litter, sat by watching them, and expecting, perhaps, to see some of them drop down dead.

To our surprise three or four of them appeared greatly agitated, writhing about and making hideous faces, but we felt very sure that this was the result of imagination ; and even these soon recovered, while the rest remained standing, and doing their best to smile and convince the king and their friends of their innocence. The effect on King Quagomolo was almost instantaneous, and before evening he declared himself perfectly recovered. To prove this, he summoned his liege subjects to attend a dance in honour of the event. No great preparations were required, and that very evening was fixed for the event. The king's wives, of whom he had no small number, and all the dames and damsels from far and wide, came trooping in, and arranged themselves in the large open space in the centre of the village. The men sat on the opposite side, with a line of musicians in front. These were mostly drummers, who beat their huge tomtoms with right good will, making the most fearful and deafening din. Others had brass kettles, and others hollow pieces of wood, which assisted greatly in the uproar; while at the same time both men and women sang, shouted, and shrieked, until we, who stood at a little distance off, could scarcely hear each other's voices. The barbarous overture being brought to a conclusion, the king, who had been seated amongst his wives, rose, and springing into the centre of the circle, began snapping his fingers, twisting and turning in all sorts of attitudes, leaping from the groun ', kicking up one leg, then another, and throwing his arms round until it appeared that he would swing them off.

"Here am I, my friends," he shouted. "Once I was ill, now I am well; and if our white friends here will stay with us, I never expect to be ill again."

He danced and shouted until we thought he would have dropped. Presently he managed to spring back, exhibiting the utmost agility to the last, until he sat down again in the midst of his better halves, who had been amongst the most demonstrative of his applauders. Several of his chiefs then followed his example, but took good care not to surpass the king either in the time they danced or the activity they displayed. Before they sat down, several women sprang up, who, not being influenced by the same motives as the courtiers, contrived to twist and turn themselves in a way which was neither creditable to their modesty, nor pleasant to look at. We had good reason to be satisfied with this commencement of our intercourse with King Quagomolo. He presented us with abundance of food, and the hut built for our accommodation was clean and comfortable.

In a short time, by careful treatment, Tom's ankle completely regained its strength, and he declared himself ready to continue the journey to the northward. We arranged, therefore, to start immediately, but we calculated without our host. When we told Aboh of our intentions, and asked him to accompany us, he made a long face, and shaking his head, said, "King no let go, want fight;" by which we understood that Quagomolo intended to detain us in order that we might assist him in some predatory excursion he was meditating against a neighbouring tribe, we having firearms in good order, while he and his people had among them only a few old muskets, many of which were destitute of locks, and could only be fired by means of matches applied to the touch-holes. On obtaining this information, we agreed that it would not be wise to show any mistrust of the king, but quietly to take our departure, with or without his leave, whenever it might suit us to do so.

As we were well treated, we were in no hurry to get away, besides which we had abundance of sport in the neighbourhood, and seldom went out without bringing back eight or ten brace of ducks and other wildfowl. However, at length we thought it time to tell the king that we must be going.

We took the opportunity when he was in a good humour, having just quaffed a few bowls of a sort of palm-wine of which he was especially fond.

"Stay, my dear friends, stay a few days longer, and you shall go forth with honour, and each of you shall take a wife with you and a hundred attendants."

Charley assured his majesty that we must decline the wives, and that our own rifles were the best attendants we desired, with the exception of one or two intelligent men to act as guides.

"You shall have your will, you shall have your will," answered the king, "but stay one day longer, just one day."

We accordingly, hoping to have no obstruction offered to our departure, agreed to stay, but when the evening arrived the king sent a messenger to say he wished to see us.

"What, my friends," he began as we entered his hut—"do you want to go and leave me all forlorn, stay another day, stay another day."

Such was the tenor of his address which Aboh translated to us.

"Tell him that to-morrow we must go," said Charley.

The king smiled benignantly, so Harry declared, although he appeared to me to make a very hideous grimace.

The next day, early in the morning, we all four loaded our muskets, and asked Aboh if he was ready to accompany us."

" King, he give him leave, him go at once," he answered.

No sooner did we quit our hut than we saw all the men of the village, fully armed, collected at the outlets, evidently resolved to stop us by force. Although we might have fought our way through them, we could not have done so without bloodshed. Again we resolved to make a virtue of necessity, and remain until we could find a favourable opportunity of escaping.

Several days passed by, and every morning, when we were prepared to set out, we found the village guarded as before. When, however, we left our packs behind us, we were allowed to ramble at perfect freedom. Besides Aboh and Shimbo we found a party always ready to accompany us and act as beaters.

Not wishing it to be supposed that we intended to leave that morning, we quietly returned to our hut, and undoing our knapsacks again went out, simply with our rifles in our hands, as if we intended to have a little shooting before breakfast. We had not gone far when we saw a woman near the shore of the lake apparently hunting about and calling out to some one in tones of distress.

" Who is she? and what is it all about? " I asked Aboh.

" She king's wife. Go bathe, lose piccannany."

We hurried on until we met the poor woman. She then explained that while she was bathing in a sheltered pool she had left her little boy on the bank of the lake to play about and amuse himself, but when she came out of the water she could nowhere find him. Of course it at once occurred to us that a crocodile must have carried him off, but Aboh averred that if such was the case the mother would have heard him cry out. He might have slipped into the water and have been drowned, but that he might possibly be hiding from her, for the sake of playing a trick.

" In that case she will soon find him, I hope," I observed.

Scarcely had I spoken than I saw a huge crocodile crawling out of the bank not twenty yards from us. The next instant, stooping down its head, it lifted up a little black boy by one of his legs.

At the sight the mother shrieked out, "My son, my son !"

The fate of the child seemed certain. As the huge creature turned to run, I saw that its neck was exposed. Fortunately, having loaded my rifle with ball, I fired. By a miracle it seemed, the crocodile let the child drop, and after making a faint attempt to recover it, gave a few convulsive struggles, and rolled off the bank perfectly dead, for we could see it lying on its back in shallow water.

The poor mother rushed forward and picked up the little boy, who, although fearfully bitten about the leg, was still alive. It had not before uttered a sound, but now it began to cry as it saw the blood streaming from the wounded limb. As far as I could judge, no vital part had been touched, and I told Aboh to say to the mother, that if she would let us doctor it we would do so, as I had hopes of its recovery. Having washed it then and there in cold water, we stopped the blood, bound up the wounds, and gave it to the mother to carry back. Quagomolo was, we found, especially fond of the child. It was six or seven years old, and, being in a healthy condition, by the evening appeared no worse, At the end of three days, as lock-jaw had not set in, and the wounds looked healthy, we assured the king of our belief that his son would in time get well. Quagomolo and his wife both appeared very grateful.

"Whatever you shall ask you shall have," he said ; "half my kingdom, half of my wives, or half of my children, or half of my people for slaves."

"Tell his majesty that we are much obliged to him," answered Charley ; "but the only favour we ask is the loan of a couple of his faithful subjects, and permission to proceed on our journey to the northward, where we expect to fall in with some of our countrymen. We are friends to Africa and the Africans, and wish to do the people all the good we can, but that if he keeps us here, our plans will be defeated."

The king replied "that he would consider the matter, but that perhaps he knew what was for our good as well as we did ourselves, and that if we wished to benefit the Africans we should remain and exercise our skill on him and his people."

This answer was anything but satisfactory. We had accordingly, as before, to shrug our shoulders and submit for the present, not intending, however, much longer to comply with the fancies of the sable monarch.

CHAPTER X.

DAY after day passed by, and still King Quagomolo made some excuse for not allowing us to proceed on our journey. He could well afford to support us, for, savage as were he and his people in most respects, they possessed an unusually large plantation of plantains, on a piece of level ground a short distance from the lake. He took special pride in it, and invited us to pay it a visit. We could not calculate how many trees there were, though there must have been upwards of twenty thousand. The trees stood about five feet apart, and the bunches of plantains which each tree produced weighed from thirty to fifty pounds, those from some of the larger trees much more. There were several varieties even in the same grove. The king informed us that some of these trees bear fruit six or seven months after the sprouts are planted, others, again, take two or three months longer before they bear fruit ; and what we may consider the finer species do not begin to bear until about eighteen months after the sprouts are put into the ground, but these last bear by far the larger bunches. This plantain grove was one of the pleasantest sights we had witnessed since we had landed on the shores of Africa. No cereal on the same space of ground, however highly cultivated, could afford the same amount of food.

We complimented the king, through Aboh, on the beauty and size of his plantation, and the fruit it contained.

"Very good for eat, but no good for trade," was the answer. His majesty had, it was evident, an eye to commerce, and we discovered that the article which he could obtain with the least difficulty, and sell at the highest price, were elephants' tusks. His hunters, we found, frequently went in chase of the monsters for a twofold purpose,—to obtain ivory, and to keep them at a distance from the plantain grove, among which two or three elephants in a few hours might have committed immense damage. He had arranged a grand elephant hunt, not having taken part in one since his illness. He had made up his mind that we should accompany him, believing that our rifles would be the means of securing more ivory than could his own people with their darts and spears. We hoped that if we complied with his wishes, he would be more ready to allow us to take our departure. We accordingly agreed to accompany him. Tom wished to go also, but, although he was able to walk, Charley advised him not to run the risk of again spraining his ankle, feeling sure that great activity would be required from the experience we had already had in getting out of the way of elephants.

"But I've been thinking, sir, that we might have a chance of making our escape while we are out hunting. We could easily slip away from the natives, and push on fast in the direction we want to go."

" There are two objections to that," answered Charley. " In the first place, the natives can travel through the forest faster than we can, and would soon overtake us; then, as we could not go out hunting with our packs, we should have to leave them behind us; besides which, I would rather leave the king who has treated us so hospitably, in an open fashion, with his goodwill, instead of stealing off like deserters."

"I dare say you are right, sir," answered Tom, "but we shall look very foolish if the king, after all, insists on our stopping with him."

"Should such be the case, we can but take up our packs and march off, and should any attempt be made to stop us, fight the black fellows."

"That's the sort of plain sailing I like," said Tom.

We were surprised next morning at the extent of the preparations made for the hunt. We found nearly four hundred men, armed with spears and javelins, assembled in the great square of the village, a large number having come from the neighbouring hamlets. The king soon came out of his palace—for so I may call it, although it was but a rude hut, thickly thatched with palm leaves. He was dressed far more elaborately than we had hitherto seen him, with a circle of feathers on his head, and a kilt of long-grass round his waist secured by a belt, to which hung a number of fetiches or charms. The skin of a leopard hung over his shoulder, to which was suspended a gun, while he carried also a long spear, ornamented with a tuft of hair at the end. The rest of the huntsmen were attired as usual, in nothing but the waist cloth, which is worn by the most savage tribes.

The king divided his force into six different parties and desired us to accompany the one commanded by himself. He then gave the order to march. We all set out. Before long we reached the forest, through which we proceeded for several hours, occasionally having to cut our way where the thick vines which hung from all the trees impeded our progress. Towards evening we arrived at the spot where the king had determined to halt. His people immediately set about forming the camp, by collecting wood and putting up shelters, which consisted of lean-to's. Two poles with forked ends were stuck in the ground, on the top of which rested an horizontal pole ; against this a number of others were placed, when large palm or other leaves were secured above them, so that the hardest rain was turned off, the roof, of course, being placed on the side against which the wind blew. A large one was built for the king, who invited us to share it with him. It was of the same construction as that of the rest. In front a large fire was kindled. We had no reason to complain of our entertainment, for the king had brought an ample supply of venison as well as plantains, and other vegetables and food. We also slept securely, as we knew that the hunters would keep a look-out during the night for any savage animals which might come prowling round the camp.

At early dawn we were on foot, and the king marshalling his forces, sent them off in different directions, so that they might form a large circle and drive in any elephants to a common centre, where we were given to understand some pits had been dug especially for the purpose of entrapping them or any other wild beasts. In that part of the forest there also grew a vast number of strong climbing plants or vines, some extending to the very tops of the tallest trees, twisting and turning among the branches. With these also the natives formed traps for elephants, by weaving them in and out among the trunks in such a way that should an elephant once get in he would be unable to extricate himself before the hunters were upon him.

" Now," said his majesty to us, through Aboh, who was kept by his side to act as interpreter, " we will start and show you what real sport is." I don't mean to say that Aboh used those very words, but he said something to that effect. We looked to our rifles and commenced our march, keeping close behind the sable monarch, whose spirits seemed to rise as he found himself once more in the midst of the wilds in which he had achieved renown as a hunter. No one uttered a word for fear of giving warning to any elephants who might be feeding near at hand, and who would break away should they hear our voices. Before long, however, we came upon traces of several animals; young saplings being trampled underfoot, bows torn down, and hanging vines dragged away. The king made a sign to us to proceed even more cautiously than before. We expected every moment to be in sight of a herd of the huge animals. Presently we heard a loud trumpeting, not fifty yards away from us.

" Be on the look-out, Dick," cried Charley, "the beasts will be coming this way perhaps. Get up a tree, but don't attempt to run."

He remembered how very nearly he had been caught, indeed, Harry and I had not forgotten the fright the beasts had given us. The blacks, however, by their movements did not seem to expect the elephants to come that way, but advanced at a more rapid pace than before in the direction whence the sounds proceeded.

"Why, that trumpeting seems to be coming out of the earth," cried Harry.

Just then the chief gave a flourish with his spear and rushed on. Presently we saw him dart his weapon with all his force, as it appeared to us, into the ground. On nearing the spot, we saw that he had hurled it into a pit at a huge elephant whose trunk was seen waving above the surface of the ground. The blacks now rushed on, each man holding a javelin in his hand, which he plunged into the back or side of the animal, now screaming with pain. Dart after dart was buried in its flesh. It was in a pit cleverly formed in the side of a hill, towards which it had been apparently making its way, the upper side much higher than it could reach even with its trunk, while the lower was of sufficient depth to prevent it scrambling out again—it was thus completely in the hunters' power. The pit had been covered over with light branches and grass, so that the animal, as it rushed along, had not seen it.

As the savages came up they continued hurling their javelins or spears into the poor beast, which was soon covered over almost to resemble a huge porcupine. As the creature's death was certain, we did not think it wise to spend powder and ball on it, indeed, we were likely to offend our fellow-hunters, as they had evidently gained a victory.

As we stood near the pit, keeping at a sufficient distance to avoid tumbling in, we watched the poor creature in its hopeless efforts to escape. While it continued on its feet, the savages in succession came rushing up and throwing their darts, each man of them seeming anxious to have a hand in its slaughter.

At length, much to our satisfaction, it sunk down on its knees, and soon afterwards rolled over on its side, dead. The blacks immediately jumped down, and began pulling out the darts, to be ready to attack a fresh elephant. We soon had an opportunity of seeing another way in which these monsters are caught. Leaving for the present the carcase of the animal we had taken, we advanced further into the forest; presently one of the scouts who had been sent ahead, came hurrying back, saying that there were three elephants not far off. The blacks now began to steal forward, keeping as much as possible under cover, and sometimes advancing on their hands and knees. We kept, by the king's desire, a short distance behind. Presently we heard a tremendous shout, and we saw two elephants before us. They looked round evidently much frightened, and then dashed forward towards one of the barriers, which had been prepared in the neighbourhood. The natives advanced rapidly, until the elephants were suddenly entrapped in a network of vines. The terrified creatures endeavoured to tear them away with their trunks and feet, but the greater their efforts, the more fatally they surrounded themselves with the tough vines. From every side the natives now appeared, completely surrounding the struggling creatures, which they plied unceasingly with their spears. Some climbed up the neighbouring trees, an example which we followed, for it seemed to us that at any moment the beasts might break away and trample us to death before we could possibly escape. The poor creatures found the darts showered down on them from above, and from every side. The more daring hunters would occasionally rush in close behind them, and dart their spears deep into their fiesh. While they were thus engaged, a third elephant, followed by another party of hunters, who had already wounded him, came tearing along. He, too, was caught in the meshes of the network. Several darts were hurled into him, but suddenly turning round, he broke away from them, and trumpeting fiercely, rushed towards a score of natives, who were still at a little distance. They endeavoured to fly on every side, but so unexpected was the attack of the beast, that all had not time to do so. Two unfortunate men were caught; in an instant they were beneath the elephant's feet, who stamped upon them with all his mighty force. In another moment they were crushed, their skulls and all the bones in their bodies being broken, then seizing one in his trunk, the monster hurled it into the air, and rushed forward in an endeavour to make his escape. The whole party, on seeing this, excited by rage, pursued the animal, shouting and shrieking, grinding their teeth, and darting their spears and javelins with all their might. I saw that the elephant had not a chance of escape, indeed, in a short time, mighty as was his strength, he sank down exhausted, with the blood flowing from a hundred wounds, and after a few struggles was dead. On this the natives rushed forward, and began cutting away at the creature with their knives, uttering curses on it for having killed their friends. The noise they had made had scared away all the other elephants—however, they appeared pretty well satisfied with the four they had killed. They now assembled round the last elephant which had fallen, while one of their fetich-men, or priests, approached and cut off a portion which was carefully stowed away in a basket; this was intended, we understood, for an offering to their idols. A dance was now commenced, and was as savage as could well be imagined. They shrieked, they leaped, they whirled their lances above their heads, and twisted and turned their bodies about in the most fantastic manner, making at the same time the most hideous faces, until, exhausted with their exertions, they all squatted down on the ground. Once more at a sign they rose, when they repeated the same dance round the fetich basket.

We were in hopes that the king would return home the next day, but the hunters brought word that there were still more elephants a short distance off, which had come to feed on the leaves of certain trees of which they are very fond. We tried to get off attending his majesty, and Charley suggested that if he made no objection we should return to the village, where, having rejoined Tom, and taken our packs, we might endeavour to make our way northward. Our friend, however, suspected the trick we intended to play him.

" King say 'No good,'" observed Aboh, while his majesty put on a knowing look; and we had to yield to circumstances.

Next day it rained, and we were compelled to keep beneath the shelter of our lean-to's, with nothing to do except to listen to the unintelligible jokes of the king, many of them we suspected at our expense, although Aboh was too polite to say so. It cleared up in the evening, but it was then too late to start.

In the morning we proceeded, after a plentiful breakfast, to the north-east. We observed that the hunters advanced in a more cautious way than before, and we soon discovered that we were entering the territory of another sable monarch, who was not likely, should he discover it, to be well pleased with our proceeding. Having advanced all the day, we at length en-camped, much in the same manner as before. Fires were lighted, and huge pieces of elephant flesh placed to cook before them. A party of carriers had followed us, bringing more delicate provisions, and among them some jugs of palm wine, with which, after the feast, the king and his more special favourites regaled themselves.

We each of us had brought some tobacco, which we thought this a favourable occasion to produce, and great was the delight of the king and his courtiers when they observed it. Pipes were brought forth, which we filled as they were handed to us. All those thus favoured collected round one fire. There are few things an African hunter delights in more than sitting round a blazing fire at night with a pipe in his mouth, and narrating for the hundredth time, perhaps, his various exploits. We regretted not having a sufficient knowledge of the language to make out what was said, but, from the shouts of laughter uttered by our black friends, the yarns were highly amusing to themselves, if not edifying to us. The shades of evening were approaching, a few rays of the setting sun penetrating amid the trees, cast a bright light on the boughs above us. A portion of the hunters were engaged in collecting wood, and bringing in bundles in order to keep up the fires during the night. The king having imbibed a good quantity of palm wine, waxed valiant, and seiz-ing his spear, advanced in front of the camp, flourishing his weapon, and addressing in stentorian tones some fetich or spirit of the air in the forest. We of course could not make out what he said, nor would Aboh enlighten us. Perhaps he was merely praying for a successful hunt the following day. After the king had thus given vent to his feelings, whatever they were, he re-turned and seated himself near us at the fire, when he ordered another jug of palm wine to be brought. One of the courtiers suggested that his majesty was taking a little too much, on which the king, who was now certainly beyond the point at which discretion is retained, told him to mind his own business, and looking in his face, swallowed down another cup. He then insisted that we should join him, wishing to show us the highest possible mark of honour ; we, to please him, took the bowls in our hands, but the moment his eyes were averted, we handed them to some of his courtiers, who had no objection to drink instead of us.

Night had now come on, but still the revels of the king and his courtiers continued. We had retired to a lean-to, hoping to find some rest, for we were all really tired after our day's excursion.

"It seems strange that the king, who ought to remember that we are in the country of one of his enemies, should not take more care to guard against a surprise," observed Charley. "I think we ought to keep watch, for very likely these African fellows will forget to do so, and even if they are not attacked by their enemies, a leopard may steal into the camp and carry one or more of them off."

Harry and I fully agreed with this ; and we drew lots, as we always did on such occasions, to settle the order in which we should keep watch. The first lot fell to me. I was on the point of arousing Harry, who was to keep the second watch, when I was startled by the most fearful shrieks bursting from every side around the camp. The next instant the whole space was filled with warriors, who leaped down into the midst of the sleeping hunters, clubbing some, piercing others with their lances, and throwing cords round the arms of others. There was no necessity to rouse up my companions, for they had started to their feet.

"Where shall we go? We are not going to fight for these drunken fellows," cried Harry.

"Into the bush then behind us," answered Charley.

Harry and I followed him as he sprung round our leafy bower ; but we had not gone many yards when we found ourselves in the presence of a dozen or more savages. The light of the fire falling upon us, revealed to them that we were white men, and instead of knocking us over with their clubs, they leaped forward and grasped our arms. We literally had not a moment to defend ourselves—indeed, from the number of our enemies, we could scarcely have hoped to have fought our way through them. If we had done so without food, and with only a limited supply of ammunition, we could not have made our way far through the country. What became of the king and his courtiers, whether they escaped or were knocked on the head, we could not tell. We were at once unceremoniously hurried off by our captors, who seemed to consider us rich prizes. As we were led off we witnessed a horrible scene. One of our unfortunate companions had been struck down, but still breathed ; when, a number of the savages rushing towards him, some seized his arms and legs, and others, drawing their long knives, plunged them in his body, taking care apparently to avoid wounding any vital part.

Several women who appeared on the scene were encouraging the men in their atrocious proceedings. The cries of the poor wretch reached our ears for some time afterwards, till, becoming fainter and fainter, they altogether ceased, and we were thankful to believe that his sufferings were over. They did not, however, deprive us of our rifles, nor were we in any way ill-treated, except that we were compelled to hurry on at a much faster rate than we liked. After travelling for several miles we saw lights ahead, and found that we were approaching the camp of the people who had captured us. Our guards uttered loud shouts, and a number of people came forth from a collection of leafy huts, which, it was evident from their slight structure, were mere temporary erections. The principal person of the crowd was a savage-looking fellow, about as ugly as King Quagomolo, and dressed much in the same fashion. His majesty, although so ugly, did not appear to have any evil intentions regarding us, but was evidently satisfied at having got us into his power. He invited us to join him at his camp-fire, and at once ordered some of his slaves to bring us food, of which we thought it prudent to partake, although we were not in reality very hungry. We had not been seated long before parties arrived, carrying the tusks of the elephants we had killed; and others followed, dragging along about thirty prisoners, among whom we recognised our friend Aboh. As soon as he saw us he shouted out to the king, who at once ordered him to be released, when he came up to us.

"Me say talkee for you," he observed, by which we understood that he had informed the king that he was our interpreter. He then had a long palaver with his majesty, who seemed well satisfied with what he heard. The intentions of the king were, we found out from what Aboh said, to make us useful to fight his battles, to assist him in governing the country, and to perform any service which he considered white men capable of doing better than his own subjects. He, by some means or other, had been informed of our being in the country, and had made the attack on Quagomolo's camp, expressly for the purpose of getting possession of us.

"What has become of your king and the rest of your people?" we asked of Aboh.

"Him no killee, me tinke run 'way," he answered.

"Things are not so bad as they might have been, so we ought to be thankful," observed Charley; "but still I am afraid that we are as little likely as before to be allowed to continue our journey."

Our chief anxiety was about Tom Tubbs. We feared that King Quagomolo was not likely to set him at liberty, nor was it probable that he would deliver up our knapsacks, even should we send for them, for though he had hitherto behaved honestly towards us, we could scarcely expect that he would withstand the temptation of appropriating their contents under the uncertainty of our fate.   Our first object then was to get Tom to rejoin us, and by some means or other to regain our property.   Our knap-sacks contained powder and shot, beads and trinkets, with which to pay our way, an extra pair of boots, and numerous other articles of the greatest value to us.   We were already more than three days' journey from King Quagomolo's village, and so much on our way to the north.   Before lying down to sleep, we con-sulted Aboh on the subject.

"Berry bad, berry bad," he answered, shaking his head, which he always did when he found a knotty point difficult to unravel. "Me say de King Sanga Tanga—me go get odder white man and him goods.   Suppose let me go, what say King Quagomolo? when him come, cut off him head me tinkee."

"We don't want you to run that risk, Aboh," said Charley ; "but still we wish you to find some other way."

"Me tinkee, me tinkee, now go sleep," answered Aboh, by which we understood that he would consider the matter and let us know the result of his cogitations in the morning.   We accordingly, as he advised, wrapt ourselves in our cloaks which we had on when we were captured, and, taking our positions as near the fire as we could, tried to sleep.   I observed that our captors kept a far more watchful look-out than had our former friends—indeed, from the little I had seen of them, they appeared to me to be a far more sagacious and keen-witted set than those we had left.   They had good reason also to be on the watch, for they might at any moment be attacked by the followers of King Quagomolo, the larger number of whom had escaped, and who would very likely rally and attempt to recover their friends and us, and revenge themselves for the sudden and unprovoked assault made on their camp.   Charley expressed a hope that such might be the case, and that we should then regain our liberty.

"I should be sorry for the bloodshed which would ensue, for our captors would probably fight desperately to detain us, and many on both sides would be killed," said Harry, who was always more anxious to obtain an object by peaceable means than by force.

"There is no use talking about the matter," said Charley, "let us go to sleep and be prepared for whatever may occur. I'll sleep with one eye open, and be ready to rouse you up should there be a chance of our escaping, only take care that the black fellows do not steal our rifles, which perhaps they may attempt to do while we sleep, although they evidently look upon them with awe, or they would have taken them from us before."

Following Charley's advice, we placed our guns by our sides, between us, with our hands upon them, so that we should be awakened should any one try to draw them away. I at length fell asleep, but I was continually fancying that something was going to occur; the camp, however, remained perfectly quiet, the only sounds heard within it being the snoring of the sleepers, and occasionally the shouts of the sentries as they called to each other.

Next morning at daybreak the whole camp was roused up by King Sanga Tanga, and the cooks set to work to dress the plantains which they had brought with them, and the elephant-meat which they had captured. A liberal portion was brought to us in a basket, but as the meat was already tainted, we preferred breakfasting on the plantains sprinkled with red pepper. We observed a dozen men or more with drawn swords standing near us as a guard to prevent our escape, though we were in no way molested. We looked about for Aboh, but he was nowhere to be seen, and without his aid we could not hope to make the king understand our wishes. I began to be afraid that he must have been removed from us, and carried away with the men of his village into slavery, or perhaps put to death.

"I don't think there's a chance of their killing him or any of the prisoners, when they can, by sending them down to the coast, obtain a good price for them," observed Charley. "If the king wants to make use of us, he will not wish to deprive us of our interpreter."

The king now shouted out to his followers, and they began to make preparations for the march, still Aboh did not appear. The farther off we got from King Quagomolo's village, the less chance we should have, we thought, of recovering our property and getting Tom to rejoin us. Charley, therefore, eagerly addressed the king, who passed near where we were sitting, and tried to make him understand by signs what we wanted. He scratched his head, but evidently did not understand either our signs or words. At last he spoke to one of his attendants, who hurried off and soon returned with Aboh, dragging him along by a rope fastened round his wrists. Poor Aboh looked very downcast.

"What's the matter?" asked Charley.

"Me try run 'way, and king bind him hands with odder prisoners."

"I'm sorry to hear that," said Charley, "it would have been better not to have attempted it. Now, we want you to ask the king to let us go back and get our knapsacks, and our companion and we will faithfully return to him as soon as we have done so."

"Me tinkee king no trust him," answered Aboh.

"What! not trust an officer in the navy, and two other English gentlemen," exclaimed Charley indignantly. "Tell him then, that one of us will remain with him, while the other two, with a sufficient guard, go back, and say that we will return as soon as possible."

"But 'spose King Quagomolo no let go," suggested Aboh.

"Then let King Sanga Tanga say, that if we are detained, he will march a large army to liberate us."

Aboh fully understood our wishes. He forthwith held a long palaver with the king. The result was more satisfactory even than we had expected. He consented to send back Charley and me with twenty men as a guard, keeping Harry as a hostage, allowing Aboh to accompany us, under the promise, however, of returning.

Thanking the king for agreeing to our proposal we begged that we might set out immediately.

"Good-bye," said Harry, "I wish that we could have all gone together, but I know you will come back for me, and I do not see how it otherwise could have been arranged."

We forthwith commenced our march. The party was under the command of Prince Ombay, the king's son, a good-natured, merry fellow, with whom Aboh seemed on very good terms. Charley and I were by this time well innured to fatigue, and our companions lightly clad were able to perform long distances each day. We met with no very interesting adventures, although I shot a deer, and Charley was fortunate enough to kill a buffalo which afforded a supply of meat to our companions, and raised us greatly in their estimation. At length we reached the neighbourhood of King Quagomolo's village, when Prince Ombay proposed encamping, and allowing Charley and me with Aboh to go forward and complete our negotiations with King Quagomolo.

We had done our best to impress upon Aboh that he must not attempt any act of treachery, and that everything must be carried on in a peaceable manner: to this he agreed, and we hoped that we could trust him. When we entered the village the people gazed at us in astonishment. Aboh did not think fit to enlighten them as to the cause of our return. We went straight to the residence of the king.

" There he is," exclaimed Charley, as we approached the house, and we found him sleeping in the shade of the rude veranda in front of it. As we were anxious to ascertain how it fared with Tom, leaving the king to finish his nap, we hurried off to our own house. Tom saw us and hastened out to greet us.

" I had given you up for lost, gentlemen, it does my heart good to see you. What has become of Mr. Harry?" he asked.

We told him in a few words the object of our visit.

" I think the chances are the king will listen to you," he answered; " he came back very much out of spirits at being taken by surprise, and at the loss of so many of his people. I don't think he has any stomach for a war with the other black king."

This was satisfactory. Accompanied by Tom we went back to Quagomolo's house. His majesty was rubbing his eyes and stretching himself after his nap. He looked greatly astonished at seeing us stand before him.

" Now tell him what we want," said Charley to Aboh; " just hint that if he doesn't agree to King Sanga Tanga's demands he may expect to have his plantain groves cut down, and his village burned, and himself and his people carried off and sold to the slave traders."

" Berry good reason for not saying No," observed Aboh.

He forthwith addressed the king in due form. His majesty scratched his head and sides and all parts of his body with much vehemence—a sign of great agitation within, if not irritation without, and replied in a long speech.

Aboh briefly translated it.

" Him no want fight, him say go when you like, but him ask ——before you away."

" Tell the king we are very much obliged to him for so readily yielding to our request, and we will certainly give him a present, and if we get safe home we will send him another, as our means at present are limited."

Whether Aboh understood this or not, I am not sure, but whatever he said made the king's countenance brighten up. As we wished to rejoin Prince Ombay as soon as possible, and put him out of suspense, we begged Tom to get ready to march at once. Returning to our house, we took out four necklaces of beads, one as a present from each of us, and also some knives and trinkets which we presented to his majesty, telling Aboh to thank him again for the kind way in which he had treated us, though he had as a mark of his favour detained us longer than we desired.

We then, shouldering our packs, and taking our rifles in our hands, bade the king good-bye, and saluting the people as we passed through the streets of the village, hastened to the spot where we had left Prince Ombay and his party. No one had discovered them, and as he thought it prudent not to remain longer than necessary in the neighbourhood, we immediately commenced our march to the north-east.

Our success had been far greater than we expected. Our bold bearing and the authoritative tone we had used, had, no doubt, considerable influence in inducing the black king to yield to our demands.

Prince Ombay was in high spirits at seeing us, and gave a hearty welcome to Tom. He proposed immediately to set out for his father's town.

" We shall now conquer all our enemies ; we shall succeed in all we undertake ; with four good guns what enemy can stand against us? The wild beasts in the forest must succumb, we shall have game in plenty, and food. What feasts we shall enjoy, what bowls of palm wine."

It was very evident from this that although the prince wished to treat us kindly, he fully intended to keep us well employed in his father's service. By this time we had picked up a good many words of the language of the people, and Aboh had also greatly improved in English, so that we were much better able to understand what was said. Prince Ombay was constantly describing to us the curious creatures of the country, and among others he mentioned some huge apes which he said were like wild men, and built houses for themselves in the trees, and were almost as big as men.

When I expressed doubt on the subject, Ombay said he would show us the houses, and the apes also. He called the animal "Nshiego." They did not live in tribes, but generally in pairs, and that the male built a house for himself, and the female for herself, close on a neighbouring tree.

Next day as we were travelling along, through a thick part of the forest, we came upon some shrubs bearing a pretty sort of wild berry. Prince Ombay at once said we should find some Nshiegoes not far off. By going a short distance from the travelling path, he pointed out what looked like a huge umbrella fixed on a large bough, about twenty feet from the ground, and close to it another of similar character, both the trees being so far removed from each other that the boughs did not touch.

"There are the houses," said the Prince. "But the Nshiegoes have either gone out hunting, or hearing us coming have hidden themselves, you see what wise fellows they are. No leopard or other savage beast can get up to them, nor could a serpent climb the trunk of that tree, as it is too large to be encircled by its body, while no boughs can fall from any neighbouring trees on their heads."

Charley, who was very anxious to examine the roof, managed to throw some stout vines over the bough, above which it was placed, by this means we climbed up. No human beings could have made the roof more neatly. It was constructed of thick leafy branches, secured together by vines, so formed that it was capable of completely throwing off the rain. Ombay told us that the male is the actual builder, while the female gathers the boughs and vines, and brings them to him; and that he builds her nest as well as his own.

As we were soon after this to pitch our camp, Ombay promised to show us some of these apes at home. We gladly accepted his offer. As soon as we had pitched our camp and had had supper, Charley and I with Aboh accompanied Ombay and two of his best hunters, set off, and after going a short distance in the woods, they told us if we would remain quiet, we should certainly see a couple of Nshiegoes under their nests in two trees close at hand. We kept perfectly quiet, scarcely daring to breathe for nearly an hour, it seemed much longer, when out of the forest came a creature which in the gloom looked almost as big as a man; presently it began to cry out "hew, hew," when another creature appeared of the same description. The first of these climbed up into one of the trees, where he sat with an arm clasped round the stem, while his feet rested on the lower branch, and his head reached quite up into the dome of the roof, so that it served as a night cap at the same time. The other Nshiego followed his example, and got into her abode, when, after exchanging a few cries, which seemed as if they were wishing good-night to each other, they both went to sleep. It seemed barbarous to interrupt so much domestic felicity, but the natives would have thought very little of us if we had not killed the Nshiegoes.

Accordingly Charley taking one, and I the other, we both fired, and both the animals fell at the same time, and the blacks taking them up, carried them back to the camp, where, by the light of the fire, we had an opportunity of examining them. We found them just about four feet high, with black skins. The back and shoulders had black hair two or three inches long, while the rest of the body was covered with short, thin, bluish hair, the top of the head being completely bald, the nose was flat, and ears remarkably large; the chin was somewhat round, some thin short hairs growing on it. As soon as we had done examining the creatures, our black escort cut them up, although, I must have been very hard pressed before I would have eaten any of the flesh.

"You think those big apes," observed Ombay, as we were marching along. "If we keep a look-out, we may see some much larger. I must warn you if you do see them to keep out of their way, for they can kill a man in a moment."

As our escort were in no hurry, having once reached their own country, we made but short journeys each day. Having hurried over our supper, we set out as we had done the previous evening. Charley advised that we should try and kill as much game as possible, to please our black companions, as well as to supply ourselves with food. I had kept on the extreme right of the party, Charley on the left, and Tom in the centre, so that we could communicate with each other. We had gone a mile or so from the camp, when I caught sight of a beautiful little deer bounding away up a glade. I followed without calling to my companions, expecting almost immediately to come up with it. It went trotting on, and feeding, and then bounding away in a playful manner, just keeping beyond the range of my gun. Now I lost sight of it, but soon again saw it before me. Thus I was led on further than I should have wished. How many turns I had made, I could not tell, but I fancied that I had gone in a straight line. After all, just as I was about to fire, the deer took flight, either at me, or something else, and bounded away.

Much disappointed, I turned to rejoin my companions. Before long, however, I made the pleasing discovery that I had lost myself. I listened, expecting to hear their shouts, but no sound reached my ears. I had gone on, some way thinking that it was in the direction where I was most likely to find my friends, when I heard voices in the distance coming through the forest. I at once endeavoured to make my way towards the spot from whence they appeared to proceed. As I advanced they sounded more strange. I kept on cautiously. They might be savages of a different tribe, for Ombay had told me of many strange people inhabiting that region. The shades of evening were already coming on. I caught the glimmer of a fire in an open glade before me, and what was my surprise on pushing aside the boughs, to see two enormous apes seated on the ground, and a couple of young ones near them.

One seated in a sort of arbour, formed by the thick foliage above the roots of the tree, appeared to be a patriarch, while just outside sat his wife caressing the youngest one, while in the front of her lay the other, warming himself before the fire. I could see the two adults were enormous creatures, as large—they appeared to me—as any ordinary human being, with huge chests and long arms. Had there been but one alone I should have felt very nervous lest he should attack me, but what would be my fate were both the creatures, aided by their infant progeny, to set upon me. I feared almost to breathe lest I should be discovered. Should I tread on a rotten branch, or brush by a bough too roughly, the noise might attract them, and they might come in chase of me. Before moving I examined my gun to see that it was ready for instant use. My hope was that I might kill one of the terrible creatures and so frighten the others and obtain time to reload.

Even the young ones were no contemptible opponents, should
they fly at my legs or seize me by the arms while I was engaged
with their parents.   This, however, they were not likely to do
unless endowed with more sagacity than the ape tribe are generally
supposed to possess.   Still if their wisdom was in proportion to
their size, they might attack me in a way which would give me
very little chance of escaping in spite of my gun.   I, however,
felt much more confidence with that in my hand than I should
have done without it.   Never did thief creep away more carefully
out of a house than did I from the bower of those terrific apes.
I had not believed that such enormous creatures existed.   Night
was rapidly coming on, for what I could tell there might be others
in the neighbourhood.   To spend a night by myself in those
wilds was anything but pleasant to contemplate.   As soon as I
could venture to move fast, without the risk of being heard by
the huge apes, I retreated rapidly.   I was not aware at the time
that I had fallen in with a family of the largest existing specimens of the ape tribe since known as the terrible gorilla,
although at that time I was ignorant of its name.   I was only
too soon to become in a terrible way better acquainted with the
creature.

As I have described I was endeavouring to get as far off as
possible from the fearful monsters, when the sun having set, it
became almost immediately dark.   The thick foliage overhead
hid the stars from my sight so that I could not tell in what direction I was going, whether to the north or south, and although I
occasionally got a glimpse of one amid the boughs, it could not
thus seen serve as a guide to me.   I pictured to myself the danger
of thus wandering through the forest by myself, for although I
might grope my way amid the trees, yet I might be pursued by a
leopard or lion, or I might tread on some venomous snake or get
into the presence unexpectedly of a herd of elephants.   For some
time I was afraid of shouting or firing my rifle, lest I might attract

the attention of those monster apes. At length, thinking I had got sufficiently far off not to bring them down upon me, and that I might after all be in the neighbourhood of my friends, I began to exercise my lungs. After I had shouted several times, I fancied that I heard an answer, but still could not be certain that the cries which reached my ears were not uttered by the monster apes or some other creatures. Then I fired off my gun. Forthwith there came a loud chattering and shrieking from out of the forest, uttered by troops of monkeys and flights of parrots. I was afraid if I fired often I might exhaust my stock of powder, which I should require for my defence if attacked either by huge apes or four-footed monsters.

Finding no answer to any of my signals, I judged that I had got a long way off from my friends; I therefore thought it prudent at once to climb a tree, hoping not to find it occupied by any arboreous ape or other creature. I therefore threw a vine over one of the lower boughs, by which means I was able to climb on to the branch. I then drew up the vine, so that I might be tolerably secure. There was still sufficient light from the sky to enable me to find my way to a part of the tree where several boughs branched off; here I could lie down with my gun by my side, without any fear of falling to the ground. Before going to sleep, however, I thought it would be as well to give another shout, hoping that, perhaps, from my lofty position, my voice would reach my friends. I listened for an answer. Silence reigned through the forest, broken now and then by a roar so terrific, so superhuman, that I involuntarily trembled. It was not like that of a wild beast, nor of that proceeding from any human throat. It seemed to come from a spot at no great distance off. What if the creature should discover me and be able to climb the tree in which I had taken shelter! What hope would there be for me then? I regretted having shouted; it would have been more prudent had I kept silence. I could only pray that the creature might not find me out, if creature it was. I did not believe that evil spirits in bodily form walked the earth, or I might have supposed that the voice I heard was that of one, so awe-inspiring was it. I now peered down from among the boughs towards the ground near the trunk of the tree, dreading every instant to see the creature approach.

At length I saw a dark form moving along, but it went on all fours. Could it be the creature that had uttered the sound? Presently it approached a small tree and then reared itself, and I saw what looked like a man of gigantic form, with a huge head, and prodigiously long arms, holding on to the tree. He seemed to look about him as if to examine the surrounding trees ; should he discover me, he evidently could with ease climb the tree on which I sat. I was afraid of moving, and yet I felt convinced that he might, with his sharp eyes, discover me looking through the boughs at him. I fortunately had the muzzle of my gun turned towards him, and could at any moment bring the butt to my shoulder. I could not expect to get a better mark than he now presented to me, but then, so human looked the creature, seen through the gloom of night, that I asked myself whether I was justified in shooting him. While these thoughts were passing through my mind, he let go the stem of the tree, and once more sank down, moving forward as before on his hands and feet. At first I thought he was coming up my tree. To my relief he turned aside, apparently satisfied that the being which had uttered the, to him, strange sounds, was not concealed among its branches. I breathed more freely. I was thankful that I had not fired, for I might only have wounded the creature, and he would then, inspired by rage, have climbed the tree to attack me. I waited, watching for an hour or more ; at length, finding sleep overcoming me, I replaced my gun by my side, and stretched myself almost at my length, for which there was ample room. My eyes closed, possibly I might have been surprised by apes, snakes, or any other tree-climbing creatures without having time to rouse myself sufficiently to offer the slightest resistance, so sound was my sleep; and yet it was not untroubled, for all night long that fearful cry occasionally rang in my ears, and I heard other shrieks and noises. Whether they were really uttered by the denizen of the forest, or created by my imagination, is more than I can possibly say.

CHAPTER XI.

A BRIGHT light streamed into my eyes—it was the sun,
just rising, sending his rays darting through the boughs.
I felt very unwilling to get up, and when I began to move I
discovered that my limbs were somewhat stiff from the hardness
of my couch. At length I rose, and, kneeling down, thanked
Heaven for the protection which had been afforded me. I now
began to feel the sensations of hunger. I hoped, however, that
I might be able to find something with which to satisfy my ap-
petite, and enable me to continue my search for my friends. It
was important to lose no time ; I accordingly descended, letting
myself down by the vine. I could now, guided by the sun, steer
a tolerably straight course. I judged that if I proceeded to the
north-east I should in time, though I might miss my travelling
companions, at all events reach King Sanga Tanga's village.
I looked about me, half expecting to see the monster who had
passed by in the evening, walk out from behind some thick
bushes which grew around. I stood close to the very tree by
which I had seen the creature supporting itself, and although I

hoped that it had gone on to a distance, I felt a disinclination to camp at that spot. I had, fortunately, some matches and a tinder-box in my pocket, so that I could light a fire as soon as I had something to cook at it. I had not gone far when a chorus of loud screams announced the approach of a flock of grey parrots, which were issuing forth from their resting-places in search of berries and nuts. Crouching down behind a bush, I allowed them to come so close to me that I shot a couple, and knocked down a third with the barrel of my gun before it had time to fly off. Slinging them over my shoulder, I trudged on until I came to the bank of a small stream. Going along it I found an open spot, in the centre of which I could kindle a fire without the risk of setting light to the neighbouring trees. I quickly had two of my parrots plucked, and by means of the usual wooden spit, soon had them roasting. Before sitting down, I looked carefully around to ascertain that no monster ape was near, likely to invite himself to the repast. I must own it, I was seized with a sort of horror of the monster apes, and as I went along I could not help every now and then looking over my shoulder, expecting to see one following. I dreaded the thought of an encounter with one of the creatures far more than I did with a leopard or lion. I hurried over my breakfast, and having taken a good draught from the bright stream, filled up my water bottle, and stowed a portion of the cooked parrot in my wallet that I might not be delayed by having to cook a mid-day meal, I pushed on. The forest in many places was more open than I expected to find it, and I made good progress.

I did not wish to expend my ammunition by firing signals, but I occasionally shouted at the top of my voice, hoping that my friends would hear me. I was disappointed, however, and another evening found me still in the forest. I was certain, by the course of the sun, which I had carefully noted, that I had kept a tolerably correct course, and I calculated that by the end of a couple of days at most, I should reach King Sanga Tanga's town. My chief regret was, that my non-appearance would cause anxiety, and that Charley and Harry would be delayed in searching for me—still that could not be helped. Had I gone in any other direction, I might naturally have lost my way, whereas I now felt sure that they must ultimately come up with me. I have not described the various animals I met with. Now and then a buffalo passed at a distance, and several species of antelopes. Once I saw a leopard stealing by, but he did not see me, having some other game in view. There were also hyenas, but I had no reason to be afraid of them, as they seldom attack a human being unless they find them asleep. There were numerous small monkeys, as well as big apes of several species. The most curious monkey was a small frolicsome little animal which, whenever seen, indicated that water was not far off, as they have an especial fondness for water. They are great friends with a pretty bird, which is constantly found in their company. They are often seen playing together, whether it is that they are attracted by the same object, or really have a mutual affection, I am unable positively to determine.

The country teeming with animal life, and producing numerous berries as well as large fruits, I had no fear of suffering from hunger, provided my stock of ammunition should hold out. Without it, in the midst of abundance, I might have starved. Although I determined, as on the previous night, to sleep up a tree ; I lit a big fire, at which I could cook my supper, on the ground near at hand. While the birds were roasting, I threw a vine over the bough, by climbing up which I could gain a place of safety. The birds I had shot being cooked, I was discussing my supper, washing it down with draughts from my water bottle, when looking up, I saw the shadow of a creature moving some fifty yards off ; a second glance convinced me that

It was a leopard. The fire kept him at bay, but he stood gazing at me, and probably scenting the odour of the roasted birds from afar. I saw him creep nearer and nearer. I might have shot him, but might have missed, so considering discretion the better part of valour, I caught hold of one of the birds by the leg, and holding it in my mouth, I swarmed up to the bough, where I was in perfect safety. I had before this fixed on a spot where I could rest for the night, and at once made my way to it, intending to start at daybreak the next morning. However, I could not resist the temptation of watching the leopard. He walked round and round my fire, but as long as it blazed up was afraid of approaching. As, however, the flames sank down, and only the bright embers remained, he made a dash at the portion of the birds I had left behind, and gobbled them up in a moment. I then threw him the bones of the one which I had been gnawing. He looked up very much surprised, wondering where it came from. I was greatly inclined to shoot him, but there was no object in doing so, as I should very likely only have wounded him, and sent him off to die miserably. At last, finding there was nothing more to be got, and possibly forgetting all about me, the leopard took his departure. I slept as soundly up the tree as I did the previous night, and coming down in the morning, immediately pushed forward in the direction I had before been travelling. I was able to make good some eight or ten miles before the air had become heated with the sun. Another day passed so like the former, that I could scarcely distinguish one from the other. Another evening was coming on. I fully expected by this time to have reached my destination, but I had met with no plantations, or any other signs to show that I was approaching an inhabited spot, I therefore supposed that I must be still some way off.

I was travelling along when I heard the sound of voices—they were those of females, several with baskets on their heads,

while others were busily employed in plucking wild fruits, which
grew in abundance in an open glade in the forest. Some thick
bushes sheltered me from view. I was thankful to see them, as
I hoped that they belonged to the village of Sanga Tanga, and
that my long solitary journey was now nearly over. Still I
thought that should I appear among them suddenly I might
alarm them—I was, therefore, determined to remain concealed,
and to follow them when they should return homeward, being
sure that they would lead me, if not to the village of which
I was in search, to another where I might hope to be well
received. The girls were all scattered about, plucking the fruit
from the bushes, when I heard a fearful scream, and looking in
the direction from whence it came, I saw one of those dreadful
monsters which had for days haunted my imagination, approaching two of the girls. The creature was too far off to allow me to
fire with a certainty of killing him, and should I merely wound
him, I should probably only make him more savage ; I therefore
crept forward as rapidly as I could, hoping to get close enough
to shoot him before he could seize either of the girls. One,
overcome by terror, seemed scarcely able to fly, or make an
effort to escape, the others fled shrieking away. Before I
could get sufficiently close to make sure of my aim, the hideous
monster seized the hapless girl round the waist with one of his
long arms, and immediately began to make his way towards a
neighbouring tree. I dashed forward. Should he once get to
any height up the branches, nothing could save the girl, for even
should I shoot him she might be killed by the fall. I knew
that by firing I ran the risk of shooting her, but that risk must
be run, her death was certain should he escape with her. He
had reached the first branch of a tree, scarcely more than twelve
feet from the ground, when I brought my rifle to bear on him.
I fired, aiming at his breast.

As the bullet struck him he uttered a terrific roar ; but at the same moment opening his left arm, which had encircled the girl, he let her fall, fortunately on a bed of leaves. She was senseless. I was afraid that the monster would fall upon her, and if so in his struggles he might tear her with his teeth and claws, but he held fast to the bough, roaring loudly and striking his breast. Under other circumstances I think that I should have put a considerable distance between myself and the beast, but the life of a fellow-creature was at stake. Summoning all the coolness I could command, I reloaded and then shouted to the other girls to come back and take their companion away. They all seemed to dread approaching the monster. I was afraid that, should I go under the bough, he might spring on me, and that the only safe mode of proceeding was to keep him covered by my rifle, so that, should he make any movement, I might again shoot. Presently I saw him swaying backwards and forwards as if his strength was leaving him ; still he growled as fiercely as before. I moved slightly, so as to get a better aim at him. He thought, perhaps, that I was about to fly, for he stepped on to another bough.

Now was my opportunity; I fired, and down he came with a crash, breaking away several rotten boughs, until he reached a quantity of dead wood, where he struggled in vain to rise. Having reloaded, I dashed forward, and, lifting the girl in my arms, bore her towards a party of her friends, who had stopped, gazing horror - stricken at what was taking place. They received her with loud cries of grief, supposing her to be dead. She, in a short time, began to breathe, and, opening her eyes, gazed round with a scared and terrified look, then she clung to her companion, shrieking out, as she caught sight of me standing by—"Save me, save me !" Apparently she for a moment supposed that I was the being who had carried her off. Her friends, however, were apparently doing their best to reassure her ; and at length, pointing to me, they made her understand that I was the person who had saved her from the grasp of the monster ape, which they pointed out lying dead beneath the tree. They then all came round me, and I had no doubt from the signs they made and their looks, that they were expressing their gratitude for the service I had rendered them in saving the young girl.

I tried in return to make them understand how glad I was that I had done so. I was now able more particularly to remark the appearance of the damsel. She was young, and for a negress remarkably pretty. As she recovered she took my hand and placed it on her head as a sign, I supposed, that she was much obliged to me for saving her. I tried to make out whether the girls belonged to King Sanga Tanga's village. When I mentioned his name they all clapped their hands and pointed to the girl whom they called Iguma. In consequence of this action I began to hope that she was in some way related to him, perhaps his daughter, in which case my friends and I were likely to be better treated than we could otherwise have expected.

As far as I could judge from the signs the girls made, I understood that the village was not far off. Having picked up the baskets and refilled them with the fruit which had been strewn on the ground, they prepared to return. Four of them carried Iguma, who placed her arms round the necks of two, while the others supported her legs. Before setting off I was anxious to secure the skin of the huge ape—if ape it was, for it looked to me, as it lay stretched on the ground, more like some savage human being of the forest. I pointed it out to the girls, who, I believe, fancied that the creature had made its escape into the wood. As soon as they saw it and knew from the signs I made that it was dead, they began to advance cautiously in the direction where it lay. I went first, with my knife drawn ready to flay it. They now crept forward, two or three of the bolder ones in front of the rest, when they would stop and gaze at the creature, talking to each other, even now apparently having some doubt whether it was dead or not. Then, as I got nearer to it and at last gave it a kick or two with my foot, they came crowding around with more confidence, crying out loudly and chattering away to each other. I was about to begin to flay it when it struck me that they would perhaps be unwilling to carry the skin, and I certainly had no wish to bear it on my own shoulders all the way to the village, even although the distance might not be great. I tried to make them understand that if they would send some young men I should be very much obliged. They, after a little time, took in my meaning, and two of them, handing their baskets to their companions, set off running.

As I was not particularly anxious to skin the creature myself, remembering that if I did so I should not be in a very fit state to be presented to the king and the inhabitants of the village, I accepted the invitation of the girls to accompany them at once.

Leaving the dead ape to any fate which might befall it, I set off with my new friends, who now surrounding me, formed themselves into a sort of triumphal procession. First went Iguma and her supporters, then followed four of my attendants, then I came with two on either hand, the rest bringing up the rear, all shouting and singing impromptu verses in praise of me, for I could tell by certain words that such was the case. The words were to this effect—

"The king's daughter with her maidens went out to pick berries, then came a huge ape, and they fled with fright. The monster seized the maiden, the pride of her father's heart, and bore her off to a cruel death. Already he had reached a tree, the cries of her companions availed her not. In another moment she would have been beyond our reach, when a pale-faced stranger appeared with a wonderful thunder maker in his hand. He made thunder, and the ape, huge as it was, fell dead at his feet. The beautiful Iguma was saved. He who had saved her has won our hearts, we will do him honour, we will do all he asks of us. The king will rejoice, he will weep with joy over his child, and he will give her to the young stranger as a reward. He will become our prince and live with us, and lead our young men to battle. We will serve him gladly."

As the meaning of these last expressions dawned upon me, I began to feel somewhat uncomfortable. I was very happy to have saved the young lady, but had no wish whatever to become the husband of a black beauty, however charming she might be in the eyes of her countrymen. I was puzzled to think how I might get out of the difficulty without offending her or her father, or her female companions, who had so unreservedly bestowed her on me without being asked. I could only hope that the maidens were indulging in poetical license, and that they did not really mean that I should marry their mistress. At all events, I determined to put the best face on the matter I could, hoping that they might not insist on the event coming off immediately.

At last I caught sight of some magnificent palm trees, rising in the midst of a number of houses. In a short time we entered a broad street which led into the square, and in the middle were the palm trees I had just before observed. It struck me as an exceedingly picturesque place, and very neat. On each side of the square two other streets branched off. Every house had a veranda in front of it, and an open space between it and the road. I should have said as we approached we met a party of young men running at full speed, who, after exchanging a few words with the girls, hastened on in the direction whence we had come. On entering the town we saw a number of persons approaching, several playing on tomtoms and various musical instruments, and others shouting and singing. In their midst walked their king in full costume, which I suspect he had put on in a hurry, for his head dress was rather awry. Coming forward, he embraced his daughter, tears falling from his eyes as a mark of his paternal affection ; then he came up to me, and saluted me in the same fashion, a ceremony I would gladly have avoided. He then poured out expressions which I took to signify how deeply grateful he was to me for saving his daughter from the huge ape. He then asked me what had become of my companions, and how it was that I was there all alone. I may have been wrong, but this, I believe, was what he said to me. I tried to explain by signs rather than words, how I had been separated from them while out hunting, that I had looked for them in vain, and then made my way towards his village, where I fortunately arrived in time to do the happy deed which I trusted would guild my humble name in the eyes of his majesty and his subjects. I do not know whether the king understood what I said, but as I put my hand to my heart and looked very much pleased, I was sure that he understood, at all events, that I wished to say something civil. From what I heard the girls say, I confess that I was somewhat afraid that his majesty would propose bestowing his daugther on me at once, and was greatly relieved when I found he had not in any way alluded to the subject. Having seen her carried into one of the huts by her attendants, the king took my hand and led me towards another hut on the opposite side of the square. It was a very well-constructed building, of fair size and height and look, remarkably neat and clean. Behind it was a plantain grove ; a garden with lime and other trees, and shrubs of beautiful foliage, with an enclosure in which were a number of goats and fowls.

Many of the inhabitants were clothed in robes of bongo, a species of cloth made from the delicate cuticle of palm leaflets, which are stripped off and ornamented with feathers. These are woven very neatly, many of them are striped, and some made even with check pattern. The pieces of cloth are then

stitched together in a regular way with needles, also manufactured by the natives. I saw in the town a number of men
sitting at looms in the middle of a hut with a wood fire burning
near them. The weavers were smoking their long pipes, the
bowls of which rested on the ground, and shouting to each
other as they worked merrily away. Some of the king's attendants brought in cushions and mats, which they placed on
the floor. He then, begging me to be seated, placed himself
by my side, and tried to enter into conversation, but I must
confess that I had great difficulty in making out what he said.
I tried, however, to look very wise, lest his majesty might
lose patience, for there was something in his countenance which
showed me that he might be apt to do so, as is often the case with
persons who have been accustomed to have their own way.

We were still carrying on this somewhat unintelligible conversation, when loud shouts were heard, and the king and
I going to the door of the hut saw the young men who
had been sent to bring in the dead ape, four carrying the
skin, with the head stuck on a pole, and the arms stretched
out, and the rest bearing the body, cut up into portions.
From the way the king licked his lips, I suspected that he
intended to enjoy a feast on the flesh of the beast. I should as
soon thought of eating a human being, so human did it look in
many respects. They halted before us, and asked what they
were to do with it. I, in reply, merely claimed the skin, at which
they appeared well satisfied, and marched off with the remainder
to the king's house at the other side of the square. I hoped, by
hanging up the skin, we might be able to clean it, and preserve
it sufficiently to carry it with us to the coast, for I was sure that
otherwise no one would believe that so enormous an ape existed.
I managed to make the king understand what I wanted, and he,
with several other persons whom he summoned, assisted me in
hanging it up to a branch of a tree, my intention being to light a

fire under it, and try to cure it by smoking. I was thus employed
when I heard several shots. The king and his attendants rushed
out to the front of the house, and I followed. They were evidently in a state of agitation, wondering what the shots could
mean. Presently we heard shouts. In a short time a number
of persons appeared at the further end of the town. As they
drew near, to my great joy I recognised Charley and Harry with
Tom Tubbs and Aboh, accompanied by Prince Ombay. On
seeing me they all hurried forward, eager to know how I had
been separated from them and found my way to the village.
While I briefly narrated my adventures, Prince Ombay learned
how I had rescued his sister. He now came forward and embraced me, telling me that I was his brother, that we should
never part.

Calling Aboh, I begged him to say everything civil he could think
of; but, at the same time, not to commit me by making any
promises on my part. The king in his generosity would have
appropriated a house to each of us, but we begged that we might
be allowed to live together in the one he had fixed on for me,
which was amply large enough for all of us. We could thus, we
agreed, defend ourselves should the feelings of the people assume
any unpleasant change towards us; or we could, if necessary,
better arrange for making our escape should the king take it into
his head to detain us. At present everything appeared as
pleasant as we could desire.

Soon after we had taken possession of the house a number of
girls appeared with baskets of provisions on their heads, and
bowls of farina. There was flesh and fowl and fruits of all
descriptions. We told Aboh that we should be very glad if he
would bring us some big bowls of water in which we could wash
our feet, and as he had before seen us perform that operation, he
at once understood what we wanted. Hastening out, he quickly
returned with a large gourd full of cool water, supplied by a

spring which ran from a hill close to the village. We were about
to perform our ablutions, when a damsel appeared carrying a
basket of fruit on her head. She approached accompanied by a
white-haired old gentleman clothed in one of the robes I have
described. Looking up I recognised Iguma. I asked Aboh
who the old gentleman was, suspecting that he had come with
some object in view.

"That's her grandfather," he answered, looking very knowing.
We, of course, rose to greet the young lady, and to receive and
open the basket she had brought. The ebon damsel then
said something, and stood with her hands clasped before her.
What it was about I, of course, could not exactly make out,
and Aboh did not appear inclined to translate it. Her vener-
able grandsire then made a long speech. It was even more
unintelligible to us than were the words which had dropped
from Iguma's lips. At last we were obliged to apply to Aboh
for information.

"Him say makee her wife," said Aboh at length. It was
certainly a great abridgment of what had been uttered by
the old man, although probably it contained the pith of the
matter.

"Tell him," said Charley, pointing to me, "that I am his elder
brother, that he cannot marry without my leave, and that I consider him far too young to think about taking upon himself the
responsibilities of matrimony. That he must come home first,
then, if he gets our parents permission, that he will come back
with chains and beads and looking-glasses, and ornaments of all
sorts for the young lady, and guns, powder and shot, and a
variety of other articles for her papa. Make this very clear,
if you please, for I must have no misunderstanding on that
point."

Aboh, who understood the chief part of what Charley had said,
immediately translated it to the old gentleman, with a good many

additions of his own. Iguma pouted a little at the thought, I suppose, of having to wait so long, on which I told Aboh to remind her of the quantity of beads I was to bring when I got our father's leave to marry a black wife. I must own I had my doubts how far we were justified in using this deceit, but our position was a difficult one and might become dangerous, and just then we did not consider the consequences which might result from the artifice we had resorted to. I tried to make Iguma understand how much I was obliged to her by eating some of the food she had brought, and assuring her how very nice I found it. At last she appeared tolerably well satisfied, and as it was getting late she and her grandfather took their departure. We were now left alone, with only Aboh and Shimbo to attend on us.

"Things have turned out much better than I expected, and we are very jolly here," observed Charley; "but I wonder whether Mr. Sanga Tanga will let us proceed on our journey."

"To my mind I am afraid that, now he has got us, he intends to keep us," observed Tom. "These nigger chiefs fancy that white men can do everything, and as we have arms and ammunition, the king will, I suspect, take it into his head to try and conquer all the country round him. King Quagomolo, as he calls himself, is evidently afraid of him, or he would not have given me and our traps up so easily."

"We, however, must try and get away," observed Harry; "we may be jolly enough, as Charley says, just now, but we shall soon get weary of the life."

"We must first try fair means, and endeavour to persuade the king to let us go home to ask our father to allow Dick to marry Miss Iguma, as I propose," said Charley; "that appears to me to be the safest plan to pursue."

"But suppose the king says no, and insists on your brother marrying his daughter with or without your father's leave, what's to be done then?"

"We must cut and run," I exclaimed ; "I should be very sorry to treat the young lady ill, but if her father insists on my marrying her, I shall regret having been the means of saving her from the wild man of the woods. I certainly thought that he would be grateful to me for what I had done, but I confess that he exhibits his gratitude in a very awkward manner as far as I am concerned. However, there is no use talking about the matter any longer, I'm getting very sleepy, and should be glad to turn in and get a quiet snooze, after spending the last three nights up trees."

My companions were ready enough to follow my advice, and we all wrapped ourselves up in the pieces of matting with which our new friends had supplied us, and went to sleep.

WE were allowed a day to rest after our long journey, and were supplied with abundance of food, but we soon found that our entertainers had no intention that we should eat the bread of idleness. Prince Ombay, as we called him, came to see us early the second morning after our arrival, and began talking away at a great rate. We nodded our heads to show that we were listening, but as we could not understand more than every tenth word he uttered, Charley summoned Aboh.

" Him say go out hunting, kill big beast horns on head."

" I suppose he means buffalo," observed Charley.

" Or deer," suggested Harry.

" Are the animals he speaks of big and hairy, or slight and thin, with very long horns ? " I inquired of Aboh.

Aboh put his thumbs up above his head, and then with his hands described a fat animal with long hair, and made a bellowing noise.

" Ah, he means buffalo, there is no doubt about that," observed Charley.

"Tell our friend we shall be happy to accompany him, and if he can show us the buffalo, we will do our best to shoot them."

Ombay, on this answer being interpreted to him, appeared well satisfied. Taking his departure, he in a short time returned accompanied by about twenty young men armed with spears and javelins—the prince and a few of his companions of more exalted rank having hangers, mostly rather the worse for wear. We got our guns ready, and a sufficient amount of ammunition for the day, and placing our knapsacks and other valuables under the charge of Shimbo, who promised that he would allow no one to steal them; we announced that we were ready to set off. Ombay kept Aboh by his side, that he might converse with us whenever he pleased. We had a long march before we stopped to dine, but the party had brought a good supply of provisions, and we had as much food as we required. We then again set out, and continued our way until near sunset; when we arrived at the edge of a wide prairie, bordered by the forest through which we had passed.

"Here big beast soon come," observed Aboh.

According to the custom of the country, our companions immediately began to set up screens of branches, behind which we were to take our post. Harry and I were together, Charley and Tom were stationed behind another screen, at a little distance off. We had to wait there for some time, when I heard Aboh, who was with us, whisper something. Presently my ears caught the sound of the trampling of hoofs, and directly afterwards I saw by the light of the moon, just then rising, a herd of thirty or more magnificent animals emerging from the forest, and scattering themselves widely over the grassy plain in front of us. We were fortunately to leeward, or our shelter would have availed us nothing.

We had now to wait patiently until some of the herd might make their way to our screen. How soon they would do this it was impossible to say. At all events, there was a prospect of our patience being severely tried. We remained as silent as death. In a short time the buffalo, who seemed not to apprehend danger, began gamboling and sporting with each other. As there appeared no chance of their coming close to us, Ombay made a sign to Harry and me to accompany him, and showed us how we were to crawl along the grass until we got near enough to have a shot. We were prepared for this, and gladly undertook to do as he proposed. Just then the moon was obscured by a cloud, and taking advantage of this he set out. We followed close behind him, creeping along with our heads just raised above the grass. We stopped whenever he did, on seeing the buffalo look towards us. Presently we were close enough to obtain fair shots. I was afraid, should we attempt to get nearer, that the animals might take alarm and scamper off. I therefore signed to Harry to shoot one, while I aimed at another no great distance from us. Without waiting for a signal from Ombay, we rose to our knees and fired. The two animals at which we had aimed lept into the air at the same moment, and fell over dead. Ombay, who had not expected us to make such excellent shots, on this shouted with delight. The rest of the herd of course galloped off, and were soon lost to sight amid the trunks of trees on the opposite side of the prairie. The hunters on seeing this rushed out, and instantly began flaying the animals, and cutting them up.

Each man having loaded himself with as much as he could carry, we returned to a spot inside the forest, previously chosen by our leader. Fires were lighted, and our companions were soon making merry over the buffalo meat. We found it fairly flavoured, but rather tough. Our camp was formed in the usual manner with lean-to's, beneath which we sheltered ourselves, and fires in front of them, the smoke of which contributed to keep off the stinging insects which abounded, and the bright light was calculated to scare the savage animals of the forest. We had now become so familiarised to this sort of life, that we thought nothing of it. Early in the morning Ombay called us up and told us, through our interpreter, that buffalo were again likely to be feeding in the prairie, and that we might have a chance of killing two or three more. Of course we were ready for the sport,—indeed, the more animals we killed, the more likely we were to propitiate the chief and his son. We felt all the time that we were prisoners, although not actually in chains, and that our masters might, at any time, change their conduct and ill treat us.

Jumping up from our bed of leaves, we shouldered our guns, and accompanied by Aboh, we attended the prince and his party—a few of the men only remaining to look after the camp and buffalo meat. As we were making our way through the forest, we got somewhat separated from the chief, of whom we caught a sight just as we were nearing the prairie. We were hastening to overtake him, when a rending and crashing sound reached our ears, followed by the most tremendous bellowing I ever heard. Then came a sharp bark—so it sounded—and a roar such as I had heard proceeding from the huge man ape I had encountered in the forest. The next instant a buffalo burst from the cover. To its back was clinging one of the monster creatures I have just mentioned. It clung on with its powerful legs and arms with a tenacity against which all the efforts of the buffalo to free itself were unavailing. Maddened with terror, on dashed the buffalo, which was making its way directly towards Ombay, who stood seemingly paralysed by fear or astonishment. No tree which he could possibly climb up was near at hand. I saw that in a few seconds the buffalo would be upon him, and that he would be either gored to death or trampled under foot by it; or that the ape, springing from its back, might, with its savage jaws and hands, tear him to pieces. I, for a moment, was doubtful whether to kill the buffalo, or the still more savage creature which bestrode it. I decided on aiming at the buffalo; I might stop it in its mad career, and, rolling over it might crush the creature on its back, or else I might have time to reload before the ape could reach me. I took good aim, the buffalo's shoulder was presented to me, I fired, and the huge animal, after bounding forward three or four yards, came to the ground with a tremendous crash, catching the leg of the ape beneath it as it rolled over on its back. Without a moment's loss of time I reloaded, for the ape was not likely to be much injured. Scarcely had I done so, when the monster, quickly extricating itself, and catching sight of Prince Ombay, with a terrific roar, striking its breast, made towards him. In another instant the young black would have received a blow from its tremendous paws, or have been seized by the fearful grinders which, giving a savage growl, it exhibited as it opened its mouth. I could not have imagined a creature with a more diabolical countenance. Human as it looked, I had no hesitation in killing it. I fired, and my bullet striking it in the breast, it fell flat on its face, emitting, as it did so, a hideous death-cry, half roar, half shriek, which echoed through the forest, and was repeated, it seemed to me, by others of the same species. Ombay, who had been fully aware of his danger, quickly recovered, and springing forward, dealt a blow with his hanger at the neck of the monster, which nearly severed the head from the body. He then, seeing me advancing, hastened forward to express his thanks, and I believe that he really was grateful to me for saving his life, although I fancy he wished to gain the credit of having killed his assailant himself. The uproar had frightened away all the other buffaloes, so, with the bodies of the one I had killed, and the ape, we forthwith returned to the camp to enjoy a hearty breakfast. The natives cut up the body of the ape, and ate it with as little compunction as they would have done mutton or beef. Charley and Harry, who were close behind me when I fired, declared that they had never seen better shots in their lives.

"I felt that much depended on my taking good aim," I replied.

"I was anxious to save the life of a fellow-creature, besides which, I hope, that by rendering him a service, we may have a better chance of being allowed to proceed upon our journey."

I wished that we had had our knapsacks and could have at once set off, without the pain of taking leave of King Sanga Tanga and the lovely Iguma.

We told Aboh that we should like to secure the skin of the ape, but he replied that none of the young men would like the trouble of carrying it. On our way back we met with several beautiful antelopes, and two or three kinds of gazelles, which bounded away before we could get near enough to obtain a shot at them. There was one of a bright orange colour with a chestnut patch between the horns and eyes, below which was a white crescent-shaped mark, while its body was completely covered with stripes from head to tail, of a lighter colour than the rest of the skin.

Although somewhat heavily built, it was graceful in its motions and exceedingly swift of foot, so that in little more than a minute the herd near to which we had got bounded out of sight. We saw two leopards, but they took good care not to come near us, they were certainly upwards of five feet in length. Tiger-cats, some of unusual size, abounded, and would have been dangerous to encounter unarmed. Charley shot an iguana, which, ugly as it looked, afforded us a pleasanter meal than the buffalo meat. As to the monkeys, they were innumerable.

On passing over a stream we caught sight of several beautiful little monkeys, not bigger than rats, frisking about among the boughs just as we had seen them on a previous occasion. Near them were some birds, which kept hopping to and fro on the same branches, apparently on the most intimate terms with these diminutive quadrumana. By putting up screens and waiting patiently, we managed to kill several antelopes and other animals, so that we returned to the village laden with meat. On entering, we found the inhabitants in a state of commotion in consequence of the arrival of a person of importance, who was then said to be having an audience with the king, but who he was, or what he had come about, we could not learn. By this time we had expended all our ammunition, and we hastened to our house to replenish our stock, in case, by any chance, we might have to use our arms. We felt that our position was critical, for at any moment our capricious masters might turn upon us, and we might have to fight for our lives. We had cause, however, to be grateful to Heaven for our preservation, and for the many dangers we had gone through safely, as also that we had been enabled to retain our health, which, in spite of the heat and fatigue we endured, was excellent. I suspect, however, that had we not been well supplied with wholesome food and pure water, the case would have been different. On arriving at our house, we found Shimbo keeping faithful watch and ward over our property. By his account more than one attempt had been made to steal it, but he had driven away the thieves, so he said, by presenting a stick at them, which they mistook for one of our guns. He could give us no information as to the visitor, nor could Aboh, who went out, learn more than his brother. There was some mystery about the matter, that was certain. We were tired and glad to take the supper which was brought to us already cooked, and consisted of plantains dressed in a variety of ways, and venison, one dish roasted and another stewed in lemon juice. Very excellent both were.

Rolling ourselves in our mats, we went to sleep. We had not closed our eyes long when I heard Charley, who was close to the door, cry out lustily. At the same instant I felt myself bitten by numberless creatures crawling over me. Harry and Tom were treated in the same manner. We all sprang to our feet, and, striking a light, discovered that the room was full of ants. They came in battle array, a numerous army pouring in through the door. We rushed out into the garden, where fortunately we found a spot free from them. Immediately lighting a fire, we formed it into a wide circle, in the middle of which we took up our posts. Then helping each other, we were able to relieve ourselves from our venomous assailants, and as we plucked them off we threw them into the flames. We soon found that the whole village was attacked, and that the inhabitants were turning out to defend themselves. They came not in thousands but in millions, covering the streets and forcing their way onwards. We saw that fires were lighted in all directions, but whenever there was no time to collect fuel and kindle it, the insects, marching onward, destroyed everything in their way. Although they fell by tens of thousands, others took their places. It was not until the morning that they disappeared, having destroyed in that short time a large portion of the provisions in the place. Fortunately they did not eat up the fruit nor the live animals, but among other things destroyed was the skin of the huge ape which we had intended to take to England to exhibit to naturalists, feeling sure it would create more surprise than anything else we could carry with us. The entire skin was devoured, and the head picked clean so that only a whitened skull remained. As we had been up all night fighting the ants, we were glad to lie down again and obtain some sleep in quiet.

We had just risen, rubbing our eyes and still feeling very drowsy, when Prince Ombay came in and invited us to accompany him on another hunt, observing that it was necessary to replenish the stock of provisions destroyed by the ants. We, of course, could not refuse.

"I would advise, gentlemen," said Tom, when he heard

through Aboh what the prince wished, "that we carry our knapsacks on our backs, and then, if we have the chance, we can take French leave of our friends. They would scarcely attempt to stop us by force; and one can make them understand that we must be off."

"Tom's advice is good," said Charley. "Let us clap on our packs as a matter of course."

We had a scanty breakfast, as the whole of the village was on short commons. We hoped before long to get some venison, on which we could feast before taking to flight. When, however, the prince saw what we were about, with a smiling countenance he said—

"Hang up your fetiches again, you can do without them when hunting, and when you come back you can worship at your leisure."

From this we found that our knapsacks were looked upon as objects of worship, perhaps this accounted for their not having been stolen. Charley tried to persuade the prince that we should kill more game if we took them, but he either suspected our intentions, or thought that they were safer in our houses, and insisted that we should leave them behind us. We had let Aboh understand what we had been doing, for we knew we could trust him, but we thought it wise not to say anything to Shimbo until the moment had arrived, when Aboh would tell him of our intentions, feeling sure that he would be ready to accompany us.

In vain we tried to persuade Ombay that we should be more successful if we carried our knapsacks. He, putting on a knowing look, again refused, and we were finally compelled to set off without them.

"We must wait for another opportunity," said Charley; "it will come some day or other, and it is very evident that we shall have to practise no small amount of patience."

"I have been thinking seriously that I could make my way down to the coast alone,' said Tom, "and if I could fall in with an English vessel, I might form a party of men to help you. I know that there is some danger, but it matters very little if Tom Tubbs loses his life, although it would be a sad thing for you three young gentlemen to be kept prisoners by these black fellows for the rest of your lives."

"No fear of that," answered Charley. "We may find ourselves free sooner than you expect. There must be rivers to the north of us, and if we could once get to the banks of one of them, we could make our way down to the sea in a canoe. The longer we remain with King Sanga Tanga, the more confidence the people will have in us. At present we have only Hobson's choice, stop here we must."

On this occasion the prince was accompanied by three times as many hunters as before. We were expected to take an active part in the sport. We proceeded nearly a couple of days journey, when we formed a camp, and the hunters went out prepared to kill either elephants, buffaloes, deer, or wild pigs; indeed, for some object or other, they seemed anxious to accumulate a large supply of food. The first day they killed two elephants, much in the same manner as I have before described. The following day Charley, Harry, and I killed two buffaloes and three deer, while the natives were not nearly so successful. Parties arrived from the village to carry home the game we had already shot. We were shortly afterwards joined by a number of strangers, who came in, we found, from the different villages at a distance, though all under the government of King Sanga Tanga, each party bringing a large net, a similar net having arrived from our village. On examining them, we found that they were made from the fibre of the pine apple plant and that of other trees twisted into thick thread. Each net was about seventy feet long, and nearly five feet in height.

The villagers—I should have said—were accompanied by packs of little sharp-eared dogs, who gave vent to loud yelps. Accompanied by these dogs, about twenty men, taking between them one of the nets, of which there were altogether about a dozen, set off to a spot fixed on, where there was a clearing in the forest. Not a word was spoken as the men crept along, followed by the dogs, which were kept close together, and seemed to understand that they were not to bark. On reaching the ground, the hunters commenced stretching the nets, fastening them up to the lower branches of trees and shrubs, forming altogether a semi-circle, upwards of half a mile in length. A party was stationed at both ends of the nets thus arranged, armed with their spears and darts, to prevent any of the game escaping ; the rest of the men, whom we accompanied, then extended themselves in another semi-circle on the concave side of the net, at the distance of a mile or more from it. Thus we advanced, the dogs barking, and the men shouting, while we held our guns ready to shoot, and the natives had their darts prepared for instant action. We might fall in with an elephant, or buffalo, or leopard, which would of course laugh at the nets, but the belief appeared to be that no such animals were likely to be found within the space we embraced. It was often difficult work making our way through the dense forest, and the natives had to hew paths for themselves with their hangers. Getting in sight of the nets, we saw, stopped by them, half a dozen gazelles, and antelopes of different species, two very large ones of the latter description, which I should have thought would have forced their way through the net had they made the attempt. We fired, and brought them down. Two gazelles were caught in the net, and others were knocked over by the natives. Altogether, the haul was considered a very good one. As soon as the animals were secured, the nets were collected, and the party moving off to another part of the forest, again spread them in the same way.

Altogether, in the course of the day we killed thirty head of game of different species, when we returned in triumph to the capital of King Sanga Tanga, who came out to meet us, and was especially civil to us, his white guests, who had so greatly assisted in supplying him with this large amount of game. On coming back to our house we asked Aboh if he could explain why the king wished to obtain this large amount of game, as all the inhabitants together could not consume it.

Aboh looked very knowing, "Him daughter goin' take husband," he answered.

A feeling of dread came over me as he said this. What if the king intended to make me, *nolens volens*, marry his daughter. It seemed impossible. I expressed my fears to Charley.

"I wish that I could relieve your anxiety," he answered. But I tell you what, perhaps Tom would not mind so much. We may ask the king to take him instead of you."

"But the young lady, she would object to that," I said, in a tone which made Charley fancy that my vanity was wounded. He laughed heartily, and Harry joined him. "Perhaps you think Tom is too old for the young woman," he added.

"Oh! no, no," I answered, "he is heartily welcome to her for that matter."

However, the next day the business was settled in a more satisfactory way than any of us expected, or supposed possible. It appeared that the prince, or the heir-apparent of a neighbouring kingdom considerably to the northward, had seen (I must not call her the "fair ") Iguma, and had fallen desperately in love with her. He had arrived during our previous absence with a large party of followers, bringing treasures of all sorts, elephants' tusks, rolls of matting, and various other articles. The king having observed my unwillingness to become his son-in-law, and the young lady being piqued at my indifference, had accepted her black suitor. Indeed, the treasures he offered were far greater than any we possessed, which probably weighed chiefly with his majesty. We hitherto had not seen the happy bridegroom, Prince Kendo, who had been living since his arrival in a hut by himself. The ceremony was to take place that very day, when the various gifts, or the amount he was to pay for his bride, were to be openly presented in the square of the village. At the hour fixed on, the prince made his appearance at the door of the house, his head decked with coloured feathers, a panther robe over his shoulders, his hunting knife stuck in his belt, to which also was fastened a sort of kilt of coloured matting, ornamented with feathers, while his whole body was freshly oiled and painted. His attendants, who bore his goods, were habited in a somewhat similar manner. As soon as he appeared, the king came forth leading his daughter. I cannot say that she was over-encumbered by robes, but her arms and ankles were encircled by rings. Her head was decked with coloured beads, and a chain of beads and charms hung round her neck. Prince Kendo, ordering his attendants to place the goods he had brought in front of the king's palace, advanced, carrying a big tusk, the last article of value which he had agreed to pay for his bride. On the king receiving it, the prince stretched out his hand and took that of the lady's, when Sanga Tanga gave her his paternal blessing, and apparently a large amount of good advice, the only ceremony, as far as we could discover, performed on the occasion. She had now become the bride of the prince, and I must own that I breathed more freely when I saw him lead her away, and felt satisfied that the king would no longer insist on my becoming her husband. The ceremony, such as it was, being concluded, the people began to shriek and shout at the top of their voices, congratulating the prince on becoming the possessor of so lovely a bride. Tom-toms were heard beating in all directions, and horns sounding, and the whole capital was in an uproar. The feast then began, and the cooks, who had been busily employed all the morning in roasting.

stewing, and boiling, produced the result of their labours in baskets and dishes, which were spread out in front of the king's house, which was on this occasion to serve as a banquet hall. The guests quickly assembled, the bride and bridegroom taking, if not the head of the table, the post of honour, while King Sanga Tanga, the heir-apparent, and the old grandfather and other members of the family, placed themselves on either side. At first matters were conducted quietly enough, the guests eating to their heart's content ; but when the palm wine began to circulate freely, they, like persons in more civilised communities under similar circumstances, became uproarious. The old grandfather tumbled not under the table, but at full length on the ground ; King Sanga Tanga cried out that it was time to commence dancing, and he himself starting up, set the example, and the crowd forming a circle, he performed a series of eccentric evolutions, similar to those exhibited on a previous occasion by his brother monarch King Quagomolo ; when at last, overcome by his exertions, he sank down on the ground close to the royal portion of the circle, the bride and bridegroom springing up went through a like performance. Their places were taken by a number of courtiers and the ladies, if I can so describe them of the royal household, but for obvious reasons I will not describe the style of their dancing. It was barbarism run mad, and our chief feeling was disgust that human beings should so degrade themselves.

"Abominable !" cried Charley. "It is wrong to sanction by our presence such doings, and if we retire to our house, and afterwards tell Sanga Tanga why we did so, it may perhaps open his eyes to the true character of what is going forward."

"Well," exclaimed Tom, "I've seen many a rum sight, but this beats even the worst I ever beheld in a seaport town in England, or elsewhere, and that's saying a good deal."

With these words Tom turned his back on the performers, and followed us to the house. So absorbed were the spectators in the dancing—if dancing it could be called—that they did not perceive our departure. We could hear the shrieks and shouts of laughter and applause, the drumming on tomtoms, and the sound of the horns until a late hour in the night. We had evidence of many barbarous customs of the natives, which I have not mentioned. I do not say that they are more savage, or rather fierce, than people of other parts of the world ; indeed, in some respects they are less so, but their barbarism is the result of their ignorance and debased condition. They have no religion—properly so called—their only belief is in what we denote fetichism, which is a word taken from the Portuguese *feticeira* or witch. They have idols, but they can scarcely be said to worship them, and they believe that power resides in serpents and birds, as well as in inanimate objects, such as mountain peaks, in bones, and feathers, and they believe also that good and evil spirits exist, and that charms have a powerful influence, as likewise that dreams signify something, but in many of these respects they really do not differ materially from their white brethren of more civilised countries. The ignorant people of many European nations believe in charms. They bow down before statues, certainly more attractive in appearance than the African's fetich god, but still things of stone. The people we met were certainly superstitious in the highest degree, but they nearly all differed in their ideas, as did even the people of the same tribe. As far as we could ascertain, they have no notion of the immortality of the soul, although they fancy that the spirit exists for a short time after it leaves the body. They dread such spirits more than they reverence them, and believe that they are rather inclined to do them harm than good. They therefore place offerings at their graves, for the sake of propitiating them, sometimes offering up a human sacrifice for the same purpose—some unfortunate slave who is of little value to them. In our village we saw a large idol in a house built expressly for the purpose. It was a hideous, ill-constructed monster, and it seemed scarcely possible, ignorant as the people were, that they could really worship such an object, but they did so if they wanted to gain benefit, either to obtain victory in war, or success in the chase. On such occasions we saw them presenting food, and then dancing and singing before it. Many of the people also had small family idols which they worshipped much in the same manner ; but if they did not obtain what they wanted from the idol, they were very apt to send it away in disgrace. They have also a belief in the power of certain doctors or medicine men, who exorcise evil spirits, and concoct charms. In these charms they have more faith than anything else. They are generally done up in the skins of animals, and consist of bones, or feathers, or ashes, or the skins or bones of snakes. The manufacture of these charms brings a large revenue to the doctors, who constantly encourage their use, just as do the priests of certain white nations, who make their dupes pay for the trumpery leaden figures or images, which they persuade them to wear round their necks.

"On my word, I do not see much difference after all, between the belief of the ignorant Russians, or Spaniards, or Portuguese, or other European people, and these unhappy blacks," exclaimed Harry one day when we were discussing the subject.

The fearful curse of the country, however, is the belief in witchcraft. When a person is seized with illness, he always believes that some enemy has caused it, and is not satisfied until the witch or wizard is discovered, who is immediately compelled to swallow poison, or is barbarously put to death in some other way. I prefer thus giving a short account of the superstitions of the people, and the evil which results from them, to detailing the abominations and horrors, which on various occasions we witnessed during our wanderings through the country. That evening we came to the resolution of endeavour ing to make our escape as soon as we possibly could. We believed that we could depend upon Ahoh and his brother, and that they would influence several of their tribe who had been captured, but were allowed to go at liberty.

As we could not sleep, owing to the hideous noise going on in the village, so we sat up to a late hour, discussing our plans for the future.

CHAPTER XIII.

THE bride and bridegroom had taken their departure
northwards. We tried to ascertain the exact position
of their village in order that we might avoid it, rather than pay
the young couple a visit. As soon as the game we had taken
was exhausted, the king wanted us once more to start on a
hunting expedition, but we had come to the resolution of going
as seldom as possible, that we might avoid the expenditure of
our ammunition. It was necessary to husband that, as we
should certainly require it on our journey. Although we were

apparently allowed our liberty, we were conscious that we were narrowly watched, and that, therefore, we should find great difficulty in making our escape by stealth.   Tom Tubbs having completely recovered his strength, and we three being in good condition, we determined to go to the king and boldly request guides and an escort to the northward as far as his jurisdiction extended, at the same time, to demand the release of Aboh and Shimbo, who were willing to accompany us instead of returning to their own village.

Taking Aboh with us, when we knew the king was at home, we proceeded together to his palace.   His majesty was seated under the veranda in front on a pile of matting, with a huge pipe in his mouth, attending to the affairs of state, for several of his counsellors were seated on either side of him.   Harry, who had learned more of the language than either Charley or I, and looked considerably older than either of us, was deputed to be spokesman, having the aid of Aboh as an interpreter, should he come to a standstill for want of words on his part, or from not being able to comprehend the meaning of what the king said. He acquitted himself, as far as we could judge, wonderfully well. He pointed out that we had been made prisoners when travelling peaceably through the country, and been compelled to accompany his people, that we had since then enjoyed our liberty, and that we had made good use of it.   In the first place, by saving his daughter from the wild man of the woods, then preserving his son from the charge of the buffalo, that we had killed enough game to support ourselves, and should have been ready to assist him in any other way in our power, but that we now desired to return to our own country.   That we should be obliged to his majesty if he would furnish us with the means of proceeding on our journey.   The king, who seemed to understand perfectly what was said—Aboh aiding with a few words here and there—gave a smile and replied—

"That he would consider the matter, that he esteemed us very much, that we were good hunters, and had brought peace and prosperity to the country, as no enemies would dare to attack his people while we remained with him. But, if you go away, what will become of me?" he asked.

"What shall I say to that?" asked Harry, turning round to Charley and me.

"Tell the king that he must manage as he did before we had the honour of making his acquaintance," answered Charley; "that we are very glad to have been of service to him hitherto, still, that now our hearts are yearning for home, and that if he detains us against our will, our spirits will sink, and we shall no longer be able to help him."

The king grinned horribly, and said something of which neither Harry nor any of us could make out the meaning.

"What did he say?" we inquired of Aboh.

"Him say, cut him head off," answered Aboh; "me tinkee him mean it too."

This was unpleasant information, but we thought it as well not to take notice of it, but it convinced us plainly that the king would not agree to our request.

"Endeavour to bribe the king with promises of the things we will send him," said Charley; "tell him we will pay him handsomely."

"I'll try," replied Harry, and forthwith he began to pour out all the native words he could recollect. It is just possible that he put in two or three by mistake, which had a very contrary meaning, for the king looked sometimes surprised, then angry, then highly amused, but yet he would not give the permission we requested.

"Try again if he can't be bribed," said Charley. "Promise that we will send him all sorts of things from England, if he will tell us how they are to be transmitted."

Harry did his best to carry out Charley's wishes, Aboh interpreting the words of the king. He said that a bird in the hand was worth two in the bush, that if we got away we might forget the promise we had made, or that if we sent the things, they might be lost long before they could reach him.

"Now try him on the threatening tack," said Charley; "tell him what a great man our king is, that ten of his soldiers would put to flight a whole army of his blacks, and that if he does not let us go, our king will send two or three hundred men, who will be landed from our ships, and march up the country to look for us."

"They have not yet arrived," said the king, with another of those sardonic grins in which he often indulged. "It will take them some time to get here, and when they do come, they will have to fight us if they come as enemies."

"Tell the obstinate old fellow that they will come notwithstanding, and will blow him and his village up to the top of the mountains," exclaimed Charley, who grew impatient at the king's refusal.

Harry did not say this, however, for two reasons. In the first place, he thought it would be imprudent, and in the second, he could not find words to express himself. He said something equivalent to it, however, which had no apparent effect on the king's mind. At last we were obliged to leave his majesty, determined notwithstanding, as Tom advised, to take French leave, and go on the first opportunity. Our condition after this became much worse than it had been before. We were compelled to go into the plantations, and to dig and hoe the ground. We at first refused, declaring that we were hunters and not cultivators of the soil. We expostulated again and again reminding the king how we had saved his daughter and son from death. He only answered "that his daughter did not now belong to him, and his son must answer for himself."

This convinced us that the black king had not a spark of

gratitude in his composition. We, however, addressed ourselves to Prince Ombay, who appeared more inclined to accede to our request than was his father, but he told us he dared not interfere with his authority.

Week after week went by, and we were kept in a state of vassalage. When we went out hunting, the king, suspecting that we might make our escape, always kept one of the party at home with our knapsacks. During the whole time, however, neither we, our knapsacks, or our guns were interfered with, the people evidently looking on them as fetiches, not daring to touch them. They also believed us to be something above the common, or we should not have been treated so civilly by them. At last we could bear it no longer.

"Come with me, we must fight our way out of this," exclaimed Charley.

"That is more easily said than done. Although we might kill a few people we should be overwhelmed with numbers," observed Tom.

"Let us try if we cannot deceive them by pretending to be reconciled to our lot," said Harry; "or if one of us shams to be ill, they'll think we cannot move under the circumstances; such a trick would be perfectly justifiable."

"Of course it would," said Tom, "and I'll be the one to sham ill, you'll see how I'll howl and shriek, until the people will be glad to get rid of us for the sake of peace and quiet."

The next evening Tom put his proposal into execution. No sooner had the villagers turned in than he began howling and shrieking in the most fearful manner.

"I think you are overdoing it," observed Harry, "we shall not get any sleep either."

"Never mind that for a few hours," answered Tom, "I must howl on until they come and see what's the matter."

He got some white earth with which he bedaubed his face, and which made it of an ashy paleness as he now lay covered up with mats on one side of the house.

The noise had been heard by the prince, who, with several other persons, came to know what was the matter. Tom made no answer, but howled and shrieked louder than ever, as if racked with pain.

Aboh, who had not, however, been let into the secret, informed the prince that the white man was very ill, and that he was afraid we should all catch the same complaint. This was an addition of his own that we had not thought of.

Just as he was speaking the king with a number of his wives came in to know what was the cause of the noise. When Aboh told him the same story he darted off with great speed, calling on his son and the rest of the people to beat a retreat from the infected place, and out they all rushed helter skelter, Tom hastening them by another series of shrieks and cries. After this we were left unmolested for the remainder of the night, although Tom once in each watch shrieked and shouted, as he said,

" Just to keep the people from forgetting us."

Though no one came into the house for several days after this, Aboh was allowed to go out and purchase provisions for us, which we were frequently able to do, with some of the beads and trinkets we possessed.

At length one day he came back, looking very much alarmed, saying that the king himself was taken ill, and having declared that some one had bewitched him, had sent for the witch doctor to find out who it was, and if the rascally doctor fixed on one of us we should have to drink the Mboundow poison.

Of course we all declared that we would do no such thing, and laughed at Aboh.

" But, I tell you what, perhaps they'll make you or your brother, or one of the rest of your people do so," observed Charley, " the wisest thing you can do is for you all to come to us to-night and we will fight our way out of the village."

Aboh agreed, fully believing what Charley said; indeed, there was every probability that he or some of his people would be fixed on by the witch doctor, when they would to a certainty be put to death.

" I'll make them suppose that I'm as bad as the king, or worse," said Tom.

As soon as it was evening Tom repeated his howls and shrieks, with even more vehemence, if possible, than before. Just about midnight, when all the people were in bed, Aboh sallied forth. We anxiously waited his return. At last he came back with Shimbo, followed by a dozen of his tribe, who had managed to possess themselves not only of bows and arrows, but of spears and hangers, and were altogether very well armed. Not a moment was to be lost. We had strapped on our knapsacks, and shouldering our muskets we sallied forth as noiselessly as possible. Fortunately no dogs barked, nor, as far as we could tell, had any of the inhabitants heard us. Not a light was burning in any of the houses. The king and his witch doctor were probably also asleep. Had an enemy attacked the village, the whole of the inhabitants might have been slaughtered before they had time to unite and offer the slightest resistance.

We began to congratulate ourselves that we should get a good distance from the village before our flight was discovered. Already we had reached the north end of the high street, and were about to emerge into the open country, when we heard a shout uttered by a single voice.

" Who speaks ? " I asked of Aboh, who was near me.

" Him doctor," said Aboh, " sleep one eye open."

" Don't answer him," said Charley, " push on ; if we get a good start, they are not likely to follow us in the dark."

Fearing that our native allies might be ready to yield, we told them to go on, while Tom and I dropped to the rear to defend them should we be attacked. We now heard several other voices. In a short time the whole village was in an uproar, men shouting, dogs barking, women screaming, fancying, perhaps, that the place was attacked. We feared, of course, that the true state of the case would soon be discovered, and that we should be followed. Whether Ombay and his people would venture to molest us was the question. We marched on steadily, but we had not gone far when we knew, by the increasing noise, that some of the people were on our track. Charley advised us not to fire unless it should become absolutely necessary. The shouts and angry cries of the savages drew nearer and nearer. It was evident that they were rushing on pell mell, still, as long as no arrows were shot at us, we were resolved not to fire. Just then the moon, though waning, rose above the horizon, and showed us a mass of dark forms, waving their weapons, shouting and howling, not a hundred yards off. Tom and I turned round and presented our rifles, shouting loudly to them to keep back. The moonbeams gleaming on the barrels showed the blacks what we were about, and the mob halting we rejoined our companions; again we pushed on. The number of our pursuers increased, we had, however, made up our minds not to yield and not to return; as soon as they saw us again moving on, they began to scamper towards us, shouting as before.

"They beat me at that," observed Tom, "but if they don't look out, I'll give them some cause to shriek."

Soon after he had spoken an arrow flew near our ears, but fortunately did not strike any of the people ahead of us, another and another followed, at last one of the blacks was hit, as we knew by the cry of pain he uttered.

"If that's your game, my lads, you shall have enough of it," exclaimed Tom, turning round and firing a shot into the midst of the savages. Who was struck we could not tell, but they all

Immediately stopped, though they continued shouting as before. Tom reloading, we ran on.

"The next time we must both of us stop and fire," he said.

For several minutes we began to hope that the savages had given up the pursuit, but as we could not long keep up the pace at which we were going, we began to slacken our speed. They again overtook us, and shooting a flight of arrows, Tom was hit in the leg, and another black man in the back.

"It's your own fault," cried Tom, facing about, when we both fired with evident effect, for we could see the savages rushing back instead of pursuing, well knowing that we had two more muskets amongst us. In consequence of having so frequently gone out on hunting excursions, we all knew the road well. In some places it was rather winding, and we were afraid that the blacks, by cutting off angles, might get on our flanks. However, that could not be helped, and we kept our eyes open to be ready for them at any moment they might appear. Fortunately, Tom's was merely a flesh wound, and it did not occur to us that the arrow was poisoned. The wound bled pretty freely, but there was no time to stop and bind it up. Our pursuers seemed to think that they might have to pay too dearly for the attempt to recover us, and we were now allowed to go on without molestation, we could still hear them, however, shouting in our rear. This only served to make us increase our speed, until our poor slave companions, who well knew that they would in all probability be put to death if we were overtaken—though the people might be afraid to kill us—were on the point of sinking from fatigue. At last, finding that Tom appeared to be suffering from loss of blood, we shouted to Charley and Harry to halt. They were glad enough to do so, both of them coming to assist me in binding up Tom's wound.

"I don't think it's anything, and it doesn't hurt me much, if

I can keep moving I don't mind," remarked Tom, as we finished the operation.

As we were all very tired with our run, which must have carried us six or seven miles, we were proposing to rest, when again we heard the cries in our rear. This made us jump to our feet and push on as before. We remembered a spot on some hilly ground, where the rocks cropped up in a curious fashion, and Charley had observed to me at the time that it was very like a fortress. It was still some miles off, but we determined to make for it as fast as we could go, and there take up our position. Listening attentively, we could occasionally catch the sound of our pursuers' voices coming from a considerable distance, showing that we had got a good way ahead of them, while the light of the moon enabled us to see our way. It was very rugged, now up hills, now down into valleys, though generally through thick woods, when the darkness rendered our progress still more difficult. All the time we dreaded lest some of the more nimble of our enemies might, by cutting across the country, get on our flanks and attack us with their spears, or send a flight of arrows amongst us from behind the trees. There was a chance, too, of our meeting with elephants, which might obstruct the road, or a leopard might spring out upon us. We were all well aware of the dangers to be encountered, but no less resolved were we to face them boldly. Charley and Harry kept calling to me every now and then, to ascertain that we were keeping up with them. The way in which we marched encouraged our black companions, and prevented any of the more faint-hearted among them from deserting. Indeed, it would have been folly in them had they done so, for they would to a certainty have been discovered and slaughtered.

At length we reached the hill where we had determined to make a stand, for we were so knocked up by this time, that we could not have proceeded further without rest. It was exactly the sort of place we had expected to find, a collection of rocks forming almost a circle, somewhat resembling the remains of Druidical temples in England. The space where there was no rock was occupied by trees, which would serve as shelter should we be surrounded. We hurried in among the rocks. Our first care was to examine the opening, and the spot where each of us should stand, and then to place our black allies between us. This done, we looked about to try and discover any broken pieces of timber or loose rock, with which we might still further fortify our position. Neither Sanga Tanga nor Ombay were likely to be thirsting for our blood—whatever some of their people might do, whose friends we had killed—their object being rather to recover us and keep us in slavery, to answer their purpose of frightening their enemies, by the idea that having white men among them they were invincible. Should we, therefore, be able to make a bold stand, we hoped to sicken them of the attempt to recover us.

" Reserve your fire lads," cried Charley, " don't pull a trigger until you are certain of your man. If we can manage to knock over half a dozen or so, before they get close up to our fortification, the rest will probably run away and give up the pursuit."

We were still engaged in stopping up gaps here and there, when we caught sight through the gloom, for day had not yet broken, of a dozen or more dark figures at the foot of the hill. They were apparently looking about to ascertain what had become of us. They seemed to suspect where we were, but were still uncertain. Some then went on ahead to see if we had gone in that direction, while the rest remained where we first discovered them. We might have shot four of the first party, as they were full in our view ; but Charley told us in a whisper to refrain from firing, as they were not actually attacking us, and might, it was possible, be peaceably disposed. We could see them clearly enough in the open, although they could not perceive us, sheltered as we were, by the rocks and brushwood. The sky was now becoming brighter towards the east, and in a short time the sun would rise, and we should probably be seen. Just then the men who had gone on returned, and shouting to their companions told them that we were not ahead. Others were also coming up from the southward, we could count nearly fifty of them, while further reinforcements could be perceived in the distance. It was evident that they were resolved on an attack. Bending their bows, they sent a flight of arrows against the rock. We received it with a well-directed fire, which killed four of our opponents, whom we saw tumbling down the hill. This checked the advance, but others who had hitherto been in the rear, pushed on with loud shouts and cries, urging on the van to a renewed attack. We had quickly reloaded behind the rock, and waiting until another flight of arrows had been harm- lessly showered on it, we jumped up, and again we all fired together with the same effect as before. Without stopping to see who was killed, our enemies rushed pell mell down the hill, tumbling over each other, while the more prudent ones, who had kept in the rear, also turned and took to flight.

"Give them another volley," cried Charley; and having again reloaded, we fired into the retreating masses. It had the desired effect of expediting their flight. Away they went howling and shrieking, and we, our own blacks joining us, uttered a loud shout of triumph.

"They'll not come back again," said Charley, who had been watching them from the top of the rock. "I don't believe Sanga Tanga or his precious son are with them, and although he may despatch them again when they get back to the village, it will be a hard matter for them to overtake us. We must have some breakfast and a couple of hours' rest, and then make our way onwards, until we can find another secure place for a camp."

We had brought some provisions I should have said, and not far off was a stream of water issuing from the hill. Having despatched our meal, three of us lay down, with all the blacks except Aboh, who undertook to keep watch with me for a portion of the time. I was then to call up Harry, who was to be succeeded by Charley. We agreed that Tom, who was suffering from his wound, should be allowed the full period to rest. Shimbo was to succeed his brother, for we did not wish to trust any of the other blacks. The moment my watch was over, and Harry had taken my place, I was fast asleep. No one came near us, and at the time agreed on we recommenced our march. Our chief anxiety now was about Tom's wound. The poison, if poison there had been, we hoped had been scraped off by the arrow going through his clothes, while the blood which flowed from the wound yet further prevented any dangerous effects. We had gone on for some hours, when having got beyond king Sanga Tanga's country, we came in sight of a village. We could not tell whether the inhabitants might prove friendly. Not to run any risk, we turned off to the right through a thick part of the forest, until we reached a small open space. Here we determined to wait until dark before passing the village. The provisions we had brought with us were nearly exhausted, but we had sufficient for another meal, and we hoped to be able to provide for the next day by our guns, when we should be at such a distance from human habitations that we might kill some game without the fear of the report of our firearms being heard.

The rest was very acceptable. It enabled Tom, especially, to regain some of the strength he had lost. As soon as we calcu-lated that the people in the village would be asleep, we decided again to make our way onward. The moon gave us sufficient light to discover the path, and also guide us in the right direc-tion. Next morning Charley fortunately killed a deer, which gave us an abundant supply of food for that day, while our native allies found a number of berries and other fruits. As they ate them readily, we gladly followed their example, for a meat diet, especially under the burning sun of Africa, is far from satisfactory. Thus for several days we went on, occasionally seeing natives, but keeping out of their sight, and avoiding the villages in which we were more likely to find enemies than friends. We were mounting a high hill, when Harry, who had just reached the top, cried out—

"Hurrah, there's a river, I caught sight of the bright stream between the trees."

We hurried forward, and could see here and there among the dark foliage the glitter of water in little patches, which extended a considerable distance to the westward. We had great hopes that this really was a river by which we might reach the sea. The scene was a beautiful one. Although the country was chiefly occupied by forests, there were open spaces visible, looking like green meadows, and to the right, downs which reminded us of our own dear England. While we were gazing at it a herd of graceful deer bounded across one of the nearest meadows. In another open space I could see a couple of elephants plucking the leaves with their huge trunks from the trees, and a small baby elephant frolicking near them. As far as we could ascertain, there were no human habitations, but they might be concealed by the forest, and the distance to the river, where villages were likely to be found, was considerable. Our great object now was to secure two or three canoes, in which we might make our way down the river to the sea. We were, we calculated, a couple of hundred miles at least from the mouth, and with the windings the stream probably took it might be half as much again, still, as we should have the current with us, the navigation might be easily performed. Our chief danger of interruption would arise from the inhabitants of any of the villages on the banks, who might take it into their heads to stop us. However, we hoped by running past these at night, we might avoid them without having to fight our way.

Ten days had passed since leaving Sanga Tanga's village. Our shoes and clothing were, as may be supposed, in a slightly dilapidated condition, but we were all in good health, and Tom had recovered from his wound. On descending the hill, we made our way through the forest towards the nearest point where we saw water. We had still some beads and trinkets left, and we hoped, should we meet any natives to purchase canoes from them. If not we agreed to try and build them, as Aboh told us that he and his companions were well able to do so. We were in high spirits at the thought of so soon terminating our journey, forgetting that months might elapse after we reached the coast before a vessel made her appearance.

We were pushing eagerly on through the forest, with less caution than usual, when we came suddenly upon a large body of armed blacks, who were out evidently on a hunting expedition. Among them was a chief who, by his dress, we saw was a person of importance. It would have been useless to have attempted to escape them, so, telling our blacks to keep behind us, with the exception of Aboh, who came as interpreter, we all advanced towards the chief. Neither Quagomolo or Sanga Tanga were beauties, but this fellow was about the ugliest black we had yet come across, with a most savage expression of countenance. He was very tall and big, with a wonderful muscular development. He inquired who we were, where we had come from, and whither we were going. Harry, who always acted as spokesman, replied that we had been shipwrecked, and were travelling through the country towards the mouth of the river, where we expected to find a ship to carry us back to England. We wished to be friends, and begged him to assist us with canoes, as we desired to prosecute our journey without delay."

Whether or not he understood what Harry said was uncertain. He uttered a loud hoarse laugh, as if he thought that it was a very good joke. We waited some time for a further reply, but the savage did not deign to say anything. At last he exclaimed in a harsh voice, " You must come along with me."

" We must have some guarantee that our liberty is not inter‹ fered with if we do that," said Harry.

I do not remember the exact terms Harry used to express him‑ self, but the savage only grinned.

" We must keep clear of this fellow," said Charley; " fall back on our men, he intends mischief."

Before, however, we had time to follow his advice, the savage, springing on him, wrenched his gun out of his hand, while the black fellows pressing round us prevented us from using our weapons. Aboh, Shimbo, and the other blacks, seeing that we were overcome, were about to take to flight, but they were immediately surrounded by a large body of enemies, our whole party thus being made prisoners. We were at once hurried unceremoniously along until we reached a large village not far from the bank of the river which we could see flowing tantalisingly by us. We had no time to exchange remarks with each other, or to speculate as to what was to be our fate. At first we fancied that the ugly black was the king of the place, but this we soon discovered was not the case, for, as we were dragged up the main street, we saw issuing from a house of more pretentions than its neighbours another black wearing a red regimental coat on his back with huge epaulets, and a round hat, battered and otherwise the worse for wear, on his head, the insignia of royalty, as we well knew.

Our captor made a speech and described to the king how he had taken us prisoners.

" Him tell‧ big lie," whispered Aboh, who stood near me. " Him say great fight, we run 'way, him kill us."

" What's the fellow's name ? " I asked, meaning that of our first captor.

" Him callee Mundungo."

" And the King ? "

" Him King Kickubaroo."

His majesty seemed perfectly satisfied with his general's statement. It tickled his vanity that his forces should have conquered four white men and an army of blacks, as was the description given of our attendants. In vain Harry tried to explain who we were, and how the affair had happened. The general, on hearing him speak, began vociferating so loudly as to drown his voice. All the efforts we made were fruitless. The louder Harry spoke, the louder Mundungo and his followers shouted. At last the king issued an order, and we were once more surrounded by guards and marched away to a house on the other side of the square, into which we were unceremoniously thrust.

" I wonder what these fellows are going to do with us," said Tom. " I say, old fellow," he exclaimed, " give me back that rifle," and he made a spring at one of the men who had possession of his weapon, and snatched it out of his hands. " Tell them that they are fetiches, Mr. Harry," cried Tom, " they'll not dare to keep them."

Harry shouted out as advised, and we made a simultaneous dash at the men who had possession of our guns. So unexpected was our onslaught, that we were enabled to wrench them from their hands. Before they could regain them we had sprung back into the house. Though the guns were all loaded, they fortunately did not go off in the struggle. From the easy way in which they delivered them up it was very evident they were not acquainted with their use.

" Shall we attempt to fight our way out and reach the river?" exclaimed Charley; " perhaps we may find a canoe there. Before these fellows have recovered from their astonishment we may be able to get beyond their reach."

" No, no!" cried Harry; " we should to a certainty lose our lives, though we might kill a few of them, and very probably, on reaching the river, we should find no canoe, when we should have to yield at discretion. Since we have recovered our weapons, it will be wiser to remain quiet, and watch for a favourable opportunity. Something or other may turn up, or when the people are off their guard, we can steal away as we did from Sanga Tanga's village."

Charley saw the soundness of Harry's advice. We therefore, without making further demonstration, allowed the door to be closed on us. By this time the people outside were shouting and howling and rejoicing over the mighty victory they had gained.

"I am sure we acted for the best," said Harry, when we found ourselves alone. "Probably the ugly fellow in the round hat will find out soon that there is no use in keeping us prisoners, and will let us go."

"Can't say I agree with you quite," observed Tom. "I don't trust these niggers. They may take it into their heads to cut off ours, or offer us up before one of their abominable fetich gods. The sooner we can get away the better."

Aboh, who had been shut up with us, looked very much cast down, and he seemed fully to agree in the fears expressed by Tom. The hut consisted of a single room about twelve feet square, without windows, the light being let in through openings between the walls and the eaves. This served also the purpose of ventilation. There was no furniture, not even a mat, and the floor was anything but clean. As we were tired, we were anxious to lie down, but hesitated to stretch ourselves on the dirty earthen floor. On looking round the room, we, however, discovered two pieces of board, or rather what are called shingles, being portions of a log of wood split by a wedge. Using these as spades, we managed, with considerable trouble, to scrape a space clear of dirt, of sufficient size to enable us all to sit on the ground. We were going to place our backs against the wall, but Aboh warned us that some ill-disposed fellow might thrust his spear through it, and that it would be much safer to take up a position near the centre. Our knapsacks had not been taken away, as our captors possibly suspected that they were part of ourselves; fortunately within them we had stored the remainder of the deer and several birds we had shot the previous days, and which we had cooked for breakfast; we therefore had abundance of food. This was indeed providential, for no provisions were brought us; we had also enough water in our leathern bottles to quench our thirst. We waited until it was dark before we attacked our meal, that the natives might not discover that we had eaten, and would give us credit for a wonderful power of endurance. By economising the food we were able to save enough for breakfast the next morning. At last we lay down to sleep, keeping our rifles by our sides ready for use. We all resolved that should we be attacked to fight to the last. To avoid being surprised, one of us, as usual, kept awake as if we were in camp. Until a late hour we heard the people outside shouting and making a great noise, for a dance was being given in honour of the victory obtained over us.

We were left alone during the whole night, and as soon as it was daylight we sat up and ate the remainder of our food, waiting for anything that might occur. It was past noon when the door opened, and the king appeared.

" Are you hungry ? " he asked, with a grin on his countenance, for he expected to find that we were starving.

" Not particularly," answered Harry. " We should not object to a dish of plantains, or some goat's milk, if you will be good enough to send them to us."

" You are wonderful men, you don't look as if you could easily be exhausted," observed the king. " My general Mundungo must be a brave warrior to have overcome you."

" He's a big knave, at all events," answered Harry. "But that's not to the point at present, what we want now are some plantains and milk, or venison."

I don't mean to say that Harry used these exact words, but with the aid of Aboh he thus signified our wishes.

After some further conversation, the object for which the king had come being gained, he left us again to ourselves.

It was not until near evening that the door opened, and two damsels appeared with baskets on their heads. They placed them on the ground before us, when, much to our satisfaction, we discovered a quantity of plantains, some roast venison, and yams, and also a couple of large gourds, the one containing goat's milk, the other water.

"We are much obliged to you for bringing these," said Harry. "And who may I ask, sent them."

"A friend," answered one of the girls. "But we were forbidden to tell you who she is. Eat and be satisfied." On this, the girls evidently acting as they had been directed, left the hut, and the door was immediately closed.

"I thought, when I saw the baskets, some young woman must have sent the food," observed Tom. "They're alike all the world over, to my mind, the same sort of heart beats inside a black skin as a white one. Things don't look so bad after all."

We had provisions enough to last us—if they would keep good—for several days. We agreed to husband them, not knowing when more might be brought us. To prevent any creatures getting into them, we hung them up to the rafters of the roof. Next day we were left entirely alone. We were, as may be supposed, getting impatient, and had good reason to dread what might next happen. Observing the light coming through under the roof, we concluded that we might get a look through the opening, to see what was going forward outside. Towards the back, and one of the sides, the walls of other houses prevented us obtaining any view, but on the other we found that we could look right down the street.

I must pass over several days, during which we were kept in confinement. Only once in three days was any food brought us, our benefactor, or benefactress, who sent it, probably not having opportunities for doing so oftener. We could gain no information from the slaves who brought the baskets, nor could we learn anything from the people who were occasionally sent in to clean out our hut. We were now growing very anxious—moreover, our health was suffering. All sort of dreadful ideas occurred to us, and we fancied that the king was reserving us for some great festival, when he might, as Tom had suggested—sacrifice us to his fetich gods. At last we agreed that, to save ourselves from a worse fate, we would run the risk of breaking out, and fighting our way down to the river.

We had been imprisoned for nearly a month, and had settled one evening, that the very next night we would make the attempt. The following day we expected to receive our usual supply of provisions, which we intended to carry with us. Early next morning, as the first gleam of light stole into the room, I climbed up as usual to have a look out, and ascertain whether anything was occurring in the village, when, what was my surprise to see a white man with a gun on his shoulder, and holding by a chain in his left hand a bull dog. Another glance at the dog, and I recognised him as Growler, while the man bore a strong resemblance to Captain Roderick. He had then escaped with his life. I could scarcely suppose that, bad as he was, he would refuse to assist in setting us free. He was evidently at liberty himself, or he would not have walked along in the independent manner he was doing. Guessing that Growler would recognise me, I whistled. The dog immediately pricked up his ears, and began to look about him. Captain Roderick started.

"What is it, Growler," I heard him ask.

I again whistled, and called to my companions. They started to their feet.

"Captain Roderick," I shouted out, "will you assist some of your countrymen in getting away from these black fellows who have imprisoned them?"

"Who is that who calls me by my name?" asked the captain in a tone of astonishment, looking up to the place from which my voice proceeded, although he could not distinguish my features under the eaves of the house. Coming to the door, he without further ceremony withdrew the bars which secured it.

"Who are you?" he exclaimed, with a look of astonishment, as he saw us ready to rush out.

"Don't you remember us, Captain Roderick?" I asked. "I don't wish to claim it as a merit, but we set you at liberty when your ship was wrecked, and enabled you to save your life."

"I wish that I had lost it," answered the captain with a gloomy look.

"Perhaps you may live to be thankful it was preserved. At all events, we acted desiring to do you a good service, and all we beg is, that if you have the power you will assist us in making our escape from this village, in which for some reason the king seems inclined to keep us prisoners. Why he does so I cannot ascertain."

"I can solve the mystery then," he answered; "I confess that I have been the cause of your detention. I have been living with the chief almost ever since I got on shore, having made my way up here immediately, and I am in high favour with him. Two rascals, former followers of mine, while I was out hunting came to the village—intending to remain here, I conclude—but finding by some chance that I had made it my headquarters, they bolted. As I had no wish to have them prying into my proceedings, I charged the king to keep them until my return, as I was on the point of starting up the country on a trading expedition.

"That of course accounts for our being kept here," exclaimed Charley.

From the description of the men given by Captain Roderick we had no doubt that they were the two pirates who had escaped when we were recaptured.

"Now, Captain Roderick," said Charley, "if you will facilitate our return to the coast, we will report favourably of the service you have rendered us, and it may be of some use to you should you ever wish to go back to England and any accusation be brought against you."

"As to that, sir, I have no intention of ever returning to my native land," answered the captain in a gloomy tone, but as I have no grudge against you, I will help you to make your escape, although the rascal who calls himself king here is an eccentric character, and it may not be so easy as you suppose. He gets drunk for six days in the week whenever palm wine is to be procured, and the seventh amuses himself by cutting off the heads of his faithful subjects and playing other vagaries. Still I have taught him to respect me, and as I have been the means of supplying his treasury, I do not doubt but that he will be ready to do what I ask him in the hopes of retaining my services. I now intend, if he is not too drunk, to rouse him up and tell him to supply you with a better house, and ample food, and a supply of water that you may wash yourselves, for you look remarkably dirty."

This I have no doubt we did. Charley thanked the captain in the name of us all. Captain Roderick then told us to remain in the prison while he went on to the king and obtained our release in a formal manner; it would be better, he said, than running the risk of offending the king, who would probably be displeased should we walk out without his permission.

We accordingly returned and sat ourselves down to wait the arrival of the pirate captain and the king's officers. Strange to say, all this time Captain Roderick had not recognised Harry, nor had he me as the clerk who had overheard the accusation brought against him by Captain Magor. Perhaps had he done so his conduct might have been different. We were all getting very hungry, having eaten nothing since noon the previous day; we were also becoming more and more impatient, when we heard footsteps approaching, and Captain Roderick, accompanied by the king himself and several of his attendants, opened the door. The king made a speech, intending, as we supposed, to apologise to us. He then led the way to another house, far superior to the hut we had occupied. It was clean and airy, with a veranda in front and a garden full of fruit trees and vegetables behind. Shortly afterwards an ample supply of all sorts of provisions was brought to us, and what we valued in no less degree, some huge bowls of water. I shall not forget in a hurry the satisfaction of washing, though we each of us had only a pocket handkerchief with which to dry ourselves, and that none of the cleanest.

After breakfast, we summoned the slaves who had brought us the water to procure a further supply, in which we washed our under garments, hanging them up afterwards to dry in the garden. This they did in a very few minutes, for the sun in that latitude does its work with marvellous rapidity.

In consequence of meeting with Captain Roderick we abandoned our idea of attempting to get off by stealth, thinking that it would be wiser to take our departure openly with the leave of the king. We had not been long in the house when Captain Roderick, accompanied as he always was by Growler, came to see us and advised that we should remain indoors. "I have a rival here in that ugly rascal Mundungo. He is jealous of the favour shown to me by the king, to whom I have recounted the true history of your capture, and I told his majesty that, instead of being taken after a tremendous fight, you were surprised and surrounded before you had time to defend yourselves. Mundungo has found that I have told the king the truth, and he is exceedingly indignant, although he is too much afraid of me to say anything. He will not, however, scruple to injure you if he has the opportunity."

While he was speaking, Mundungo himself appeared, his countenance exhibiting the hatred which raged in his bosom.

"Beware what you are about," he exclaimed. "You have attempted to malign me to the king. Remember I possess the most powerful fetich in the world."

"A fig for your fetich!" exclaimed the captain, drawing his huge dagger. "I possess a more potent fetich than you do. Look at that, and then look at this animal. What do you think of him? In two minutes, if I were to tell him, he would tear you limb from limb, and your wretched fetich could not help you. Now go and talk to your silly countrymen about your fetich, but don't come and attempt to impose such nonsense on me," and the captain turned aside with a haughty air.

Mundungo was defeated. Muttering and growling he walked away along the street towards his own residence. The captain set up a loud laugh in which we could not help joining, while Growler uttered one of his terrific barks, which made the brave general take to his heels and scamper away as hard as he could go.

Captain Roderick again burst into a loud laugh. "I have settled the fellow for the present, but depend upon it, if he can he will do you and me harm, we must guard against that. I have hitherto, since I came among these people, kept the upper-hand, partly by my independent bearing, and partly owing to the fears they entertain of Growler; who, on several occasions, has given me timely warning when Mundungo and his supporters have attempted to murder me, which they have still a strong desire to do. Although I have obtained your liberty, I cannot answer for your safety. If they fail to shoot you with their arrows, or to spear you, they may try the effects of poison, and against that you must be specially on your guard. Fortunately, they are no great adepts in the art, but it will be safer to take only such food as it cannot be mixed with, such as eggs, birds, and plantains, and fruit, and joints of meat."

We thanked Captain Roderick for his advice, which we promised to follow as long as we remained in the place.

"But," continued Charley, " as you may suppose, we are very anxious to get away as soon as possible. We believe that if we could obtain a good-sized canoe, we could easily navigate her down the river."

" You may depend upon it, gentlemen, that I will do what I can to persuade the king to allow you to go, and I have no wish to have any one interfering with my proceedings here, which you probably might be tempted to do were you to remain."

" But we have no wish to interfere with you, Captain Roderick," said Charley ; " we are grateful for the service you have already rendered us, and should be very glad if you would accompany us down the river, for I am very sure you will soon get tired of living among these savages."

" I shall never return to civilised life, at all events in my own land," answered Captain Roderick gloomily. " Do not mention the subject to me again. I will help you more on my own account than on yours, for I would rather be alone with these black fellows than herding with white men. Let me advise you to remain in your house at present, until I have time to talk with the king, who is at present too drunk to understand me. I cannot promise that you will immediately obtain leave to go, or be furnished with a canoe for the purpose, but it will not be my fault if, in the meantime, you are not well treated."

As we agreed that it would be wise to follow the pirate's advice, we re-entered our house, intending to remain there until summoned by him to pay our respects to the king, when his majesty had recovered sufficiently to give us an audience. Behind the house was a garden of sufficient size to enable us to enjoy some fresh air under the trees without the risk of being molested by the natives.

CHAPTER XIV.

WE had now been six months in Africa, and, wonderful to relate, none of us had been ill or even hurt, with the exception of Tom. We, however, often felt sad, not on our own account, but on that of the loved ones at home, who, we knew, would be suffering intense anxiety about us, even if they did not suppose that we had lost our lives. As Tom remarked, we knew very well where we were and what we hoped to be able to do, but those at home knew nothing, but that ship after ship arrived and no tidings of us reached them.

A thick, black wall, as it were, intervened between them and us, through which their loving eyes could not penetrate. How we longed for some bird of rapid wing to carry home a message for us.

Captain Roderick did not come near us for the remainder of

the day. The following morning, however, he appeared, saying that the king would not hear of our going away, as he wanted to employ us for elephant hunting, under the belief that with our rifles we should obtain a far greater number of tusks than could his own people.

"You will be well fed, and as the sport is highly exciting, I don't think you have any cause to complain," said the Captain.

"That may depend upon circumstances," observed Charley. "When are we to set out?"

"To-morrow, or perhaps the next day; as soon as the hunters are ready. They only returned from an expedition a few days ago and require time to rest."

While the Captain was speaking, I saw him eyeing Harry and me in a far more searching manner than he had done before. Suddenly he asked me my name. I told him without hesitation, —indeed, I supposed all along that he must have known it. He then turned to Harry, and I saw his countenance change as Harry replied, " My name is Bracewell."

The Captain started as Harry spoke, and as he looked at him a frown gathered on his brow.

"I might have known you before, but your dress and sunburnt countenances deceived me. When I first saw you on board the ' Arrow ' "——

"Captain Roderick, let bygones be bygones!" exclaimed Charley, who had heard from me all that had happened in England between Captain Roderick and my friend—"Do not let us refer to the past. Here we are, five Englishmen together among savages If we quarrel our destruction is certain. We can help you and you can help us."

The captain's features resumed their usual look, showing that he was somewhat moved by this address.

"I have no quarrel with any of you, and have already shown you my readiness to render you assistance. I have told you that

I will exert my influence with the king to procure your release, and I intend to keep my promise."

Captain Roderick did not long remain with us ; he went away, as he said, to have a talk with the king.

" My idea is, that that fellow wants us to stop and hunt for him," observed Charley. " Depend upon it he would take possession of the tusks of the elephants we killed. It may be wise in us, however, to do so for the sake of procuring our liberty."

" He has got a hand over us at present, and as we cannot help ourselves, we had better make the best of a bad job," observed Tom.

Accordingly, the next morning, when we saw a number of people collecting in the square, armed for the chase, we agreed that, if invited, we would accompany them without showing any objection. We had just taken our breakfast, when we saw a young man approaching, who by the ornaments he wore on his arms and ankles, the chain round his neck, and the circlet of feathers on his head, we knew to be a person of consequence.

"Why, I believe he's no other than the young fellow who married Miss Iguma," said Tom ; "and if so, he ought to help us, for if it hadn't been for you, Mr. Westerton, the young lady would have lost her life."

Prince Kendo at once knew us, indeed, I suspect he was well aware of our being in the village, but had kept out of the way, supposing that we were enemies of Captain Roderick's, and not wishing to offend him. He now, however, came forward in a friendly manner, and invited us to accompany him on the hunting expedition of which he was to be the leader.

As agreed, we accepted it and joined his party of about fifty men. Soon after leaving the village a couple of hundred more, coming from various quarters, united with us, until we formed quite a little army. We marched along for a whole day, however, without seeing any elephants, although we came upon smaller game, of which, for the sake of the meat, we killed several. Charley was fortunate enough to knock over a buffalo, and Harry and I each killed a deer. Tom shot two hogs—curious-looking creatures, the most active of the pig species. Those which made their escape leapt over the trunks of trees several feet high, and a stream five or six yards broad. They were enormous creatures, having red bodies and white faces, on which were several lumps between the nose and the eyes, which latter were surrounded by long bristles, while their ears were exceedingly long, having at their tips tufts of coarse hair. We knocked over several monkeys, and a huge ape, just as it was about to strike a man who had approached and had had his spear snatched out of his hand.

Prince Kendo complimented us, and evidently looked upon us as great hunters. After encamping for the night, as was usual, we again set out, and just as we reached the edge of the forest, beyond which was a plain, we caught sight of a huge elephant standing by himself, while he kept flapping his ears and whisking round his tail. As we watched him the trees around him looked like mere shrubs, so vast was his size. Charley insisted on shooting him. Kendo, as he looked at the animal, whispered that he was afraid that he would make for the open plain should his own men attempt to kill him. On this Charley volunteered to shoot the huge creature. I felt very anxious about it, but he said that he was confident, unless his rifle failed him, that he should kill the beast. Having ascertained the way the wind was blowing, we made a slight round so as to get to leeward. We got behind some trees, while Charley, imitating the native way of approaching the enormous creatures, stooped down among the grass, and began to creep up slowly towards the elephant, keeping himself entirely concealed, while only occasionally could we get a glimpse of him to assure us that he was moving on. I regretted that I had not insisted on accompanying him, to fire in case he should miss, though he himself had no apprehensions on that score. For several minutes we could perceive no motion in the long grass. Not a word was spoken. No sound came from any part of the forest, except that we fancied we could hear the flapping of the elephant's ears. For a few seconds even that ceased, and then there came a sharp report, ringing through the forest and across the plain. I dashed forward and saw the elephant raise its trunk in the air, and move on as if about to destroy its enemy, but the instant afterwards the trunk dropped, the huge animal staggered, and down it came with a crash on the shrubs and rotten wood beneath the trees. Charley started up scarcely three yards from where the creature fell. Numbers of monkeys and birds shrieking and screaming clambered chattering away amid the branches, or flew off across the plain at the report of Charley's rifle, while the blacks came rushing forward, shouting and congratulating him and us on the success of his shot. Never had they seen an animal brought down so suddenly. This was the first elephant we had killed on the expedition. Charley killed two others from the ground, while Harry and I each shot one while we were perched on a tree, a far safer, if not so honour able a position. All the natives together had, in the meantime, only killed three, by piercing them with their spears, and they had lost two men crushed by the monsters' feet. Altogether, Kendo acknowledged that it was the most successful hunting expedition he had ever engaged in, while our success raised us greatly in the estimation of the blacks, but also made them more anxious than ever to retain us. We were well aware of this, and came to the conclusion that if we were to get away, it must be by stealth, as we had escaped from the other savages. On approaching the village, we were met by some women howling and wailing, and on inquiring the reason, we were informed that queen Hugga Mugga, the favourite wife of the king, was desperately ill, and had been bewitched, and that the king had sent for a learned sorcerer to discover the guilty persons. On inquiring for Captain Roderick we found also that he, during our absence, had been away. We saw him, however, coming along the street. Charley and I went out to meet him, advising Harry to keep in the house. He appeared to be in a very different humour to that in which we had before seen him. He appeared greatly out of spirits. Seating himself in our veranda, without attempting to enter the house, he turned to Charley.

"You have been more successful even than I expected," he said, "and I have to compliment you on your skilful hunting. You might remain out here and make your fortunes in a very short time, but I suspect that your lives would not be safe in this place. You have already excited the jealousy and hatred of Mundungo, and he is, I have discovered, a friend or relative of the fetich doctor who has been sent for, and will probably accuse you of causing, by your incantations, the illness of Kickubaroo's wife. Come here," and he approached a palm tree which grew on one side of the house, from which he cut a long branch. "If I ascertain that you are in danger, I will find means to send you a similar branch to this, in the basket with your provisions, in which case do not leave the house until nightfall, then, as soon as the people have gone to their houses, and are asleep, make your way directly to the bank of the river, where I will cause two canoes to be prepared with paddles and food in them. Embark at once, and make your way down the stream. You must not ask why I did not long ago follow the course I advise you to take."

I was struck by the man's melancholy countenance and the mournful tone in which he spoke, so different to his usual overbearing confident language.

Charley and I expressed our thanks, feeling more pity for him than we had ever done before. Keeping the palm branch in his hand, he resumed his seat in the veranda, then turning to me he said—

"If you ever reach home, tell my brother that you met me, and that I asked his forgiveness for my conduct towards him. I do not suppose that he will withhold it, when he knows that I intend never again to resume my former mode of life. I wish I could feel as certain that all my sins are forgiven."

I pointed out to him the only way by which man's sins can be forgiven. He turned his head from me, and said abruptly to Charley—

"You must be surprised at the change you perceive has come over me."

"For some reasons I am glad of it," answered Charley, "although I hope it is not because you feel yourself suffering from illness."

"No," answered Captain Roderick, "I am as well as ever, still I believe that my days are numbered. My enemies here have succeeded in destroying my faithful dog Growler. While you were away I missed him while out shooting, and after some time he crawled back to me with a poisoned arrow sticking in his ribs. I drew it out, hoping that the flow of blood would prevent the poison taking effect. In less than ten minutes he was seized with violent convulsions, between the paroxysms of which he endeavoured to lick my hand, and gasped out his last breath in the attempt. He was the only friend I ever had in the world in whom I could truly trust."

After sitting some time, Captain Roderick took up his gun and hat, which he had placed by his side while enjoying the shade of the veranda, and proceeded towards the house he inhabited, close to that occupied by the king. Going in we told Harry what Captain Roderick had said.

"He exhibits very little true remorse and sorrow for his misdeeds," said Harry; "like many men with fierce, ill regulated minds, he is overcome with superstitious fears, and probably his present temper will not last very long. I only hope he will give us warning in due time, and enable us to make our escape, we shall then have good reason to thank him."

We were now expecting the arrival of the witch doctor, who, however, we discovered lived at a considerable distance, and might not make his appearance for two or three days. We scarcely supposed, however, that he would accuse us of bewitching the queen. We felt, indeed, rather a curiosity to see how he would proceed, than any fear of bad consequences to ourselves. Soon after Captain Roderick's visit, Prince Kendo appeared, and invited us to accompany him that evening on another shooting expedition. Some elephants, he said, had been seen a short distance off up the river, and as there was plenty of the food they liked thereabouts they would not probably have gone away. As we were glad of something to do, we accepted the offer, and all four of us, with Aboh and Shimbo, set out with the party the prince had already collected, and who were waiting at the outskirts of the village. It was too dark, however, by the time we reached the part of the forest where the elephants had been seen to go in search of them. We therefore encamped, and lighted a fire to cook the provisions we had brought with us. Soon after we had begun supper, two figures appeared from amidst the brushwood surrounding the open spot we had selected for our camp. The gleam of the fire fell upon them. We saw by their dress and faces that they were white men. Their haggard countenances showed that they were suffering from hunger. Tom Tubbs, who had started to his feet, advanced a few paces towards them—

"Why, as I live," he exclaimed, "I think I know you fellows."

"Like enough you do, mate," answered one of the men, "like enough you do, but before you have any palaver, just hand us out some of that grub, and a drink of water or anything stronger if you've got it, for we are well-nigh famished."

"So you look," said Tom; "sit down, the gentlemen here will be glad enough to share their provisions with you, so will this nigger prince, and after that we will hear what you have got to tell about yourselves."

The men without uttering another word sat down close to the fire, and eagerly seizing the food we offered them, began munching away in a style which fully confirmed the account they had given of their famished state.

Looking at their countenances more narrowly, I at once recognised the two seamen, Caspar Capar and Herman Jansen, who had escaped during the massacre of the Frenchmen.

The two men exhibited a marked contrast, and it seemed surprising that they should have associated together. Caspar seemed a good-natured, honest fellow, and as soon as he had satisfied his hunger, he began to laugh and joke with Tom, and to describe the adventures they had gone through, while Jansen sat moody and silent, a frown on his brow, and his looks averted from us. Even when Tom spoke to him he answered only in monosyllables, or did not answer at all, holding out the gourd which had been given him for a further supply of palm wine.

"I shouldn't like to meet that fellow by myself were I unarmed in a dark place, he looks as if he would attempt to kill a man merely for the satisfaction of committing murder," whispered Charley to me; "I wonder he has not before now shot his companion, and I suspect that only the desire of self-preservation has restrained him."

I fully agreed with my brother, and we settled that we would not allow him to associate with us more than we could help. At present common humanity demanded that we should give him food, and such protection as we might be able to afford against the savages. After eating and drinking as much as he required, he got up and strolled away from the camp towards the lake, the shore of which was at no great distance.

We now spoke more freely about him. Harry suggested that hunger and privation had given him the expression we remarked in his features, and that he might notwithstanding be a useful addition to our party, and assist us, should we make our escape, in navigating our canoe down the river.

"What's the matter with your friend?" I asked, turning to Caspar.

"He's in one of his sulks," was the answer; "he is often like that, and I have been in fear of my life over and over again, but I have kept an eye upon him, and generally managed to get hold of his long sheath knife, and to hide it until he got better again. Lately he has become worse, and I would have left him had I been able to do so. My idea is, that he'll do some harm to himself, or he will try to kill some one else, and if he had a gun I should not think any one of us was safe sitting down here."

"Should there be a chance of his injuring himself, it is our duty to try and prevent him," observed Harry, "we must deprive him of his weapon, and watch him narrowly. Perhaps after he has been well-fed for a few days he may recover his temper. I think it would be as well now to go and watch him, and see that he doesn't throw himself into the lake."

I agreed with Harry, and both getting up accompanied by Caspar, we walked on in the direction Jansen had taken.

The moon which had just risen, afforded us light sufficient to make our way through the forest, which was here not so thick as in most places. We had gone some little way, when we reached an open spot or glade close to the lake.

"Stop here," said Caspar, "I think I see him coming along, it is as well he should not discover us."

We concealed ourselves behind some bushes. We could hear approaching footsteps, and thought that Jansen, having gone on some way, had turned back and intended to rejoin us at the camp. Just then I saw that the figure of the person approaching was not that of Herman Jansen, but of Captain Roderick. I concluded that he had followed us intending to treat with Prince

Kendo for the ivory we had procured, or else that he had come to warn us of some danger to which we might be exposed, should we return to the village. I was on the point of stepping out of our place of concealment to go and meet him, when another person sprang up from behind a bank where he had been concealed, with a large knife in his hand, and before I could cry out to warn the captain, the other had plunged the weapon into his breast. With one piercing cry Captain Roderick fell back, while his assailant having driven the weapon home, left it sticking in the wound, and with a howl like a wild beast plunged into the forest, which immediately hid him from our sight. We all hurried forward, eager to give assistance to the wounded man; Caspar drew out the knife.

"Yes," he said, " this was Jansen's, he had vowed vengence against the captain, and we had good reason to hate him, but this is a foul cowardly deed notwithstanding."

Harry and I meantime lifted up the wounded man ; his arms dropped downwards, not a groan, not a breath escaped him, his eyes were fixed and staring in death. The weapon had struck too deeply home for human power to save him. His spirit had fled. We notwithstanding sent Caspar back to obtain assistance, that we might carry the body to the camp.

In a short time Caspar returned with Charley and Tom and several blacks. A litter was formed, and we conveyed him to the camp. Though we had every reason to dislike the man who had been the cause of all the hardships and sufferings we were enduring, yet we felt no animosity towards him, and were horror-struck at his appalling death. Prince Kendo expressed his astonishment at the captain's death. What he said was to the effect that he thought that no human power could injure him, "but I now see that white men can die like black men," he observed with a peculiar expression which made us feel that it would be dangerous to offend the black Prince.

" But it was a white man that killed him, remember that," said Tom, "the black fellows, from what I hear, tried it very often but could not succeed."

" Yes, that was the case, but he had a friendly spirit always by to protect him, but that got killed at last, and so you see his power departed from him."

The prince alluded to Growler, whose death we thus discovered was well known, although Captain Roderick had endeavoured to conceal the fact."

" The sooner we bury the poor fellow the better," observed Charley. "While he is in their sight the blacks will be thinking about him, and being reminded how easily a white man is killed, they may take it into their heads to try and put us out of the way, and possess themselves of our guns and the contents of our knapsacks."

We accordingly asked Kendo to allow some of his people to assist us in digging a grave. Though they at first showed some indications of fear, yet on Tom suggesting that the spirit of the dead man would haunt them if they did not, they eagerly set about the work, and saved us any trouble whatever. At first they made only a shallow hole, but Tom told them that that would never do, that it was necessary to bury a white man very far down in the earth, as they had such potent spirits that they would otherwise quickly force their way up again. On this they eagerly recommenced their labours, and managed to dig a grave six feet deep. We were going to put the body into it, when Tom advised that we should examine his pockets, and take possession of any documents or valuables he might have about him. We found nothing, however, except some ammunition, a knife, and a tinder box. Not a line or document of any sort to prove his identity. Had we not witnessed his death, or discovered his body, no one would have known how he met with his untimely end. Like many another evil-doer, he would have disappeared from the face of the earth and left no trace behind him.

At a late hour we lay down to rest. By Harry's advice, however, one of us kept awake lest the blacks should attempt to play us any trick, or, as was very likely, lest they should all go to sleep, and a leopard steal into the camp and carry some one of us off, or a troop of elephants come rushing along and trample us under foot.

Next morning, although we were very unwilling to continue the hunt, judging it safer to get back to the village and attempt to make our escape without delay, Prince Kendo insisted that we should remain, promising that we should have a share of the tusks of any elephants we might kill.

We thought it wise to make a virtue of necessity, but determined, should we find a canoe on the banks of the river, to appropriate it, and without taking leave to make our way down the stream.

We had not gone far when our ears were saluted by a terrific roar which seemed to come from the depths of the forest. My companions looked at each other, wondering what animal could produce the sound. Roar succeeded roar, and I guessed it must come from one of the big man apes which I had before encountered. Charley and Harry, upon my telling them, were both eager to see the creature, and keeping our guns in readiness we approached the spot whence the fearful sounds proceeded. The roars were accompanied by a loud drumming noise, followed by a fierce bark-like yelp, which, as Harry observed, sounded like the horrible ravings of a madman. Kendo and several of the other blacks accompanied us, but kept well in our rear, ready to take to flight should we fail to kill the beast.

"There he is," exclaimed Charley, "let one fire at a time. Dick, you fire first, if you miss I'll have a shot at him, and if I miss, Tom, you must take the next shot, and you, Harry, must be in reserve. Remember that our lives will depend upon the steadiness of your aim.

These arrangements had just been made when the boughs were put aside by a pair of long arms, and the next instant a huge hairy creature, with a hideous countenance, appeared in sight, advancing slowly into the open; I could distinguish its fierce eyes glowing at us, the face black and wrinkled, and distorted with rage, as it came forward balancing its monstrous body with its long arms, while at every few seconds it stopped and beat its breast, at the same time throwing back its head to give utterance to one of its tremendous roars. We might have been excused had we really taken it for a forest demon, for nothing which the imagination of man has pictured could be more calculated to inspire its beholders with awe.

The natives ceased their chattering and drew back. The creature still advanced, but every now and then stopped to sit down and roar. One circumstance, however, showed that its power was limited. Its legs were short and slight, and unable firmly to sustain its huge body, they tottered beneath its weight. While it hobbled forward it had a somewhat ridiculous appearance, which made Tom burst into a loud laugh. This seemed to increase the creature's rage; unable to spring forward, it sat down and began to roar and beat its breast. Once more it rose with the aid of its long arms, and advanced. I waited until it was about ten yards off, when I fired, half expecting, however, to see the animal when the smoke cleared off still coming towards us. I was prepared to spring back to let Charley fire, when throwing up its arms down it came with a crash to the ground. The blacks set up a shout of triumph.

"Take care, sirs, a bite from those big teeth would not be pleasant," exclaimed Tom, as he saw Harry and me rushing forward.

The creature, however, made no movement, and the blacks coming up, turned it over without ceremony and thrust the end of their spears into its eyes to show that it was dead. They then began singing and dancing around it in triumph, as they would round the body of a dead human enemy, indeed, even now I could scarcely persuade myself that the creature had not something human in it. It was not until very many years afterwards that I ascertained that this man ape, as I have called it, was what is now known as the gorilla. When I afterwards described it in England, no one would believe that it was of the size I have mentioned, and I got credit for indulging in travellers' tales.

The natives at once skinned the beast and then cut the body into pieces, which they afterwards cooked and ate with great gusto. None of us, however, could persuade ourselves to touch it.

We later in the day killed three elephants, much in the way I have before described, and early next morning our party, carrying the skin of the ape and the elephants' tusks, with large quantities of meat, returned to the village.

CHAPTER XV.

IN the course of the morning we reached our house, which we had left in charge of Shimbo. We had the satisfaction of finding that none of our knapsacks had been touched. We invited Caspar to join us, which he, poor fellow, was very glad to do. Nothing had been seen of Jansen; we supposed that he had either thrown himself into the river, or been seized by a wild beast. We were surprised to find that the witch doctor had not yet arrived, and therefore hoped that something had detained him, and that by his not coming the people whom he would accuse of witchcraft, should he appear, might escape death. We thought that the king might possibly not have heard of the death of Captain Roderick, and after duly discussing the subject, we came to the conclusion that it would be wise while the king was still impressed with the belief of his almost superhuman powers, to request leave to proceed on our journey

As it was still early in the day, we hoped to find his majesty tolerably sober, and capable of listening to reason. We accordingly issued forth from our house with our knapsacks on our shoulders, and our guns in our hands, Harry and Aboh ready to act as spokesmen, Charley and I coming next, and Tom and Caspar with Shimbo bringing up the rear. We found the king seated in a sort of broad veranda in front of his house, which served him as an audience chamber. On one side was his fetich or idol house. At the further end was a huge hideous figure painted in various colours; with big goggle eyes, and clothed in robes of matting, and adorned with feathers of various hues. Numerous other idols were placed against the walls, most of them bearing but the very faintest resemblance to human figures—big round eyes, and marks for noses, and grinning mouths, with teeth set in them, showing for what they were intended. The king, with his round hat on his head, and his red uniform coat covering his royal body, was seated on a pile of mats with a bottle by his side, while one or two empty ones lay outside on the floor, showing how he had already been spending his morning. Several of his counsellors and other chief men sat at a little distance on either side of him, discussing, apparently, affairs of state.

We waited until there seemed to be a pause, when we advanced in a bold manner, and Harry began an address, thanking the king for the hospitality he had shown us, and the opportunities we had enjoyed of seeing some sport, and adding that now, having done all the service we could, we were desirous of going down the river, as we were anxious to get on board one of the ships of our country, which we expected to find at the mouth of the stream."

The king rolled his eyes round as Harry spoke, apparently not understanding a word; he then turned to his courtiers, desiring them to explain what the white man said.

This was more than even the most learned of his attendants could do, for, although they were more sober than their master, they also had had a pull at the bottles. Fortunately the king did not appeal to us, but again and again asked them what we had said. At length starting up he called them all by the most opprobrious names, insisting that they should interpret, then seizing a cane, which he probably thought was a sword, he ordered them to go about their business, bestowing a kick on the rear of first one, and then on another, sending them all flying away from him, the commander-in-chief, who maintained his post to the last, receiving a blow from the monarch's foot as he endeavoured to leap down the steps, which sent him flying away some fifty yards, when down he sprawled with his nose in the dust, kicking up his heels in the air. The king having accomplished this feat, no longer able to stand, rolled back in his seat, where he continued kicking out with his legs, shaking his hands, and blubbering away, exclaiming, "that he could get no wisdom out of his counsellors, who were a useless, lazy set." He then looking up, inquired in husky tones "What we wanted?"

Harry once more endeavoured to explain our object in coming, but all his efforts were vain to make the king comprehend a word he said. Aboh then tried, with the same want of success. The king, who in the meantime had taken a pull at another bottle, evidently felt no inclination to rise, and comforted himself by showering abuse on Aboh's head and ours, bestowing upon him all sorts of opprobrious epithets.

At last, as it was very evident that we could get nothing out of the monarch, we beat a retreat in as dignified a manner as possible, and retired to our house, more resolved than ever to take French leave before many days were over, should we have the opportunity.

The king's attendants wisely kept out of his way when he was in his drunken fits, and shut themselves up in their houses, or left the village, lest he might take a fancy to cut off any of their heads. We, finding the road open to the river, determined to make an excursion along the banks in the hope of discovering some canoes fit for our purpose. Keeping our guns ready for action, we sauntered along near the river, though we pretended to take that road merely for the sake of the fresh breeze which blew off the water. We spied four or five canoes; in none of them, however, could we see paddles, and without some such means of propulsion they would be useless. How to procure the paddles was the difficulty. They were probably in the houses of the owners, and it was a question whether these owners would part with the paddles, and whether it would be safe to enter into a bargain with them, lest they should betray us to the king.

"To my mind, the best thing we can do, sir, is to make some paddles for ourselves," observed Tom Tubbs.

"Of course," answered Charley; "we can work away as soon as it is dark, and have them ready by to-morrow night. Longer than that we must not stay in this horrible place, we shall have wood enough for our purpose in the building, by pulling down part of the rear of our house, where it won't be missed, or from the trees in our garden, or part of the fencing. We should have a paddle for each person, as we shall require two or three canoes to convey all our party."

This matter settled, we were about to return, when we saw a female at the door of one of the largest houses near the water, at the end of the village which we had just reached. She appeared to be beckoning to us; we went forward, and great was our surprise to find that she was no other than Iguma, the young lady I had saved from the ape, and whose marriage with · Prince Kendo I had afterwards witnessed. Feeling sure that gratitude would animate a female bosom, I asked Harry to tell her the difficulty in which we were placed, and, throwing ourselves on her generosity, entreat her to assist us in escaping. She seemed much pleased at seeing us, and at once recognised me, and said she had not forgotten the service I had done her. We then informed her how we were situated. She at once said she would do all she could to help us, but that her power, she was afraid, was very limited. She complained that her husband was constantly away on shooting expeditions, and that she held his drunken uncle, King Kickubaroo, in great awe, and that he evidently had no affection for her. She told us that we need have no fear about canoes, as her husband had three or four which were hauled up on the bank inside a yard, close to which we then were, and that by climbing over the fence we should find them at any time ready for use. As to paddles, she acknow-ledged that they were generally kept shut up in the house, to prevent the canoes being taken away, but that she would try and place them on board the following evening as soon it was dark. Thus all was quickly arranged for our attempt to escape.

As soon as we got back to our house we looked about for wood suitable to form paddles, not wishing to trust entirely to those with which Iguma might supply us. We had no difficulty in finding an ample supply of material for our purpose, although we thought it prudent not to begin working it up until darkness should prevent the risk of what we were about being discovered. We were thus employed when we heard a tremendous noise proceeding from the house in which the king's wife lay sick. On looking out we saw it surrounded by people, who were singing, and shouting, and shrieking, and dancing, with all their might; some beating tomtoms and drums; others blowing horns and shaking rattles, all uniting in a hideous chorus. The object of this, Aboh told us, was to drive out the evil spirit which was making the queen ill.

"It was a signal," he said, "that the fetich doctor, who had been so long coming, was about to arrive, and that his canoe was probably seen descending the river."

As we thought it prudent to keep out of the way of the people, we remained in the house, although we would very gladly have got to a distance to escape from the uproar. We had cooked our dinner and were eating it, when Aboh, who had been to the door, came back and told us that the doctor had arrived, and was beginning his incantations. As we were curious to see what he was about, we went a short distance from the house, where, remaining concealed behind a fence, we could observe what was going forward without ourselves being seen. The doctor had dressed himself up to look as hideous as possible. On his head he wore a huge and lofty plume of black feathers drooping down on all sides ; his face was painted white, with red stripes over his eyes, and others in different parts of his face. A case was suspended by a piece of rope round his neck, which was also adorned by a necklace of human bones, while a girdle of a similar description was fastened round his waist, to which was suspended a sort of apron. He had taken his seat on a stool, round which were hides and the horns of several animals, a leopard's skin, and more cases containing charms. In one hand he held a rattle, and in the other a wand. Near him stood two attendants, one beating a small drum, and the other a couple of sticks. For sometime he continued uttering all sorts of gibberish, which I do not think was intelligible to any even of his hearers, while his attendants played on their instruments—if playing it could be called. He then took up a horn, from which he shook a quantity of black powder in the air, and regarded it gravely as it fell. It was sad to think that human beings could be deceived by so gross an imposture, but yet it was very evident that all the people present watched the proceedings with the utmost awe and re spect. After a dead silence the people again shouted out, though what they said it was impossible to understand, but I shall never forget the alarmed looks Aboh and Shimbo exchanged.   At length the shouting ceased, when the doctor began to shriek, making his voice sound like the croaking of a whole flock of birds of prey about to descend on a dead carcase.   Then he stopped, and slowly pronounced several names.

If ever black man turned white, Aboh and Shimbo did on that occasion.   Poor fellows, they understood the meaning of what was said better than we did.   Again the people shouted and shrieked in the most savage manner, indeed, no words can describe the hideous noise they made.

"Go back to the house, go back," cried Aboh.

We followed his advice, but ere we could reach our dwelling the crowd had rushed towards us.   Unfortunately we had come out without our arms.   The infuriated blacks did not attempt to touch us, but before we could prevent it, they had seized Shimbo and dragged him off, although we succeeded, by knocking down with our fists those who came near us, in hauling Aboh into the house.   We at once shut the door, seized our rifles, and stood prepared for a desperate resistance.   Contrary to our expectations, the mob, having got possession of one of our followers, retreated with him up the street.   Scarcely had they gone than we heard a knocking at the door, and finding that there was only one person present we opened it, and Prince Kendo entered.

"Ah, white men, save my wife," he exclaimed, "the doctor has accused her of bewitching the queen, and should her majesty die, nothing will save my poor Iguma, her head will to a certainty be cut off."

We all at once exclaimed that we would endeavour to save her, if he could point out the best way we could do so.

"Shall we go to the king and ask her life?"

Aboh shook his head, and declared that it would be utterly useless.   "The king was bound to kill her with his own hand if the doctor accused her of causing the queen's death."

" The queen is not dead yet," said Harry.

" No, but she may die to-night, for she is much worse than she has been before, and frightened out of her wits by the noise the people make."

" Then what do you propose we should do ?" said Harry.

"Carry her away. You intend going yourselves, I will go too, I should like to see your country and the wonderful things it contains, and I had made up my mind to propose going, even if this had not happened. I should like to take my wife with me, for whatever you may think, I love her dearly."

On hearing this, we resolved at once to put our long projected plan into execution. Kendo's assistance would be of great value, as he had canoes at hand, and could aid us in getting away. We advised Kendo to go back and hide his wife, should he not have the means of protecting her, lest the people might come and seize her at once, and we promised to be at the house or at any spot he might appoint as soon as possible after dark.

He stopped for a moment to consider.

" Come to my house," he answered, "the canoes will be ready, and so will Iguma ; but be prepared to fight, for if the people come and find out that we are going to carry her off, they will try to prevent it. Better fight than lose Iguma."

We of course promised, unless prevented by any unforeseen occurrence, that we would do as he proposed, feeling confident that we could trust to his honesty, and that he had a real desire to save his wife from the horrible fate which threatened her. We had not in the meantime forgotten poor Shimbo. Aboh constantly cried out—

" Oh ! my brodder, my brodder."

" I say, it would be a great shame to allow these murderous scoundrels to put the poor fellow to death," exclaimed Charley. " If the old woman dies they'll make short work of him ; I propose that we set off and claim him as our servant, threatening them with the vengeance of England should a shock of his woolly pate be injured."

Aboh, who understood what was said, cried out, "Tankee, massa, tankee, no let my brodder die."

We scarcely needed this appeal from the faithful Aboh to run every risk for the sake of rescuing his brother.

"Never fear, we will do what we can to save him," said Charley, "but do you remain in the house, lest that abominable juggler takes it into his wicked head to accuse you as well as your brother."

Aboh was very thankful to follow this advice, indeed, he was scarcely fit to accompany us, so overcome was he by the fears of death for himself and his brother, increased by the superstitious dread he had of the doctor. Shouldering our arms, with our knapsacks on our backs, we left the house, closing the door behind us, and marched boldly towards the fetich house, a sort of temple situated near the residence of the king. The number of people collected round it showed that something was going forward. At the further end of the structure—a sort of temple composed of rough timber with a thatched roof—was a hideous idol standing in a shrine raised on an altar, for such it resembled, possibly imitated from the Portuguese who once held sway in the land, and established for a short period what they called Christianity, although it was in reality an idolatrous system, scarcely superior in the effect it produced on the moral and religious sentiments of the people to that which it displaced. This Christianity, however, such as it was, had long ago been overthrown, and only such slight traces as I now observed remained. I may here remark, that wherever the Spaniards and Portuguese have established their religion, the people have invariably sunk back again into the barbarism and gross idolatry of their original state, indeed, it might be safe to say that they were never really raised out of idolatry. On getting nearer we saw that the king was standing in front of the temple, with a drawn scimitar of enormous size in his hand. We were hurrying forward, when the starling cry arose, " The queen is dead, the queen is dead ! "

The multitude immediately uttered the most piercing shrieks and lamentations. Directly afterwards we caught sight of the hideous doctor, or priest, urging on a party who were dragging forward a person between them. We did not at first see the features of the latter, and it was not until he had been hauled up on the platform, where the king was standing, that we discovered him to be our friend Shimbo. His hands were tied behind his back, so that he was unable to make any movement with them. He cast an imploring look around him, for he knew but too well why he was brought there.

Harry on seeing him shouted out to the king : " Let that man go, he is our servant."

But the king, taking no notice of what was said, flourished his long sword. The multitude shouted and howled, the weapon flashed in the sunlight, and the next instant Shimbo fell, and his head rolled along the floor of the temple. The maddened cries of the superstitious mob on this grew louder, and many of the elders and chiefs of the people, rushing forward, bowed themselves before the king.

We were horror-struck at what we had seen, and we had also reason to fear, from the savage looks that the people cast at us, that we ourselves were in no slight danger. The juggler might at any moment accuse us of sorcery, and, in the excited state of mind in which the people surrounding us then were, they might set upon us, and in spite of the resistance we might make, tear us limb from limb. Fortunately for us, the names of three other persons were shouted out as having taken part in the enchantment which had destroyed the queen. As the mob were occupied with them, we beat a retreat in a dignified way to our house.

Without telling Aboh what had happened, we placed him in our midst, and avoiding the excited multitude, made our way down to the river. If we were to save Iguma, we must carry her off at once without waiting for the night, for the instant the priest had pronounced her name, the crowd, in overwhelming numbers, would rush to her house to seize her, and even Kendo himself would be utterly unable to afford her protection. All this time we knew by the hideous din that the cruel executions were going forward. As long as the people were thus engaged we might be unmolested, but should a new victim be required, they would at once come rushing towards the house of the prince. We dreaded every instant to hear their voices approaching. We had already reached the bank of the river, but could find no canoes fit for our purpose. The prince's house was, I should have said, some way along the bank. We hurried towards it. As we got near Kendo himself sprang out to meet us.

" My wife is in the canoe," he exclaimed, " quick, quick ! "

There was good reason for our hastening, for after a few minutes' cessation of the uproar, the din from the vast multitude again burst forth. Kendo was certain that they were coming towards us. Not a moment was to be lost. Several canoes were on the bank, one was already in the water smaller than the others. Kendo pointed it out to Charley and me, and entreated us to jump in, observing as he did so : "Wife dare." We thought that he was about to follow, but instead of doing so, he gave the canoe a shove off with all his might into the middle of the stream, and then assisted Harry and the rest to launch another.

As soon as we found ourselves adrift, we each took a paddle and made down with the current. If we were to save Iguma's life, we had no time to spare. Already we could see a mass of black forms coming rushing frantically towards the river flourishing their weapons, while the air was filled with the cries they uttered. Two other canoes contained the remainder of our party, Kendo being accompanied by a single faithful attendant who had acted as his henchman and companion on all our hunting expeditions. Just as they were on the point of shoving off, a white man appeared on the bank, and without apparently even asking permission, leapt into one of the canoes. Instantly she shoved off and came paddling after us. Kendo shouted to us to go on and not stop for anything; a piece of advice we saw the wisdom of following.

As Iguma was the chief object of the savages pursuit, it was of the greatest importance to get her beyond their reach. She lay all this time, I should have said, at the bottom of the boat, covered up with a piece of matting, but she uttered no expressions of terror now that she thought she was safe. Had we delayed another minute, not only would Iguma have been captured, but we should ourselves very likely have lost our lives. Scarcely had the other canoe got away from the shore, than a vast multitude of infuriated natives, uttering the most fearful yells, appeared on the banks. We naturally expected to be immediately followed, but, as we looked astern, we saw no canoes being launched. We were not aware at the time that Kendo had thoughtfully concealed all the paddles, or had so injured the canoes that they were unfit to put off.

"Paddle on, paddle on," he kept shouting to us, and we were, as may be imagined, well disposed to follow his advice. We wished, however, that he had come with us, both to act as pilot and to assist in the defence of his wife, for he was a brave fellow, and would certainly have fought to the last. Though it was still daylight, evening was approaching. We hoped during the darkness to get far beyond the pursuit of the savages, who would, we felt sure, endeavour to obtain possession of Iguma, and to wreak their vengence on our heads for attempting to carry her off.

Had the course of the river been straight, there would have been no doubt about our ultimate escape, but it made numerous bends, sometimes running to the north, then to the south, then again to the west, so that it would be a long time before we could get out of the territory owned by King Kickubaroo. Now and then also the river was very broad, extending almost into a lake. This under some circumstances might be to our advantage, but during the night we ran the risk of losing our way, for though Charley still had in his possession the pocket compass, it was so dark that we could not see it, and we did not venture to strike a light. Charley and I, however, paddled along with all our might, hoping that even should our savage pursuers again catch sight of us, they would be still unable to procure canoes in which to follow us.

The night was unusually dark, and by Charley's advice we all kept silence, that our voices might not betray our position, should there be any of the enemy near us. Although our canoe was somewhat smaller than the others, yet as they were more heavily laden, we managed to keep ahead. We must have paddled on for a couple of hours or so, when we found ourselves on a broad lake. A thick mist obscured the sky, so that not a star was twinkling over head to guide us, and we were only able to steer by ascertaining in which direction the current was running. The darkness was so great that we could not even see the other canoes, and we were afraid, for the reason I have before mentioned, of shouting to attract their notice. We thought that unless we paddled on we should be overtaken by daylight. At length, however, my strength began to fail, my arms ached, though by this time I was pretty well used to bodily exertion. Charley continued working away without uttering a word, and sometimes I wished that he would speak, for the silence oppressed me; Iguma lay perfectly still in the bottom of the canoe; it was evident she fully comprehended the danger we were in.

On we went, hour after hour passed by. Daylight broke sooner than I had expected, and yet it seemed that we had been in the canoe a long time. A mist hung over the water shrouding all objects, so that we were unable to see the land, or discover which bank we were nearest. Though we listened attentively, we could not hear the slightest splash of paddles to indicate the whereabouts of our friends. We were afraid that something had happened to them, either that they had been overtaken, or that the canoes had run on snags. We said nothing to Iguma, however, lest we should alarm her, but it was absolutely necessary that we should rest our arms and take some food, of which we had brought a supply in our knapsacks, some also had been put in the canoe. Not knowing how far off the shore we were, we allowed the canoe to drift down, while we took in our paddles and got out our provisions. We invited Iguma to take some breakfast; she, pointing to some plantains and roast yams, signified that they would satisfy her hunger.

"Come, I think we ought to take to our paddles again," said Charley, when we had finished our meal. "How do your arms feel, Dick?"

"Ready for work, though I should be glad to give them a few hours' rest," I answered—"but softly, where are we?"

As I spoke, I found that the canoe had drifted in among some tall reeds, which showed that we were nearer the shore than we expected. While we were attempting to paddle out from among them, a breeze blew the mist away, and what was our astonishment, not to say dismay, to see a number of blacks standing on the banks and regarding us attentively. They had probably heard us talking and making a splashing while endeavouring to extricate the canoe from the reeds into which it had drifted. No sooner did they discover us than a dozen of them, or more, armed with spears and lances, plunged into the water and began swimming towards us.

"Put down your paddle and take your gun," cried Charley, "these fellows mean mischief."

All this time Iguma had not moved. The blacks, seeing only two white men in the canoe, thought that they would easily master us, and swam boldly forward.

"I suppose that there are no crocodiles hereabouts, or those fellows will be picked up to a certainty by one of the beasts; we must not trust to that, however, but when the men come near enough, shoot them without ceremony," exclaimed Charley.

Standing up in the canoe we warned the blacks to go back, but they took no notice of what we said.

"Their blood be on their own heads—fire, Dick."

We both pulled our triggers, one black threw up his arms and floated down the stream wounded, another dived, still I felt sure that I had hit him. The rest, undaunted, came on while we were reloading. Three were close upon us, and several others were not far behind them; one had actually got hold of the gun-wale of the canoe, while Charley was aiming at another a short distance off. He fired, the black letting go his spear, threw up his arms. The first, however, might in another instant have climbed into the canoe, when Iguma, springing up with an axe in her hand, dealt him a blow on the head; without a cry he dropped back and sank immediately. I fired, and the rest seeing the fate of their companions, turned about and made for the shore. This gave us time to reload and be ready should any fresh ones come off to renew the attack. They appeared, how-ever, to have had enough of it, and we, putting down our rifles, again took to our paddles and urged the canoe further out into the river, which was here very broad and the current slow. Still it ran at a sufficient speed to enable us to ascertain the direction we were to take. We now had time to look-out for our com-panions. They were nowhere to be seen, and we were still in doubt as to whether they were ahead or astern of us. Charley thought they must have paddled on and gone ahead, and if so, we should overtake them before long. We were, however, still followed by other bodies of our enemies along the shore, for those we had encountered were evidently only a small party, and, probably, others would be waiting for us close to the banks.

CHAPTER XVI.

BELIEVING that our friends were ahead, we paddled on with all our might. It was of the greatest importance that we should join them before we were again attacked, for, united, we might set at defiance any number of our pursuers likely to assail us. As may be supposed, our arms ached, and though we paddled on mechanically, I felt very sleepy, and occasionally my eyelids closed. As the sun got up the heat became excessive, but we did not dare to stop even for a few seconds under the trees which shaded the banks, lest any of our enemies might be lurking near, and might pounce down upon us. At last Iguma, who had been sitting watching us, offered to take my paddle. At first I felt ashamed to let her have it.

"Give it up to her," said Charley. "I daresay she understands how to handle it as well as you do, and we shall make better way."

I at length consented. When she had the paddle in her hand I lay down in her place at the bottom of the canoe, and I soon saw that she was working away with far more energy than I had lately shown. I watched her for a few minutes admiring the grace and dexterity with which she plied the paddle, and then my eyelids closed, and in another instant I was fast asleep. I do not think I ever enjoyed a more sound slumber, lulled by the ripple of the water on the side of the canoe as we glided rapidly along. Charley, being older and more inured to labour, was able to keep up better than I was, and I knew that he would not give in while there was any necessity for his exerting himself. I had pulled the matting over my head to preserve myself from the heat of the sun, which struck down with great force on the calm water.

"There they are, there they are!" I heard Charley shouting out.

His words awoke me, and starting up I could distinguish two dots on the water right ahead.

"Are they our friends, though?" I asked Charley, after I had gazed at them a few seconds.

"I hope so," he answered. "I felt sure that they were ahead of us, for, thinking that we were before them, they have been paddling on, expecting all the while to overtake us."

"What does Iguma think?" I said, and tried to make her understand that we wanted to know whether the canoes we saw were those of our friends. To my great satisfaction she appeared to have no doubt about the matter.

I then begged that she would let me have the paddle again, but she smiled and replied that her arms did not ache, and advised me to take my brother's paddle.

"I don't mind if you do for ten minutes or so, I will then

resume it and try if we cannot come up with the other canoes," said Charley.

"How long have I been asleep?" I asked him, as I took his place.

"Three or four hours, I suspect," he answered, "though I have not had time to look at my watch."

As I thought would very likely be the case, no sooner did Charley lie down than he dropped off into a sound sleep. As after my long rest I felt very capable of work, I determined not to arouse him, treating him as he had treated me.

Iguma and I made the canoe glide rapidly over the water. A light breeze had sprung up, somewhat cooling the air and enabling us to increase our exertions. I eagerly watched the canoes ahead, and felt sure that we were gaining on them. I wondered, however, that no one on board saw us, and could only suppose that those who were not paddling were asleep, while, of course, the paddlers had their backs towards us, and believing that we were ahead did not trouble themselves to look astern.

At length I thought that they were near enough to make them hear me. At first I thought of firing my rifle, but the sound would, to a certainty, show our whereabouts to our enemies should they still be pursuing us, whereas my voice could be heard to any distance along the water alone. Acting on the impulse of the moment, I shouted out at the top of my voice. Charley started up, thinking that something was the matter. On seeing the canoes he joined his voice to mine.

At length they ceased paddling; as they did so I cried out:

"I fear, after all, they are enemies. See, those are black fellows standing up in the canoe nearest us."

"If they are we must fight our way past them," observed Charley; "they have no firearms, and we can knock over several of them before they get up alongside, and should they do that we must fight them hand to hand; Iguma has shown that she is well able to defend herself; at all events, a few minutes will settle the matter."

We again took to our paddles, and I, making a sign to Iguma to sit down again in the canoe, took her place. We had not gone far before Charley shouted out, "Hurrah! it's all right, I see Harry's and Tom's broad-brimmed hats, and I make out two white men in the other canoe."

We were soon up to our friends, who greeted us warmly, they all along having fancied that we were ahead, and under that belief having paddled on, incited to exertions by occasionally hearing the voices of their pursuers as they cut off the bends of the river. They were of opinion, however, that we were now well ahead of them,—still we agreed that, during the remainder of daylight, it would be safer to continue our course.

The river now narrowed considerably, and the current became much more rapid than it had been hitherto. Kendo and his henchman, with Harry and Tom, led the way.

We were gliding quickly on, when suddenly Kendo's canoe spun round, and filling was driven against some rocks whose black heads rose above the foaming water. We narrowly avoided the danger, and as we shot by had just time to help Harry, who held on tight to his gun, on board, while Kendo, striking out, got up along side us, and with the aid of Iguma also scrambled in.

"Never mind me," cried out Tom, who was standing on the half sunken canoe, "I'll get into the other. Steer over this way, mates," he shouted out to the men in the other canoe.

We had no time to render him assistance, and had to exert our skill to prevent our canoe running against some more rocks which appeared ahead.

In less time than it has taken to describe the occurrence we were again in tranquil water, when looking round we were thankful to see Tom and Kendo's henchman safely seated in Caspar's canoe. The wrecked canoe was in the meantime dashed to pieces, so as to be rendered perfectly useless. We were some-what crowded, but that could not be helped, and we hoped that we should not meet with more rapids in our course ; although we might manage to swim on shore, should any accident occur, we should probably lose our rifles and knapsacks, and at all events damage our ammunition. We waited until Tom's canoe came up with us. I now recognised the stranger who had got on board just as they were shoving off as Herman Jansen, the murderer of Captain Roderick. His countenance wore the same gloomy expression as before. By his manner, however, he appeared not to be conscious that we were witnesses of the fearful deed he had committed, and under the circumstances we were placed, Harry and Charley agreed with me that it would not be wise in any way to allude to it. He had brought a rifle with him, how procured we could not tell. That would, of course, be of assistance should we be again attacked. From what we could learn from Kendo, we had too much reason to fear that we should meet with numerous enemies on our way down the river, who would only be restrained from attacking us by seeing our means of defence.

He advised that we should keep our weapons ready for instant use.

Another night was approaching. It was absolutely necessary that we should seek some place of shelter where we could rest for a few hours, as it would otherwise be impossible to paddle on during another day. We had fortunately a sufficient supply of cooked food, so that we had no need to go on shore and light a fire. Seeing a wooded point on the south bank of the river, where the trees overhung the water, we agreed to paddle in and secure the canoes. After supper it was arranged that some of us should lie down while the rest sat up and kept watch, so that we might be ready to defend ourselves against either human foes or any savage creatures which might be on the look-out for prey.

We had remained at rest a couple of hours, when as Harry and

I were sitting up while the remainder of the party were sleeping, we heard voices approaching, and looking out we saw a number of black forms gliding through the forest. From the way they approached, however, the savages could not have expected to surprise us, we therefore concluded that they were entirely ignorant of our whereabouts. Presently they came to a halt about a couple of hundred yards from where our canoes lay. We saw a light struck and they soon had a fire kindled, around which they seated themselves. In a short time other blacks arrived, and they all began to cook the provisions they had brought with them. It was very evident they had not forgotten a supply of palm wine, which they must have quaffed pretty freely, as ere long several of them got up and began dancing away furiously. Others joined them, until the greater number were dancing round and round the fire, snapping their fingers, kicking out their legs, and giving vent to the most hideous yells and shrieks of laughter, the sounds echoing through the forest being answered by the jabberings of monkeys and the cries of night birds. Whether these were our pursuers or some other tribe indulging in a night orgie we could not tell. Kendo touched Charley's rifle as a sign for him to fire. My brother shook his head and answered—

" We none of us wish to injure any of the poor fellows unless compelled to do so in self-defence. The sooner we get away from this the better. We shall not be discovered while all this uproar is going on, and may be far down the river before the blacks recover their senses."

Kendo rather unwillingly took his paddle, and Charley setting the example, we cautiously cast off from the branch to which we were moored and got up to the other canoe. Telling Tom that we were going to continue our course down the river, we paddled on.

"Let's have a shot at the niggers," I heard Jansen say to his companions; "we might knock over a dozen before they could get near us."

"Pull on, mate," said Tom; "what would be the use of injuring the people? they can do us no harm."

Aboh seeing us going ahead, took his paddle, Tom doing the same, compelled the others to do so likewise. As I looked round I saw them following us. We continued our way during the greater part of the night, Kendo being sure that we were keeping the right course. We were thankful, however, once more to bring up, when we believed that we had put sufficient distance between ourselves and our pursuers, and that there was now no longer any fear of our being overtaken by them. We had another enemy, however, to contend with. As we lay moored to the bank we heard grunting sounds, and a splashing which proceeded, we well knew, from hippopotami, and from the frequency and loudness of the noises we had good reason to believe that a number of the creatures were either sporting about or feeding near us. However, they seldom attack canoes so as to injure them intentionally and are generally greatly afraid of human beings either when on shore or in the water.

Huge and awkward as they are, they can run, and manage to make good progress over the ground, which they do when in search of grass, the food they live on. The bodies of those we saw were fully as large as elephants, although, having short legs, they were of a very different height, indeed, their bellies almost sweep the ground as they walk. Their feet are constructed in a very curious manner, to enable them to walk among the reeds and over the mud, as also to swim with ease. The hoof is divided into four short unconnected toes, which they can spread out like the feet of the camel when moving over the soft mud, or when swimming. The skin, which is almost entirely hairless, except in a few spots, is of a yellowish colour, the lower part assuming almost a pinkish hue. The head is hideous in the extreme, and armed with huge crooked tusks, the object of which is not so much for defence, as to dig up grass from the bottom of the river. These tusks afford the whitest ivory to be procured. There must have been thirty or forty of these creatures gamboling about around us. In spite of their noise, "those who had the watch below," as Charley called it, slept as soundly as tops.

As soon as the sun rose the next morning, we went on shore for the first time since we had embarked, but no enemies were in sight, and we ventured to breakfast comfortably on the bank; Harry and I having shot several birds which contributed to the repast. As soon as breakfast was over, we continued our course, as we were anxious to get into a district where people were accustomed to white men, and were likely to assist us.

Our canoe was leading, Tom being a little astern. We were just rounding a point where the water was somewhat shallow, when I heard a cry from the canoe astern. Upon looking round, I saw it lifted high in the air, and turned bottom upwards, while beneath it appeared a huge hippopotamus, which was making after one of the men; another man was on the point of being pitched on the creature's back, the two blacks, with their legs in the air, were falling into the water, and one of the men, who seemed to have sprung on shore, was scrambling up the bank. I saw all this at a glance, the next instant a fearful shriek escaped the swimmer, the huge hippopotamus had pierced him with its tusks, and seemed bent on venting its rage upon him.

For an instant I feared that the victim was our friend Tom, but his voice reassured me, and I saw the good boatswain making for the bank, which his other companion had gained. The two blacks quickly followed. Just then catching sight of the countenance of the man attacked by the hippopotamus, I recognised Jansen, the murderer of Captain Roderick.

Before either of us could raise our rifles to fire at the beast the miserable man had been dragged down beneath the water by the infuriated monster. We were on the point of returning to try and secure the canoe, when the hippopotamus again rose, and seizing the side in his huge mouth, crushed it to pieces, and we were thankful to paddle off to save our canoe from a like fate. We had now to consider what was to be done. We could not possibly take all the party into our canoe, nor could we leave any of them behind us. The blacks would to a certainty have been seized and carried off into slavery, unless protected by us. We were still, we calculated, a hundred miles or more from the coast; our only mode of proceeding, therefore, was for one party to continue along the shore, while the other paddled the canoe, and to relieve each other at intervals. We continued on in this fashion the greater part of the day, not meeting with another canoe or any habitations.

As evening approached, having reached an open spot, we agreed to encamp there that we might shoot some game, as our stock of provisions was reduced to a very low ebb.

Tom and Caspar, who had been walking the greater part of the day along the bank, were glad to take charge of the camp, while Charley, Harry, and I, with Kendo, went out in search of game. We were fortunate in killing two deer, several birds, and a couple of monkeys, and on our return we found that Iguma had not been idle, and had collected a supply of fruits and nuts, which, with the remainder of the plantain, gave us an abundant meal. There was still some time before dark, which we occupied in building a hut for the young lady, while we put up shelters for ourselves, and collected a large supply of sticks, so that we could have a blazing fire during the night. This was very necessary, as we had seen traces of wild beasts, and we might have otherwise very likely been visited by some of them. All of us required as much sleep as we could get. As soon as supper was over, we set the watch and lay down under our lean-to's, which were, I should have said, at a sufficient distance from the water to avoid the risk of any of us being carried off by a hungry crocodile. I had been some hours asleep, forgetting entirely where we were, when I was awakened by a tremendous crash of thunder. Starting up, I heard crash succeeding crash, while vivid flashes of lightning darted from the sky, and went playing round us like fiery serpents. The wind at the same time began to blow with a fury we had not encountered since we landed on the shores of Africa, but as it was off the land we were partly sheltered by the forest, and it did not send the waves up the bank. Our lean-to's were speedily blown down. In a short time the rain came down in torrents, and had we not just before made up the fire it would at once have been put out. Fortunately Iguma's hut stood, and she invited us all in to take shelter beneath its roof, which, being composed of several layers of large leaves, fastened down by vines, sheltered us from the pitiless storm. There we all sat for the remainder of the night, all huddled up like so many mummies, and a curious picture we must have presented.

Towards morning the hurricane abated, Tom and Aboh rushing out managed to scrape together the ashes of the fire which was not wholly extinguished, and again made it up. Shortly afterwards dawn broke. Uncomfortable as I was, I was actually dozing when I heard Tom cry out—

" The canoe, the canoe, where is she?"

We all of us jumped up and hurried to the beach, when what was our dismay to find that the tree to which the canoe had been made fast had, riven by the storm, fallen and crushed it to pieces. On examining it we saw at once that to repair it would be hopeless, and we had now only to make up our minds once more to continue our journey overland.

Fortunately we had still enough ammunition remaining to kill game for our support, but it was necessary carefully to husband it. Charley at once called a council of war.

" One thing is certain. We must not delay," he observed, " for even when we do reach the coast, we don't know how long we may be detained, and unless we fall in with friendly savages we may find it difficult to procure food; or, perhaps, indeed have to fight our way. We are bound also to protect the blacks who are trusting to us, for depend upon it, every attempt will be made by the slave-trading rascals on the coast to detain them."

Every one agreed with Charley, and without loss of time we commenced our march. I have already described travelling in Africa, so that I need not enter into the details of the journey we performed. We passed through the neighbourhood of several villages, from the inhabitants of which, with the remainder of the beads and the trinkets we possessed, we purchased food so that we were able to husband our powder and shot. Two attempts were made to carry off our black friends, but by showing a bold front and by pushing on, we prevented them from being made prisoners.

The health of all the party was wonderfully preserved, indeed the climate, though so close under the line—from the nature of the soil—is superior to that further north. At length to our great joy we caught sight from a rising ground of the blue ocean sparkling in the distance.

We had been two weeks performing the journey. We found that we had hit the shore some way to the south of the river, at a spot where a fine sheltered bay afforded a tempting harbour to any ships cruising off the coast, and the clear sparkling stream, which flowed down from the hill side at which vessels could obtain water, made it still more a likely spot to be touched at.

We accordingly determined to pitch our camp there, near a wood from which we could obtain materials for building huts, and an ample supply of fuel for our fires as well as game for our food. It seemed surprising that no blacks should have taken up their abode in what appeared to us so fine a situation. We lost no time in erecting our huts, and making ourselves, as Tom called it, "at home."

Of course we could not tell how long we might be detained there. Day after day passed by, no ship appeared in sight. At length Charley proposed proceeding to the northward, but Harry and I urged him to wait patiently a little longer.

That same evening my brother and I had strolled out from our camp to enjoy the freshness of the breeze along the sea shore. A light wind played over the water, the stars shone forth with wonderful brilliancy. We were tempted to sit down on the rocks, where we remained talking over our prospects for some time, when Charley exclaimed—

"Look there, Dick, look there! a vessel, as I'm alive, she's standing into the bay. She's no stranger to it, or she would not come here during the dark. We must make a signal and try to attract her attention, though it is pretty certain that she will send a boat on shore early in the morning, yet it will be trying to have to wait until then to know what she is."

There was abundance of drift wood on the beach which we quickly collected, and Charley having fortunately a tinder box in his pocket, we had no difficulty in kindling a blaze. As soon as we got a brand burning I took it up, and swinging it round my head threw it high into the air. A second and a third time I did the same, when as I threw up a fourth brand, the signal was answered by a rocket which rose from the vessel.

Before many minutes were over we heard the splash of oars, and could distinguish a boat. We both shouted, our hail was answered by an English voice. In another five minutes the stem of the boat touched the beach, and a person sprang on shore.

"Who are you? where do you come from?" exclaimed a

voice which I well knew. It was that of Captain Magor. The next instant we were all warmly shaking hands.

Harry and Tom hearing our shouts had hurried down to the beach. Our surprise and satisfaction were mutual. We very quickly told him our adventures, and he then informed us that he had played the same trick on the pirates which they had played on Lieutenant Hillton, and that having recaptured the " Arrow " he had carried her safely back to England, and that he had now just arrived on the coast, the only misfortune which had happened to him being the death of a young man who had come out as super-cargo.

" You may therefore still be of the greatest assistance to me," he said, " and having now learned something of the language, and being acclimatised, you will be able to transact business with the natives far better than you could otherwise have done."

We then told him of our black followers, who would, we believed, be of still greater assistance in procuring the articles we required, and disposing of the goods we had brought.

Iguma and Kendo were somewhat alarmed at first at the thought of going on board a ship, but we soon overcame their fears, and the next morning we all went on board, bidding farewell to our encampment, and once more trod the deck of the " Arrow."

Harry and I resumed our berths on board, as did Tom Tubbs, for the boatswain who had come out had already fallen sick and was unable to do duty.

Caspar entered as one of the ship's company, as did Aboh. Captain Magor arranged to carry Kendo and Iguma with their followers to England, if they preferred going there to being landed at one of the English settlements on the coast.

I must now bring my tale rapidly to a conclusion. Kendo and his wife—wisely, I think—determined not to go to England.

A week afterwards we fell in with the " Rover." when Charley rejoined his ship, taking the blacks with him, the captain kindly promising to land them at Cape Coast Castle, where they would be properly treated and looked after. With the information we had gained, we were so well able to conduct our transactions, that our voyage was the most successful ever made by the "Arrow," and we had the satisfaction of meeting with the approval of our employers, and receiving substantial acknowledgments.

Of course our disappearance had caused very great anxiety to our friends, though they had been buoyed up by the hope that we would surely return.

Harry and I having married the young ladies to whom we had so long been attached, entered the firm, and on the death of that kind and excellent man Mr. Swab, we found that he had divided his fortune between us.

THE END.

Nelson's Books for Boys.

THE *Books below are specially suitable for Boys, and a better selection of well-written, attractively-bound, and beautifully-illustrated Gift and Prize Books cannot be found. The list may be selected from with the greatest confidence, the imprint of Messrs. Nelson being a guarantee of wholesomeness as well as of interest and general good quality.*

Many Illustrated in Colours.

"CAPTAIN SWING."	*Harold Avery.*	5s.
HOSTAGE FOR A KINGDOM.	*F. B. Forester.*	5s.
FIRELOCK AND STEEL.	*Harold Avery.*	5s.
A CAPTIVE OF THE CORSAIRS.		5s.
	John Finnemore.	
THE DUFFER.	*Warren Bell.*	5s.
A KING'S COMRADE.	*C. W. Whistler.*	5s.
IN THE TRENCHES.	*John Finnemore.*	5s.
IN JACOBITE DAYS.	*Mrs. Clarke.*	5s.
HEADS OR TAILS? (A School Story.)	*H. Avery.*	5s.
JACK RALSTON. (Life in Canada.)	*H. Burnham.*	5s.
A CAPTAIN OF IRREGULARS. (War in Chili.)		5s.
	Herbert Hayens.	
IN THE GRIP OF THE SPANIARD.		5s.
	Herbert Hayens.	

T. NELSON AND SONS, London, Edinburgh, Dublin, and New York.

NELSON'S BOOKS FOR BOYS.

HELD TO RANSOM. (A Story of Brigands.)   3s. 6d.
F. B. Forester.

RED, WHITE, AND GREEN. (Hungarian   3s. 6d.
Revolution.)   *Herbert Hayens.*

THE TIGER OF THE PAMPAS. *H. Hayens.*   3s. 6d.

TRUE TO HIS NICKNAME. *Harold Avery.*   3s. 6d.

RED CAP.   *E. S. Tylee.*   3s. 6d.

A SEA-QUEEN'S SAILING. *C. W. Whistler.*   3s. 6d.

PLAY THE GAME!   *Harold Avery.*   3s. 6d.

HIGHWAY PIRATES. (A School Story.) „   3s. 6d.

SALE'S SHARPSHOOTERS.   „   3s. 6d.
A rattling story of how three boys formed a very irregular volunteer corps.

FOR KING OR EMPRESS? (Stephen and   3s. 6d.
Matilda.)   *C. W. Whistler.*

SOLDIERS OF THE CROSS. *E. F. Pollard.*   3s. 6d.

TOM GRAHAM, V.C. *William Johnston.*   3s. 6d.

THE FELLOW WHO WON. *Andrew Home.*   3s. 6d.

BEGGARS OF THE SEA. *Tom Bevan.*   3s. 6d.

A TRUSTY REBEL. *Mrs. Henry Clarke.*   3s. 6d.

THE BRITISH LEGION. *Herbert Hayens.*   3s. 6d.

SCOUTING FOR BULLER.   „   3s. 6d.

THE ISLAND OF GOLD. *Dr. Gordon Stables.*   3s. 6d.

HAROLD THE NORSEMAN. *Fred Whishaw.*   3s. 6d.

MINVERN BROTHERS. *Charles Turley.*   3s. 6d.

IN DAYS OF DANGER. *Harold Avery.*   3s. 6d.

LADS OF THE LIGHT DIVISION.   ·   3s. 6d.
Colonel Ferryman.

A LOST ARMY.   *Fred Whishaw.*   3s. 6d.

DOING AND DARING. *Eleanor Stredder.*   3s. 6d.

T. NELSON AND SONS. London. Edinburgh, Dublin and New York.

NELSON'S BOOKS FOR BOYS.

BAFFLING THE BLOCKADE.   3s. 6d.
J. Macdonald Oxley.

TOM BROWN'S SCHOOLDAYS.   *Hughes.*   3s.

HEREWARD THE WAKE. *Charles Kingsley.*   3s.

THE "LONE STAR" SERIES.

Handsome Gift Books at a moderate price. Uniformly bound and well illustrated.

UNDER THE LONE STAR. *Herbert Hayens.*   3s. 6d.

CLEVELY SAHIB.   ,,   3s. 6d.

AN EMPEROR'S DOOM.   ,,   3s. 6d.

A VANISHED NATION.   ,,   3s. 6d.

A FIGHTER IN GREEN.   ,,   3s. 6d.

THE DORMITORY FLAG.   *Harold Avery.*   3s. 6d.

KILGORMAN.   *Talbot Baines Reed.*   3s. 6d.

IN THE WILDS OF THE WEST COAST.   3s. 6d.
J. Macdonald Oxley.

EVERY INCH A SAILOR. *Dr. Gordon Stables.*   3s. 6d.

AT THE POINT OF THE SWORD.   3s. 6d.
Herbert Hayens.

RED, WHITE, AND GREEN.   ,,   3s. 6d.

A HERO OF THE HIGHLANDS. *E. E. Green.*   3s. 6d.

HELD TO RANSOM.   *F. B. Forester.*   3s. 6d.

T. NELSON AND SONS, London, Edinburgh, Dublin, and New York.

NELSON'S BOOKS FOR BOYS.

VICTORIES OF THE ENGINEER. 3s. 6d.
A. Williams.

Recent engineering marvels graphically described and fully illustrated.

HOW IT IS MADE. *A. Williams.* 3s. 6d.

HOW IT WORKS. „ 3s. 6d.

Splendid books for boys, telling them just what they want to know. Profusely illustrated.

IN FLORA'S REALM. *Edward Step, F.L.S.* 3s. 6d.

A NATURALIST'S HOLIDAY. „ „ 3s. 6d.

Two books by one of the most popular of living writers on natural history subjects.

THE "ACTIVE SERVICE" SERIES.

FOR THE COLOURS. *Herbert Hayens.* 2s. 6d.
A Boy's Book of the Army.

YE MARINERS OF ENGLAND. 2s. 6d.
Herbert Hayens.
A Boy's Book of the Navy.

TRAFALGAR REFOUGHT. 2s. 6d.
Sir W. Laird Clowes and Alan H. Burgoyne.

AUTOBIOGRAPHY OF A SEAMAN. 2s. 6d.
Abridged from Lord Dundonald.

ADVENTURES IN THE RIFLE BRIGADE. 2s. 6d.
Sir John Kincaid.

FOR THE EMPEROR. *Eliza F. Pollard.* 2s. 6d.

T. Nelson and Sons, London, Edinburgh, Dublin, and New York.

NELSON'S BOOKS FOR BOYS.

THE GOLD KLOOF.	*H. A. Bryden.*	2s. 6d.
SEA DOGS ALL!	*Tom Bevan.*	2s. 6d.
THE FEN ROBBERS.	,,	2s. 6d.
RED DICKON, THE OUTLAW.	,,	2s. 6d.
HAVELOK THE DANE.	*Charles W. Whistler.*	2s. 6d.
KING ALFRED'S VIKING.	,,	2s. 6d.
THE VANISHED YACHT.	*Harcourt Burrage.*	2s. 6d.
A splendid story of adventure.		
MY STRANGE RESCUE.	*J. Macdonald Oxley.*	2s. 6d.
DIAMOND ROCK.	,,	2s. 6d.
UP AMONG THE ICE-FLOES.	,,	2s. 6d.
CHUMS AT LAST.	*Mrs. G. Forsyth Grant.*	2s. 6d.
MOBSLEY'S MOHICANS. (A Tale of Two Terms.)		2s. 6d.
	Harold Avery.	
KNIGHTS OF THE ROAD.	*E. Everett-Green.*	2s. 6d.
ROBINSON CRUSOE.	*Defoe.*	2s. 6d.
WON IN WARFARE.	*C. R. Kenyon.*	2s. 6d.
THE WIZARD'S WAND.	*Harold Avery.*	2s. 6d.
A PRINCE ERRANT.	*C. W. Whistler.*	2s. 6d.
BRAVE MEN AND BRAVE DEEDS.		2s. 6d.
	M. B. Synge.	
RALPH THE OUTLAW.	*Mrs. H. Clarke.*	2s.
THE "GREY FOX."	*Tom Bevan.*	2s.
THE JEWELLED LIZARD.	*W. D. Fordyce.*	2s.
THE CHANCELLOR'S SPY.	*Tom Bevan.*	2s.
HIS MAJESTY'S GLOVE.	*Miss Whitham.*	2s.

T. NELSON AND SONS, London, Edinburgh, Dublin, and New York.

NELSON'S BOOKS FOR BOYS.

A FORTUNE FROM THE SKY. *S. Kuppord.* 2s.

FRANK'S FIRST TERM. *Harold Avery.* 1s. 6d.

THREE SAILOR BOYS; or, Adrift in the Pacific. 1s. 6d.
Commander Cameron.

RIVERTON BOYS. *K. M. Eady.* 1s. 6d.

TRAVEL SERIES.

ADVENTURERS ALL. *K. M. Eady.* 1s. 6d.

ALIVE IN THE JUNGLE. *Eleanor Stredder.* 1s. 6d.

CABIN IN THE CLEARING. *Edward S. Ellis.* 1s. 6d.

THE CASTAWAYS. *Captain Mayne Reid.* 1s. 6d.

LOST IN THE BACKWOODS. *Mrs. Traill.* 1s. 6d.

LOST IN THE WILDS OF CANADA. 1s. 6d.
Eleanor Stredder.

THE THREE TRAPPERS. *Achilles Daunt.* 1s. 6d.

THROUGH FOREST AND FIRE. *E. S. Ellis.* 1s. 6d.

WITH STANLEY ON THE CONGO. 1s. 6d.
Miss Douglas.

T. NELSON AND SONS, London, Edinburgh, Dublin, and New York.

www.ingramcontent.com/pod-product-compliance
Lightning Source LLC
Chambersburg PA
CBHW060534030726
47498CB00004B/1189